Customer Service
1.704.898.0770

North Carolina General Statues is published by The Muliti-Media Group of Greater Charlotte in Charlotte, North Carolina. Copyright 2015 by the Multi-Media Group of Greater Charlotte. This book or parts thereof may not be reproduced in any form, stored in a retrieval system, or transmitted in any form by any means—electronic, mechanical, photocopy, recording or otherwise—without prior written permission of the publisher, except as provided by United States of America copyright law.

The records required by U.S. Code 2257(a) through (c) and the pertinent regulations 28 C.F.R. Cli. 1, Part 75 with respect to this publication and all materials associated with such records are maintained by The Multi-Media Group of Greater Charlotte, Publisher and available for review by Attorney General.

www.visionbooks.org

Copyright © 2015 by MMGGC
All rights reserved!

TID: 5109315
ISBN (10) digit: 1503254739
ISBN (13) digit: 978-1503254732

123-4-56789-01239-Paperback
123-4-56789-01239-Hardback

First Edition

090520140547

Printed in the United States of America

North Carolina Criminal Law

And Procedure-Pamphlet # 89

Printed In conjunction with the
Administration of the Courts

Chapters	Pamphlet
Chapter 1 Civil Procedure	1
Chapter 1 Civil Procedure (Continue)	2
Chapter 1A Rules of Civil Procedure	2
Chapter 1B Contribution.	2
Chapter 1C Enforcement of Judgments.	2
Chapter 1D Punitive Damages.	2
Chapter 1E Eastern Band of Cherokee Indians.	2
Chapter 1F North Carolina Uniform Interstate Depositions and Discovery Act.	2
Chapter 2 - Clerk of Superior Court [Repealed and Transferred.]	3
Chapter 3 - Commissioners of Affidavits and Deeds [Repealed.]	3
Chapter 4 - Common Law	3
Chapter 5 - Contempt [Repealed.]	3
Chapter 5A - Contempt	3
Chapter 6 - Liability for Court Costs	3
Chapter 7 - Courts [Repealed and Transferred.]	3
Chapter 7A – Judicial Department	3
Chapter 7A – Continuation (Judicial Department)	4
Chapter 7A – Continuation (Judicial Department)	5
Chapter 7B - Juvenile Code	5
Chapter 8 - Evidence	6
Chapter 8A - Interpreters for Deaf Persons [Recodified.]	6
Chapter 8B - Interpreters for Deaf Persons	6
Chapter 8C - Evidence Code	6
Chapter 9 - Jurors	6
Chapter 10 - Notaries [Repealed.]	6
Chapter 10A - Notaries [Recodified.]	6
Chapter 10B - Notaries	6
Chapter 11 - Oaths	6
Chapter 12 - Statutory Construction	6
Chapter 13 - Citizenship Restored	6
Chapter 14 - Criminal Law	7
Chapter 14 –Criminal Law (Continuation)	8
Chapter 15 - Criminal Procedure	9
Chapter 15A - Criminal Procedure Act (Continuation)	10
Chapter 15A - Criminal Procedure Act (Continuation)	11
Chapter 15B - Victims Compensation	11
Chapter 15C - Address Confidentiality Program	11
Chapter 16 - Gaming Contracts and Futures	11
Chapter 17 - Habeas Corpus	11

Criminal Justice Education and Training Standards Commission	11
Chapter 17D - North Carolina Justice Academy	11
Chapter 17E - North Carolina Sheriffs' Education and Training Standards Commission	11
Chapter 18 - Regulation of Intoxicating Liquors [Repealed.]	12
Chapter 18A - Regulation of Intoxicating Liquors [Repealed.]	12
Chapter 18B - Regulation of Alcoholic Beverages	12
Chapter 18C - North Carolina State Lottery	12
Chapter 19 - Offenses against Public Morals	12
Chapter 19A - Protection of Animals	12
Chapter 20 - Motor Vehicles	13
Chapter 20 - Motor Vehicles (Continuation)	14
Chapter 20 - Motor Vehicles (Continuation)	15
Chapter 20 - Motor Vehicles (Continuation)	16
Chapter 21 - Bills of Lading	17
Chapter 22 - Contracts Requiring Writing	17
Chapter 22A - Signatures	17
Chapter 22B - Contracts Against Public Policy	17
Chapter 22C - Payments to Subcontractors	17
Chapter 23 - Debtor and Creditor	17
Chapter 24 – Interest	17
Chapter 25 – Uniform Commercial Code	18
Chapter 25 – Uniform Commercial Code (Continuation)	19
Chapter 25A – Retail Installment Sales Act	20
Chapter 25B - Credit	20
Chapter 25C - Sales of Artwork	20
Chapter 26 - Suretyship	20
Chapter 27 - Warehouse Receipts [Repealed.]	20
Chapter 28 - Administration [Repealed.]	20
Chapter 28A - Administration of Decedents' Estates	20
Chapter 28B - Estates of Absentees in Military Service	20
Chapter 28C - Estates of Missing Persons	20
Chapter 29 - Intestate Succession	21
Chapter 30 - Surviving Spouses	21
Chapter 31 - Wills	21
Chapter 31A - Acts Barring Property Rights	21
Chapter 31B - Renunciation of Property and Renunciation of Fiduciary Powers Act	21
Chapter 31C - Uniform Disposition of Community Property Rights at Death Act	21
Chapter 32 - Fiduciaries	21
Chapter 32A - Powers of Attorney	21
Chapter 33 - Guardian and Ward [Repealed and Recodified.]	21

Chapter 35 - Sterilization Procedures	22
Chapter 35A - Incompetency and Guardianship	22
Chapter 36 - Trusts and Trustees [Repealed.]	22
Chapter 36A - Trusts and Trustees	22
Chapter 36B - Uniform Management of Institutional Funds Act [Repealed.]	22
Chapter 36C - North Carolina Uniform Trust Code	22
Chapter 36D - North Carolina Community Third Party Trusts, Pooled Trusts	23
Chapter 36E - Uniform Prudent Management of Institutional Funds Act	23
Chapter 37 - Allocation of Principal and Income [Repealed.]	23
Chapter 37A - Uniform Principal and Income Act	23
Chapter 38 - Boundaries	23
Chapter 38A - Landowner Liability	23
Chapter 39 - Conveyances	23
Chapter 39A - Transfer Fee Covenants Prohibited	23
Chapter 40 - Eminent Domain [Repealed.]	23
Chapter 40A - Eminent Domain	23
Chapter 41 - Estates	23
Chapter 41A - State Fair Housing Act	23
Chapter 42 - Landlord and Tenant	23
Chapter 42A - Vacation Rental Act	23
Chapter 43 - Land Registration	23
Chapter 44 - Liens	24
Chapter 44A - Statutory Liens and Charges	24
Chapter 45 - Mortgages and Deeds of Trust	24
Chapter 45A - Good Funds Settlement Act	24
Chapter 46 - Partition	24
Chapter 47 - Probate and Registration	25
Chapter 47A - Unit Ownership	25
Chapter 47B - Real Property Marketable Title Act	25
Chapter 47C - North Carolina Condominium Act	25
Chapter 47D - Notice of Settlement Act [Expired.]	25
Chapter 47E - Residential Property Disclosure Act	25
Chapter 47F - North Carolina Planned Community Act	25
Chapter 47G - Option to Purchase Contracts	25
Chapter 47H - Contracts for Deed	25
Chapter 48 - Adoptions	26
Chapter 48A - Minors	26
Chapter 49 - Bastardy	26
Chapter 49A - Rights of Children	26
Chapter 50 - Divorce and Alimony	26
Chapter 50A - Uniform Child-Custody Jurisdiction and	

Chapter 51 - Marriage	26
Chapter 52 - Powers and Liabilities of Married Persons	27
Chapter 52A - Uniform Reciprocal Enforcement of Support Act [Repealed.]	27
Chapter 52B - Uniform Premarital Agreement Act	27
Chapter 52C - Uniform Interstate Family Support Act	27
Chapter 53 - Banks	27
Chapter 53A - Business Development Corporations and North Carolina Capital Resource Corporations	28
Chapter 53B - Financial Privacy Act	28
Chapter 54 - Cooperative Organizations	28
Chapter 54A - Capital Stock Savings and Loan Associations [Repealed.]	28
Chapter 54B - Savings and Loan Associations	29
Chapter 54C - Savings Banks	29
Chapter 55 - North Carolina Business Corporation Act	30
Chapter 55A - North Carolina Nonprofit Corporation Act	31
Chapter 55B - Professional Corporation Act	31
Chapter 55C - Foreign Trade Zones	31
Chapter 55D - Filings, Names, and Registered Agents for Corporations, Nonprofit Corporations, and Partnerships	31
Chapter 56 - Electric, Telegraph and Power Companies [Repealed.]	31
Chapter 57 - Hospital, Medical and Dental Service Corporations [Recodified.]	31
Chapter 57A - Health Maintenance Organization Act [Recodified.]	31
Chapter 57B - Health Maintenance Organization Act [Recodified.]	31
Chapter 57C - North Carolina Limited Liability Company Act.	31
Chapter 58 - Insurance.	32
Chapter 58 - Insurance (Continuation)	33
Chapter 58 - Insurance (Continuation)	34
Chapter 58 - Insurance (Continuation)	35
Chapter 58 - Insurance (Continuation)	36
Chapter 58 - Insurance (Continuation)	37
Chapter 58 - Insurance (Continuation)	38
Chapter 58A - North Carolina Health Insurance Trust Commission [Recodified.]	38
Chapter 59 - Partnership.	39
Chapter 59B - Uniform Unincorporated Nonprofit Association Act.	39
Chapter 60 - Railroads and Other Carriers [Repealed and Transferred.]	39
Chapter 61 - Religious Societies	39
Chapter 62 - Public Utilities	39

Chapter 63 - Aeronautics	40
Chapter 63A - North Carolina Global TransPark Authority	40
Chapter 64 - Aliens	40
Chapter 65 – Cemeteries	40
Chapter 66 - Commerce and Business	41
Chapter 67 - Dogs	41
Chapter 68 - Fences and Stock Law	41
Chapter 69 - Fire Protection	41
Chapter 70 - Indian Antiquities, Archaeological Resources and Unmarked Human Skeletal Remains Protection	42
Chapter 71 - Indians [Repealed.]	42
Chapter 71A - Indians	42
Chapter 72 - Inns, Hotels and Restaurants	42
Chapter 73 - Mills	42
Chapter 74 - Mines and Quarries	42
Chapter 74A - Company Police [Repealed.]	42
Chapter 74B - Private Protective Services Act [Repealed.]	42
Chapter 74C - Private Protective Services	42
Chapter 74D - Alarm Systems	42
Chapter 74E - Company Police Act	42
Chapter 74F - Locksmith Licensing Act	42
Chapter 74G - Campus Police Act	42
Chapter 75 - Monopolies, Trusts and Consumer Protection	42
Chapter 75A - Boating and Water Safety	43
Chapter 75B - Discrimination in Business	43
Chapter 75C - Motion Picture Fair Competition Act	43
Chapter 75D - Racketeer Influenced and Corrupt Organizations	43
Chapter 75E - Unlawful Activities in Connection With Certain Corporate Transactions	43
Chapter 76 - Navigation	43
Chapter 76A - Navigation and Pilotage Commissions	43
Chapter 77 - Rivers, Creeks, and Coastal Waters	43
Chapter 78 - Securities Law [Repealed.]	43
Chapter 78A - North Carolina Securities Act	43
Chapter 78B - Tender Offer Disclosure Act [Repealed.]	43
Chapter 78C - Investment Advisers	43
Chapter 78D - Commodities Act	43
Chapter 79 - Strays [Repealed.]	43
Chapter 80 - Trademarks, Brands, etc.	44
Chapter 81 - Weights and Measures [Recodified.]	44
Chapter 81A - Weights and Measures Act of 1975.	44
Chapter 82 - Wrecks [Repealed.]	44
Chapter 83 - Architects [Recodified.]	44

Chapter 85 - Auctions and Auctioneers [Repealed.]	44
Chapter 85A - Bail Bondsmen and Runners [Recodified.]	44
Chapter 85B - Auctions and Auctioneers	44
Chapter 85C - Bail Bondsmen and Runners [Recodified.]	44
Chapter 86 - Barbers [Recodified.]	44
Chapter 86A - Barbers	44
Chapter 87 - Contractors	44
Chapter 88 - Cosmetic Art [Repealed.]	44
Chapter 88A - Electrolysis Practice Act	44
Chapter 88B - Cosmetic Art	45
Chapter 89 - Engineering and Land Surveying [Recodified.]	45
Chapter 89A - Landscape Architects	45
Chapter 89B - Foresters	45
Chapter 89C - Engineering and Land Surveying	45
Chapter 89D - Landscape Contractors	45
Chapter 89E - Geologists Licensing Act	45
Chapter 89F - North Carolina Soil Scientist Licensing Act	45
Chapter 89G - Irrigation Contractors	45
Chapter 90 - Medicine and Allied Occupations	45
Chapter 90 - Medicine and Allied Occupations (Continuation)	46
Chapter 90 - Medicine and Allied Occupations (Continuation)	47
Chapter 90 - Medicine and Allied Occupations (Continuation)	48
Chapter 90A - Sanitarians and Water and Wastewater Treatment Facility Operators	48
Chapter 90B - Social Worker Certification and Licensure Act	48
Chapter 90C - North Carolina Recreational Therapy Licensure Act	48
Chapter 90D - Interpreters and Transliterators	48
Chapter 91 - Pawnbrokers [Repealed.]	48
Chapter 91A - Pawnbrokers Modernization Act of 1989	48
Chapter 92 - Photographers [Deleted.]	48
Chapter 93 - Certified Public Accountants	48
Chapter 93A - Real Estate License Law	49
Chapter 93B - Occupational Licensing Boards	49
Chapter 93C - Watchmakers [Repealed.]	49
Chapter 93D - North Carolina State Hearing Aid Dealers and Fitters Board.	49
Chapter 93E - North Carolina Appraisers Act	49
Chapter 94 - Apprenticeship	49
Chapter 95 - Department of Labor and Labor Regulations	49
Chapter 95 - Department of Labor and Labor Regulations (Continuation)	50
Chapter 96 - Employment Security	50
Chapter 97 - Workers' Compensation Act	50
Chapter 97 - Workers' Compensation Act (Continuation)	51

Chapter 99B - Products Liability	51
Chapter 99C - Actions Relating to Winter Sports Safety and Accidents	51
Chapter 99D - Civil Rights	51
Chapter 99E - Special Liability Provisions	51
Chapter 100 - Monuments, Memorials and Parks	51
Chapter 101 - Names of Persons	51
Chapter 102 - Official Survey Base	51
Chapter 103 - Sundays, Holidays and Special Days	51
Chapter 104 - United States Lands	51
Chapter 104A - Degrees of Kinship	51
Chapter 104B - Hurricanes or Other Acts of Nature	51
Chapter 104C - Atomic Energy, Radioactivity and Ionizing Radiation [Repealed and Recodified.]	51
Chapter 104D - Southern States Energy Compact	51
Chapter 104E - North Carolina Radiation Protection Act	51
Chapter 104F - Southeast Interstate Low-Level Radioactive Waste Management Compact [Repealed]	51
Chapter 104G - North Carolina Low-Level Radioactive Waste Management Authority Act of 1987 [Repealed]	51
Chapter 105 - Taxation	51
Chapter 105 - Taxation (Continuation)	52
Chapter 105 - Taxation (Continuation)	53
Chapter 105 - Taxation (Continuation)	54
Chapter 105A - Setoff Debt Collection Act	55
Chapter 105B - Defaulted Student Loan Recovery Act	55
Chapter 106 - Agriculture	55
Chapter 106 - Agriculture (Continue)	56
Chapter 106 - Agriculture (Continue)	57
Chapter 107 - Agricultural Development Districts [Repealed.]	57
Chapter 108 - Social Services [Repealed and Recodified.]	57
Chapter 108A - Social Services	57
Chapter 108B - Community Action Programs	58
Chapter 108C Medicaid and Health Choice Provider Requirements.	58
Chapter 108D Medicaid Managed Care for Behavioral Health Services.	58
Chapter 109 - Bonds [Recodified.]	58
Chapter 110 - Child Welfare	58
Chapter 111 - Aid to the Blind	58
Chapter 112 - Confederate Homes and Pensions [Repealed.]	58
Chapter 113 - Conservation and Development	58
Chapter 113 - Conservation and Development (Continuation)	59

Chapter 114 - Department of Justice	60
Chapter 115 - Elementary and Secondary Education [Repealed.]	60
Chapter 115A - Community Colleges, Technical Institutes, and Industrial Education Centers [Repealed.]	60
Chapter 115B - Tuition and Fee Waivers	60
Chapter 115C - Elementary and Secondary Education	60
Chapter 115C - Elementary and Secondary Education (Continuation)	61
Chapter 115C - Elementary and Secondary Education (Continuation)	62
Chapter 115C - Elementary and Secondary Education (Continuation)	63
Chapter 115D - Community Colleges	63
Chapter 115E - Private Educational Facilities Finance Act [Recodified]	63
Chapter 116 - Higher Education	63
Chapter 116 - Higher Education (Continuation)	63
Chapter 116A - Escheats and Abandoned Property [Repealed.]	64
Chapter 116B - Escheats and Abandoned Property	64
Chapter 116C - Continuum of Education Programs	64
Chapter 116D - Higher Education Bonds	64
Chapter 116E -Education Longitudinal Data System	64
Chapter 117 - Electrification	64
Chapter 118 - Firemen's and Rescue Squad Workers' Relief and Pension Funds [Recodified.]	64
Chapter 118A - Firemen's Death Benefit Act [Repealed.]	64
Chapter 118B - Members of a Rescue Squad Death Benefit Act [Repealed.]	64
Chapter 119 - Gasoline and Oil Inspection and Regulation	64
Chapter 120 - General Assembly	65
Chapter 120 - General Assembly (Continuation)	66
Chapter 120 - General Assembly (Continuation)	67
Chapter 120C - Lobbying	67
Chapter 121 - Archives and History	67
Chapter 122 - Hospitals for the Mentally Disordered [Repealed.]	67
Chapter 122A - North Carolina Housing Finance Agency	67
Chapter 122B - North Carolina Agricultural Facilities Finance Act [Repealed.]	67
Chapter 122C - Mental Health, Developmental Disabilities, and Substance Abuse Act of 1985	67
Chapter 122C - Mental Health, Developmental Disabilities, and Substance Abuse Act of 1985 (Continuation)	68

Chapter 123 - Impeachment	69
Chapter 123A - Industrial Development [Repealed.]	69
Chapter 124 - Internal Improvements	69
Chapter 125 - Libraries	69
Chapter 126 - State Personnel System	69
Chapter 127 - Militia [Repealed.]	69
Chapter 127A - Militia	69
Chapter 127B - Military Affairs	69
Chapter 127C - Advisory Commission on Military Affairs	69
Chapter 128 - Offices and Public Officers	69
Chapter 128 - Offices and Public Officers (Continuation)	70
Chapter 129 - Public Buildings and Grounds	70
Chapter 130 - Public Health [Repealed.]	70
Chapter 130A - Public Health	70
Chapter 130A - Public Health (Continuation)	71
Chapter 130A - Public Health (Continuation)	72
Chapter 130B - Hazardous Waste Management Commission [Repealed.]	72
Chapter 131 - Public Hospitals [Repealed.]	72
Chapter 131A - Health Care Facilities Finance Act	72
Chapter 131B - Licensing of Ambulatory Surgical Facilities [Repealed.]	72
Chapter 131C - Charitable Solicitation Licensure Act [Repealed.]	72
Chapter 131D - Inspection and Licensing of Facilities	72
Chapter 131E - Health Care Facilities and Services	72
Chapter 131E - Health Care Facilities and Services (Continuation)	73
Chapter 131F - Solicitation of Contributions	73
Chapter 132 - Public Records	73
Chapter 133 - Public Works	74
Chapter 134 - Youth Development [Recodified.]	74
Chapter 134A - Youth Services [Repealed.]	74
Chapter 135 - Retirement System for Teachers and State Employees; Social Security; Health Insurance Program for Children	74
Chapter 135 - Retirement System for Teachers and State Employees; Social Security; Health Insurance Program for Children	75
Chapter 136 - Transportation	75
Chapter 136 - Transportation (Continuation)	76
Chapter 137 - Rural Rehabilitation [Repealed.]	76
Chapter 138 - Salaries, Fees and Allowances	76
Chapter 138A - State Government Ethics Act	76

Chapter 140A - State Awards System	76
Chapter 141 - State Boundaries	76
Chapter 142 - State Debt	76
Chapter 143 - State Departments, Institutions, and Commissions	77
Chapter 143 - State Departments, Institutions, and Commissions (Continuation)	78
Chapter 143 - State Departments, Institutions, and Commissions (Continuation)	79
Chapter 143 - State Departments, Institutions, and Commissions (Continuation)	80
Chapter 143A - State Government Reorganization	80
Chapter 143B - Executive Organization Act of 1973	80
Chapter 143B - Executive Organization Act of 1973 (Continuation)	81
Chapter 143B - Executive Organization Act of 1973 (Continuation)	82
Chapter 143C - State Budget Act	83
Chapter 143D - The State Governmental Accountability and Internal Control Act	83
Chapter 144 - State Flag, Official Governmental Flags, Motto, and Colors	83
Chapter 145 - State Symbols and Other Official Adoptions.	83
Chapter 146 - State Lands	83
Chapter 147 - State Officers	83
Chapter 148 - State Prison System	84
Chapter 149 - State Song and Toast	84
Chapter 150 - Uniform Revocation of Licenses [Repealed.]	84
Chapter 150A - Administrative Procedure Act [Recodified.]	84
Chapter 150B - Administrative Procedure Act	84
Chapter 151 - Constables [Repealed.]	84
Chapter 152 - Coroners	84
Chapter 152A - County Medical Examiner [Repealed.]	84
Chapter 152A - County Medical Examiner [Repealed.] (Continuation)	84
Chapter 153 - Counties and County Commissioners [Repealed.]	84
Chapter 153A - Counties	84
Chapter 153A - Counties (Continue)	85
Chapter 153B - Mountain Resources Planning Act	85
Chapter 153C - Uwharrie Regional Resources Act	85
Chapter 154 - County Surveyor [Repealed.]	85
Chapter 155 - County Treasurer [Repealed.]	85

Chapter 157A - Historic Properties Commissions [Transferred.]	86
Chapter 158 - Local Development	86
Chapter 159 - Local Government Finance	86
Chapter 159 - Local Government Finance (Continuation)	87
Chapter 159A - Pollution Abatement and Industrial Facilities Financing Act [Unconstitutional.]	87
Chapter 159B - Joint Municipal Electric Power and Energy Act	87
Chapter 159C - Industrial and Pollution Control Facilities Financing Act	87
Chapter 159D - The North Carolina Capital Facilities Financing Act	87
Chapter 159E - Registered Public Obligations Act	87
Chapter 159F - North Carolina Energy Development Authority [Repealed.]	87
Chapter 159G - Water Infrastructure	87
Chapter 159H - [Reserved.]	87
Chapter 159I - Solid Waste Management Loan Program and Local Government Special Obligation Bonds	87
Chapter 160 - Municipal Corporations [Repealed And Transferred.]	87
Chapter 160A - Cities and Towns	88
Chapter 160A - Cities and Towns (Continuation)	89
Chapter 160B - Consolidated City-County Act	89
Chapter 160C - Baseball Park Districts [Repealed.]	90
Chapter 161 - Register of Deeds	90
Chapter 162 - Sheriff	90
Chapter 162A - Water and Sewer Systems	90
Chapter 162B Continuity of Local Government in Emergency.	90
Chapter 163 Elections and Election Laws.	90
Chapter 163 Elections and Election Laws. (Continuation)	91
Chapter 164 Concerning the General Statutes of North Carolina.	92
Chapter 165 Veterans.	92
Chapter 166 Civil Preparedness Agencies [Repealed.]	92
Chapter 166A North Carolina Emergency Management Act.	92
Chapter 167 State Civil Air Patrol [Repealed.]	92
Chapter 168 Persons with Disabilities.	92
Chapter 168A Persons With Disabilities Protection Act.	92

jurisdiction into districts of any number, shape, and area that may be deemed best suited to carry out the purposes of this Part; and within those districts it may regulate and restrict the erection, construction, reconstruction, alteration, repair or use of buildings, structures, or land. Such districts may include, but shall not be limited to, general use districts, in which a variety of uses are permissible in accordance with general standards; overlay districts, in which additional requirements are imposed on certain properties within one or more underlying general or special use districts; and special use districts or conditional use districts, in which uses are permitted only upon the issuance of a special use permit or a conditional use permit and conditional zoning districts, in which site plans and individualized development conditions are imposed.

(b)   Property may be placed in a special use district, conditional use district, or conditional district only in response to a petition by the owners of all the property to be included. Specific conditions applicable to these districts may be proposed by the petitioner or the city or its agencies, but only those conditions mutually approved by the city and the petitioner may be incorporated into the zoning regulations or permit requirements. Conditions and site-specific standards imposed in a conditional district shall be limited to those that address the conformance of the development and use of the site to city ordinances and an officially adopted comprehensive or other plan and those that address the impacts reasonably expected to be generated by the development or use of the site.

A statement analyzing the reasonableness of the proposed rezoning shall be prepared for each petition for a rezoning to a special or conditional use district, or a conditional district, or other small-scale rezoning.

(c)   Except as authorized by the foregoing, all regulations shall be uniform for each class or kind of building throughout each district, but the regulations in one district may differ from those in other districts. (1923, c. 250, s. 2; C.S., s. 2776(s); 1931, c. 176, s. 1; 1933, c. 7; 1963, c. 1058, s. 1; 1971, c. 698, s. 1; 1973, c. 426, s. 60; 1985, c. 607, s. 1; 2005-426, s. 6(a).)

§ 160A-383. Purposes in view.

adopted comprehensive plan and any other officially adopted plan that is applicable, and briefly explaining why the board considers the action taken to be reasonable and in the public interest. That statement is not subject to judicial review.

The planning board shall advise and comment on whether the proposed amendment is consistent with any comprehensive plan that has been adopted and any other officially adopted plan that is applicable. The planning board shall provide a written recommendation to the governing board that addresses plan consistency and other matters as deemed appropriate by the planning board, but a comment by the planning board that a proposed amendment is inconsistent with the comprehensive plan shall not preclude consideration or approval of the proposed amendment by the governing board.

Zoning regulations shall be designed to promote the public health, safety, and general welfare. To that end, the regulations may address, among other things, the following public purposes: to provide adequate light and air; to prevent the overcrowding of land; to avoid undue concentration of population; to lessen congestion in the streets; to secure safety from fire, panic, and dangers; and to facilitate the efficient and adequate provision of transportation, water, sewerage, schools, parks, and other public requirements. The regulations shall be made with reasonable consideration, among other things, as to the character of the district and its peculiar suitability for particular uses, and with a view to conserving the value of buildings and encouraging the most appropriate use of land throughout such city. (1923, c. 250, s. 3; C.S., s. 2776(t); 1971, c. 698, s. 1; 2005-426, s. 7(a); 2006-259, s. 28.)

§ 160A-383.1. Zoning regulations for manufactured homes.

(a) The General Assembly finds and declares that manufactured housing offers affordable housing opportunities for low and moderate income residents of this State who could not otherwise afford to own their own home. The General Assembly further finds that some local governments have adopted zoning regulations which severely restrict the placement of manufactured homes. It is the intent of the General Assembly in enacting this section that cities reexamine their land use practices to assure compliance with applicable

(b)   For purposes of this section, the term "manufactured home" is defined as provided in G.S. 143-145(7).

(c)   A city may not adopt or enforce zoning regulations or other provisions which have the effect of excluding manufactured homes from the entire zoning jurisdiction.

(d)   A city may adopt and enforce appearance and dimensional criteria for manufactured homes. Such criteria shall be designed to protect property values, to preserve the character and integrity of the community or individual neighborhoods within the community, and to promote the health, safety and welfare of area residents. The criteria shall be adopted by ordinance.

(e)   In accordance with the city's comprehensive plan and based on local housing needs, a city may designate a manufactured home overlay district within a residential district. Such overlay district may not consist of an individual lot or scattered lots, but shall consist of a defined area within which additional requirements or standards are placed upon manufactured homes.

(f)   Nothing in this section shall be construed to preempt or supersede valid restrictive covenants running with the land. The terms "mobile home" and "trailer" in any valid restrictive covenants running with the land shall include the term "manufactured home" as defined in this section. (1987, c. 805, s. 1.)

§ 160A-383.2. Voluntary agricultural districts.

A city may amend the ordinances applicable within its planning jurisdiction to provide flexibility to farming operations that are located within a city or county voluntary agricultural district or enhanced voluntary agricultural district adopted under Article 61 of Chapter 106 of the General Statutes. Amendments to applicable ordinances may include provisions regarding on-farm sales, pick-your-own operations, road signs, agritourism, and other activities incident to farming. For purposes of this section, the term "farming" shall have the same meaning as set forth in G.S. 106-581.1. (2005-390, s. 7.)

regulates the placement, screening, or height of the antennas or support structures of amateur radio operators must reasonably accommodate amateur radio communications and must represent the minimum practicable regulation necessary to accomplish the purpose of the city. A city may not restrict antennas or antenna support structures of amateur radio operators to heights of 90 feet or lower unless the restriction is necessary to achieve a clearly defined health, safety, or aesthetic objective of the city. (2007-147, s. 1.)

§ 160A-383.4. Local energy efficiency incentives.

(a) Land-Use Development Incentives. - Counties and municipalities, for the purpose of reducing the amount of energy consumption by new development, and thereby promoting the public health, safety, and welfare, may adopt ordinances to grant a density bonus, make adjustments to otherwise applicable development requirements, or provide other incentives to a developer or builder within the county or municipality and its extraterritorial planning jurisdiction if the developer or builder agrees to construct new development or reconstruct existing development in a manner that the county or municipality determines, based on generally recognized standards established for such purposes, makes a significant contribution to the reduction of energy consumption.

(b) Repealed by Session Laws 2009-95, s. 1, effective June 11, 2009. (2007-241, ss. 1, 2; 2008-22, s. 1; 2009-95, s. 1.)

§ 160A-384. Method of procedure.

(a) The city council shall provide for the manner in which zoning regulations and restrictions and the boundaries of zoning districts shall be determined, established and enforced, and from time to time amended, supplemented or changed, in accordance with the provisions of this Article. The procedures adopted pursuant to this section shall provide that whenever there is a zoning map amendment, the owner of that parcel of land as shown on the county tax listing, and the owners of all parcels of land abutting that parcel of land as shown on the county tax listing, shall be mailed a notice of a public hearing on the proposed amendment by first class mail at the last addresses listed for such owners on the county tax abstracts. This notice must be deposited in the mail at

owner of the parcel of land to which the amendment would apply, the applicant shall certify to the city council that the owner of the parcel of land as shown on the county tax listing has received actual notice of the proposed amendment and a copy of the notice of public hearing. The person or persons required to provide notice shall certify to the city council that proper notice has been provided in fact, and such certificate shall be deemed conclusive in the absence of fraud.

(b)   The first class mail notice required under subsection (a) of this section shall not be required if the zoning map amendment directly affects more than 50 properties, owned by a total of at least 50 different property owners, and the city elects to use the expanded published notice provided for in this subsection. In this instance, a city may elect to either make the mailed notice provided for in subsection (a) of this section or may as an alternative elect to publish notice of the hearing as required by G.S. 160A-364, but provided that each advertisement shall not be less than one-half of a newspaper page in size. The advertisement shall only be effective for property owners who reside in the area of general circulation of the newspaper which publishes the notice. Property owners who reside outside of the newspaper circulation area, according to the address listed on the most recent property tax listing for the affected property, shall be notified according to the provisions of subsection (a) of this section.

(b1)   Actual notice of the proposed amendment and a copy of the notice of public hearing required under subsection (a) of this section shall be by any manner permitted under G.S. 1A-1, Rule 4(j). If notice cannot with due diligence be achieved by personal delivery, registered or certified mail, or by a designated delivery service authorized pursuant to 26 U.S.C. § 7502(f)(2), notice may be given by publication consistent with G.S. 1A-1, Rule 4(j1). This subsection applies only to an application to request a zoning map amendment where the application is not made by the owner of the parcel of land to which the amendment would apply. This subsection does not apply to a city-initiated zoning map amendment.

(c)   When a zoning map amendment is proposed, the city shall prominently post a notice of the public hearing on the site proposed for rezoning or on an adjacent public street or highway right-of-way. When multiple parcels are included within a proposed zoning map amendment, a posting on each individual parcel is not required, but the city shall post sufficient notices to

2005-418, s. 4(a); 2009-178, s. 2.)

§ 160A-385. Changes.

(a) Qualified Protests.

(1) Zoning ordinances may from time to time be amended, supplemented, changed, modified or repealed. In case, however, of a qualified protest against a zoning map amendment, that amendment shall not become effective except by favorable vote of three-fourths of all the members of the city council. For the purposes of this subsection, vacant positions on the council and members who are excused from voting shall not be considered "members of the council" for calculation of the requisite supermajority.

(2) To qualify as a protest under this section, the petition must be signed by the owners of either (i) twenty percent (20%) or more of the area included in the proposed change or (ii) five percent (5%) of a 100-foot-wide buffer extending along the entire boundary of each discrete or separate area proposed to be rezoned. A street right-of-way shall not be considered in computing the 100-foot buffer area as long as that street right-of-way is 100 feet wide or less. When less than an entire parcel of land is subject to the proposed zoning map amendment, the 100-foot buffer shall be measured from the property line of that parcel. In the absence of evidence to the contrary, the city may rely on the county tax listing to determine the "owners" of potentially qualifying areas.

(3) The foregoing provisions concerning protests shall not be applicable to any amendment which initially zones property added to the territorial coverage of the ordinance as a result of annexation or otherwise, or to an amendment to an adopted (i) special use district, (ii) conditional use district, or (iii) conditional district if the amendment does not change the types of uses that are permitted within the district or increase the approved density for residential development, or increase the total approved size of nonresidential development, or reduce the size of any buffers or screening approved for the special use district, conditional use district, or conditional district.

(b) Amendments in zoning ordinances shall not be applicable or enforceable without consent of the owner with regard to buildings and uses for

unrevoked pursuant to G.S. 160A-422 or (ii) a vested right has been established pursuant to G.S. 160A-385.1 and such vested right remains valid and unexpired pursuant to G.S. 160A-385.1. (1923, c. 250, s. 5; C.S., s. 2776(v); 1959, c. 434, s. 1; 1965, c. 864, s. 1; 1971, c. 698, s. 1; 1977, c. 912, s. 7; 1985, c. 540, s. 2; 1989 (Reg. Sess., 1990), c. 996, s. 1; 1991, c. 512, s. 4; 2005-418, s. 5.)

§ 160A-385.1. Vested rights.

(a)   The General Assembly finds and declares that it is necessary and desirable, as a matter of public policy, to provide for the establishment of certain vested rights in order to ensure reasonable certainty, stability, and fairness in the land-use planning process, secure the reasonable expectations of landowners, and foster cooperation between the public and private sectors in the area of land-use planning. Furthermore, the General Assembly recognizes that city approval of land-use development typically follows significant landowner investment in site evaluation, planning, development costs, consultant fees, and related expenses.

The ability of a landowner to obtain a vested right after city approval of a site specific development plan or a phased development plan will preserve the prerogatives and authority of local elected officials with respect to land-use matters. There will be ample opportunities for public participation and the public interest will be served. These provisions will strike an appropriate balance between private expectations and the public interest, while scrupulously protecting the public health, safety, and welfare.

(b)   Definitions.

(1)   "Landowner" means any owner of a legal or equitable interest in real property, including the heirs, devisees, successors, assigns, and personal representative of such owner. The landowner may allow a person holding a valid option to purchase to act as his agent or representative for purposes of submitting a proposed site specific development plan or a phased development plan under this section, in the manner allowed by ordinance.

(2)   "City" shall have the same meaning as set forth in G.S. 160A-1(2).

than the plan determined by the city to be a site specific development plan.

(4)   "Property" means all real property subject to zoning regulations and restrictions and zone boundaries by a city.

(5)   "Site specific development plan" means a plan which has been submitted to a city by a landowner describing with reasonable certainty the type and intensity of use for a specific parcel or parcels of property. Such plan may be in the form of, but not limited to, any of the following plans or approvals: A planned unit development plan, a subdivision plat, a preliminary or general development plan, a conditional or special use permit, a conditional or special use district zoning plan, or any other land-use approval designation as may be utilized by a city. Unless otherwise expressly provided by the city, such a plan shall include the approximate boundaries of the site; significant topographical and other natural features effecting development of the site; the approximate location on the site of the proposed buildings, structures, and other improvements; the approximate dimensions, including height, of the proposed buildings and other structures; and the approximate location of all existing and proposed infrastructure on the site, including water, sewer, roads, and pedestrian walkways. What constitutes a site specific development plan under this section that would trigger a vested right shall be finally determined by the city pursuant to an ordinance, and the document that triggers such vesting shall be so identified at the time of its approval. However, at a minimum, the ordinance to be adopted by the city shall designate a vesting point earlier than the issuance of a building permit. A variance shall not constitute a site specific development plan, and approval of a site specific development plan with the condition that a variance be obtained shall not confer a vested right unless and until the necessary variance is obtained. Neither a sketch plan nor any other document which fails to describe with reasonable certainty the type and intensity of use for a specified parcel or parcels of property may constitute a site specific development plan.

(6)   "Vested right" means the right to undertake and complete the development and use of property under the terms and conditions of an approved site specific development plan or an approved phased development plan.

(c)   Establishment of vested right.

a phased development plan, following notice and public hearing by the city with jurisdiction over the property. Such vested right shall confer upon the landowner the right to undertake and complete the development and use of said property under the terms and conditions of the site specific development plan or the phased development plan including any amendments thereto. A city may approve a site specific development plan or a phased development plan upon such terms and conditions as may reasonably be necessary to protect the public health, safety, and welfare. Such conditional approval shall result in a vested right, although failure to abide by such terms and conditions will result in a forfeiture of vested rights. A city shall not require a landowner to waive his vested rights as a condition of developmental approval. A site specific development plan or a phase development plan shall be deemed approved upon the effective date of the city's action or ordinance relating thereto.

(d) Duration and termination of vested right.

(1) A right which has been vested as provided for in this section shall remain vested for a period of two years. This vesting shall not be extended by any amendments or modifications to a site specific development plan unless expressly provided by the city.

(2) Notwithstanding the provisions of subsection (d)(1), a city may provide that rights shall be vested for a period exceeding two years but not exceeding five years where warranted in light of all relevant circumstances, including, but not limited to, the size and phasing of development, the level of investment, the need for the development, economic cycles, and market conditions. These determinations shall be in the sound discretion of the city.

(3) Notwithstanding the provisions of (d)(1) and (d)(2), the city may provide by ordinance that approval by a city of a phased development plan shall vest the zoning classification or classifications so approved for a period not to exceed five years. The document that triggers such vesting shall be so identified at the time of its approval. The city still may require the landowner to submit a site specific development plan for approval by the city with respect to each phase or phases in order to obtain final approval to develop within the restrictions of the vested zoning classification or classifications. Nothing in this section shall be construed to require a city to adopt an ordinance providing for vesting of rights upon approval of a phased development plan.

plan from subsequent reviews and approvals by the city to ensure compliance with the terms and conditions of the original approval, provided that such reviews and approvals are not inconsistent with said original approval. Nothing in this section shall prohibit the city from revoking the original approval for failure to comply with applicable terms and conditions of the approval or the zoning ordinance.

(5)   Upon issuance of a building permit, the provisions of G.S. 160A-418 and G.S. 160A-422 shall apply, except that a permit shall not expire or be revoked because of the running of time while a vested right under this section is outstanding.

(6)   A right which has been vested as provided in this section shall terminate at the end of the applicable vesting period with respect to buildings and uses for which no valid building permit applications have been filed.

(e)   Subsequent changes prohibited; exceptions.

(1)   A vested right, once established as provided for in this section, precludes any zoning action by a city which would change, alter, impair, prevent, diminish, or otherwise delay the development or use of the property as set forth in an approved site specific development plan or an approved phased development plan, except:

a.   With the written consent of the affected landowner;

b.   Upon findings, by ordinance after notice and a public hearing, that natural or man-made hazards on or in the immediate vicinity of the property, if uncorrected, would pose a serious threat to the public health, safety, and welfare if the project were to proceed as contemplated in the site specific development plan or the phased development plan;

c.   To the extent that the affected landowner receives compensation for all costs, expenses, and other losses incurred by the landowner, including, but not limited to, all fees paid in consideration of financing, and all architectural, planning, marketing, legal, and other consultant's fees incurred after approval by the city, together with interest thereon at the legal rate until paid. Compensation

d. Upon findings, by ordinance after notice and a hearing, that the landowner or his representative intentionally supplied inaccurate information or made material misrepresentations which made a difference in the approval by the city of the site specific development plan or the phased development plan; or

e. Upon the enactment or promulgation of a State or federal law or regulation which precludes development as contemplated in the site specific development plan or the phased development plan, in which case the city may modify the affected provisions, upon a finding that the change in State or federal law has a fundamental effect on the plan, by ordinance after notice and a hearing.

(2) The establishment of a vested right shall not preclude the application of overlay zoning which imposes additional requirements but does not affect the allowable type or intensity of use, or ordinances or regulations which are general in nature and are applicable to all property subject to land-use regulation by a city, including, but not limited to, building, fire, plumbing, electrical, and mechanical codes. Otherwise applicable new regulations shall become effective with respect to property which is subject to a site specific development plan or a phased development plan upon the expiration or termination of the vesting rights period provided for in this section.

(3) Notwithstanding any provision of this section, the establishment of a vested right shall not preclude, change or impair the authority of a city to adopt and enforce zoning ordinance provisions governing nonconforming situations or uses.

(f) Miscellaneous provisions.

(1) A vested right obtained under this section is not a personal right, but shall attach to and run with the applicable property. After approval of a site specific development plan or a phased development plan, all successors to the original landowner shall be entitled to exercise such rights.

(2) Nothing in this section shall preclude judicial determination, based on common law principles or other statutory provisions, that a vested right exists in a particular case or that a compensable taking has occurred. Except as

(3) In the event a city fails to adopt an ordinance setting forth what constitutes a site specific development plan triggering a vested right, a landowner may establish a vested right with respect to property upon the approval of a zoning permit, or otherwise may seek appropriate relief from the Superior Court Division of the General Court of Justice. (1989 (Reg. Sess., 1990), c. 996, s. 2.)

§ 160A-386. Protest petition; form; requirements; time for filing.

No protest against any change in or amendment to a zoning ordinance or zoning map shall be valid or effective for the purposes of G.S. 160A-385 unless it be in the form of a written petition actually bearing the signatures of the requisite number of property owners and stating that the signers do protest the proposed change or amendment, and unless it shall have been received by the city clerk in sufficient time to allow the city at least two normal work days, excluding Saturdays, Sundays and legal holidays, before the date established for a public hearing on the proposed change or amendment to determine the sufficiency and accuracy of the petition. The city council may by ordinance require that all protest petitions be on a form prescribed and furnished by the city, and such form may prescribe any reasonable information deemed necessary to permit the city to determine the sufficiency and accuracy of the petition. A person who has signed a protest petition may withdraw his or her name from the petition at any time prior to the vote on the proposed zoning amendment. Only those protest petitions that meet the qualifying standards set forth in G.S. 160A-385 at the time of the vote on the zoning amendment shall trigger the supermajority voting requirement. (1963, c. 1058, s. 2; 1971, c. 698, s. 1; 2005-418, s. 6.)

§ 160A-387. Planning board; zoning plan; certification to city council.

In order to initially exercise the powers conferred by this Part, a city council shall create or designate a planning board under the provisions of this Article or of a special act of the General Assembly. The planning board shall prepare or shall review and comment upon a proposed zoning ordinance, including both the full text of such ordinance and maps showing proposed district boundaries. The council shall not hold its required public hearing or take action until it has received a recommendation regarding ordinance from the planning board. Following its required public hearing, the city council may refer the ordinance back to the planning board for any further recommendations that the board may wish to make prior to final action by the city council in adopting, modifying and adopting, or rejecting the ordinance.

Subsequent to initial adoption of a zoning ordinance, all proposed amendments to the zoning ordinance or zoning map shall be submitted to the planning board for review and comment. If no written report is received from the planning board within 30 days of referral of the amendment to that board, the governing board may proceed in its consideration of the amendment without the planning board report. The governing board is not bound by the recommendations, if any, of the planning board. (1923, c. 250, s. 6; C.S., s. 2776(w); 1967, c. 1208, s. 2; 1971, c. 698, s. 1; 1973, c. 426, s. 60; 1977, c. 912, s. 8; 2005-418, s. 7(a).)

§ 160A-388. Board of adjustment.

(a) Composition and Duties. - The zoning or unified development ordinance may provide for the appointment and compensation of a board of adjustment consisting of five or more members, each to be appointed for three years. In appointing the original members or in the filling of vacancies caused by the expiration of the terms of existing members, the city council may appoint certain members for less than three years so that the terms of all members shall not expire at the same time. The council may appoint and provide compensation for alternate members to serve on the board in the absence or temporary disqualification of any regular member or to fill a vacancy pending appointment of a member. Alternate members shall be appointed for the same term, at the same time, and in the same manner as regular members. Each alternate member serving on behalf of any regular member has all the powers and duties of a regular member. The ordinance may designate a planning board or governing board to perform any of the duties of a board of adjustment in addition to its other duties and may create and designate specialized boards to hear technical appeals.

(a1) Provisions of Ordinance. - The zoning or unified development ordinance may provide that the board of adjustment hear and decide special and

requirement, or determination. The board of adjustment shall follow quasi-judicial procedures when deciding appeals and requests for variances and special and conditional use permits. The board shall hear and decide all matters upon which it is required to pass under any statute or ordinance that regulates land use or development.

(a2) Notice of Hearing. - Notice of hearings conducted pursuant to this section shall be mailed to the person or entity whose appeal, application, or request is the subject of the hearing; to the owner of the property that is the subject of the hearing if the owner did not initiate the hearing; to the owners of all parcels of land abutting the parcel of land that is the subject of the hearing; and to any other persons entitled to receive notice as provided by the zoning or unified development ordinance. In the absence of evidence to the contrary, the city may rely on the county tax listing to determine owners of property entitled to mailed notice. The notice must be deposited in the mail at least 10 days, but not more than 25 days, prior to the date of the hearing. Within that same time period, the city shall also prominently post a notice of the hearing on the site that is the subject of the hearing or on an adjacent street or highway right-of-way.

(b) Repealed by Session Laws 2013-126, s. 1, effective October 1, 2013, and applicable to actions taken on or after that date by any board of adjustment.

(b1) Appeals. - The board of adjustment shall hear and decide appeals from decisions of administrative officials charged with enforcement of the zoning or unified development ordinance and may hear appeals arising out of any other ordinance that regulates land use or development, pursuant to all of the following:

(1) Any person who has standing under G.S. 160A-393(d) or the city may appeal a decision to the board of adjustment. An appeal is taken by filing a notice of appeal with the city clerk. The notice of appeal shall state the grounds for the appeal.

(2) The official who made the decision shall give written notice to the owner of the property that is the subject of the decision and to the party who sought the decision, if different from the owner. The written notice shall be delivered by personal delivery, electronic mail, or by first-class mail.

of the decision within which to file an appeal.

(4) It shall be conclusively presumed that all persons with standing to appeal have constructive notice of the decision from the date a sign containing the words "Zoning Decision" or "Subdivision Decision" in letters at least six inches high and identifying the means to contact an official for information about the decision is prominently posted on the property that is the subject of the decision, provided the sign remains on the property for at least 10 days. Posting of signs is not the only form of constructive notice. Any such posting shall be the responsibility of the landowner or applicant. Verification of the posting shall be provided to the official who made the decision. Absent an ordinance provision to the contrary, posting of signs shall not be required.

(5) The official who made the decision shall transmit to the board all documents and exhibits constituting the record upon which the action appealed from is taken. The official shall also provide a copy of the record to the appellant and to the owner of the property that is the subject of the appeal if the appellant is not the owner.

(6) An appeal of a notice of violation or other enforcement order stays enforcement of the action appealed from unless the official who made the decision certifies to the board of adjustment after notice of appeal has been filed that because of the facts stated in an affidavit, a stay would cause imminent peril to life or property or because the violation is transitory in nature, a stay would seriously interfere with enforcement of the ordinance. In that case, enforcement proceedings shall not be stayed except by a restraining order, which may be granted by a court. If enforcement proceedings are not stayed, the appellant may file with the official a request for an expedited hearing of the appeal, and the board of adjustment shall meet to hear the appeal within 15 days after such a request is filed. Notwithstanding the foregoing, appeals of decisions granting a permit or otherwise affirming that a proposed use of property is consistent with the ordinance shall not stay the further review of an application for permits or permissions to use such property; in these situations the appellant may request and the board may grant a stay of a final decision of permit applications or building permits affected by the issue being appealed.

(7) Subject to the provisions of subdivision (6) of this subsection, the board of adjustment shall hear and decide the appeal within a reasonable time.

presentation of matters not presented in the notice of appeal, the board shall continue the hearing. The board of adjustment may reverse or affirm, wholly or partly, or may modify the decision appealed from and shall make any order, requirement, decision, or determination that ought to be made. The board shall have all the powers of the official who made the decision.

(9) When hearing an appeal pursuant to G.S. 160A-400.9(e) or any other appeal in the nature of certiorari, the hearing shall be based on the record below and the scope of review shall be as provided in G.S. 160A-393(k).

(10) The parties to an appeal that has been made under this subsection may agree to mediation or other forms of alternative dispute resolution. The ordinance may set standards and procedures to facilitate and manage such voluntary alternative dispute resolution.

(c) Special and Conditional Use Permits. - The ordinance may provide that the board of adjustment may hear and decide special and conditional use permits in accordance with standards and procedures specified in the ordinance. Reasonable and appropriate conditions may be imposed upon these permits.

(d) Variances. - When unnecessary hardships would result from carrying out the strict letter of a zoning ordinance, the board of adjustment shall vary any of the provisions of the ordinance upon a showing of all of the following:

(1) Unnecessary hardship would result from the strict application of the ordinance. It shall not be necessary to demonstrate that, in the absence of the variance, no reasonable use can be made of the property.

(2) The hardship results from conditions that are peculiar to the property, such as location, size, or topography. Hardships resulting from personal circumstances, as well as hardships resulting from conditions that are common to the neighborhood or the general public, may not be the basis for granting a variance.

(3) The hardship did not result from actions taken by the applicant or the property owner. The act of purchasing property with knowledge that

(4) The requested variance is consistent with the spirit, purpose, and intent of the ordinance, such that public safety is secured, and substantial justice is achieved.

No change in permitted uses may be authorized by variance. Appropriate conditions may be imposed on any variance, provided that the conditions are reasonably related to the variance. Any other ordinance that regulates land use or development may provide for variances consistent with the provisions of this subsection.

(e) Voting. -

(1) The concurring vote of four-fifths of the board shall be necessary to grant a variance. A majority of the members shall be required to decide any other quasi-judicial matter or to determine an appeal made in the nature of certiorari. For the purposes of this subsection, vacant positions on the board and members who are disqualified from voting on a quasi-judicial matter shall not be considered members of the board for calculation of the requisite majority if there are no qualified alternates available to take the place of such members.

(2) A member of any board exercising quasi-judicial functions pursuant to this Article shall not participate in or vote on any quasi-judicial matter in a manner that would violate affected persons' constitutional rights to an impartial decision maker. Impermissible violations of due process include, but are not limited to, a member having a fixed opinion prior to hearing the matter that is not susceptible to change, undisclosed ex parte communications, a close familial, business, or other associational relationship with an affected person, or a financial interest in the outcome of the matter. If an objection is raised to a member's participation and that member does not recuse himself or herself, the remaining members shall by majority vote rule on the objection.

(e1) Recodified as subdivision (e)(2) by Session Laws 2013-126, s. 1, effective October 1, 2013, and applicable to actions taken on or after that date by any board of adjustment.

(e2) Quasi-Judicial Decisions and Judicial Review. -

shall be reduced to writing and reflect the board's determination of contested facts and their application to the applicable standards. The written decision shall be signed by the chair or other duly authorized member of the board. A quasi-judicial decision is effective upon filing the written decision with the clerk to the board or such other office or official as the ordinance specifies. The decision of the board shall be delivered by personal delivery, electronic mail, or by first-class mail to the applicant, property owner, and to any person who has submitted a written request for a copy, prior to the date the decision becomes effective. The person required to provide notice shall certify that proper notice has been made.

(2) Every quasi-judicial decision shall be subject to review by the superior court by proceedings in the nature of certiorari pursuant to G.S. 160A-393. A petition for review shall be filed with the clerk of superior court by the later of 30 days after the decision is effective or after a written copy thereof is given in accordance with subdivision (1) of this subsection. When first-class mail is used to deliver notice, three days shall be added to the time to file the petition.

(f) Oaths. - The chair of the board or any member acting as chair and the clerk to the board are authorized to administer oaths to witnesses in any matter coming before the board. Any person who, while under oath during a proceeding before the board of adjustment, willfully swears falsely is guilty of a Class 1 misdemeanor.

(g) Subpoenas. - The board of adjustment through the chair, or in the chair's absence anyone acting as chair, may subpoena witnesses and compel the production of evidence. To request issuance of a subpoena, persons with standing under G.S. 160A-393(d) may make a written request to the chair explaining why it is necessary for certain witnesses or evidence to be compelled. The chair shall issue requested subpoenas he or she determines to be relevant, reasonable in nature and scope, and not oppressive. The chair shall rule on any motion to quash or modify a subpoena. Decisions regarding subpoenas made by the chair may be appealed to the full board of adjustment. If a person fails or refuses to obey a subpoena issued pursuant to this subsection, the board of adjustment or the party seeking the subpoena may apply to the General Court of Justice for an order requiring that its subpoena be obeyed, and the court shall have jurisdiction to issue these orders after notice to all proper parties. (1923, c. 250, s. 7; C.S., s. 2776(x); 1929, c. 94, s. 1; 1947,

c. 512, s. 2; 1993, c. 539, s. 1088; 1994, Ex. Sess., c. 24, s. 14(c); 2005-418, s. 8(a); 2009-421, s. 5; 2013-126, ss. 1, 2(a), 2(b); 2013-410, s. 25(a).)

§ 160A-389. Remedies.

If a building or structure is erected, constructed, reconstructed, altered, repaired, converted, or maintained, or any building, structure or land is used in violation of this Part or of any ordinance or other regulation made under authority conferred thereby, the city, in addition to other remedies, may institute any appropriate action or proceedings to prevent the unlawful erection, construction, reconstruction, alteration, repair, conversion, maintenance or use, to restrain, correct or abate the violation, to prevent occupancy of the building, structure or land, or to prevent any illegal act, conduct, business or use in or about the premises. (1923, c. 250, s. 8; C.S., s. 2776(y); 1971, c. 698, s. 1.)

§ 160A-390. Conflict with other laws.

When regulations made under authority of this Part require a greater width or size of yards or courts, or require a lower height of a building or fewer number of stories, or require a greater percentage of a lot to be left unoccupied, or impose other higher standards than are required in any other statute or local ordinance or regulation, regulations made under authority of this Part shall govern. When the provisions of any other statute or local ordinance or regulation require a greater width or size of yards or courts, or require a lower height of a building or a fewer number of stories, or require a greater percentage of a lot to be left unoccupied, or impose other higher standards than are required by the regulations made under authority of this Part, the provisions of that statute or local ordinance or regulation shall govern. (1923, c. 250, s. 9; C.S., s. 2776(z); 1971, c. 698, s. 1.)

§ 160A-391. Other statutes not repealed.

This Part shall not repeal any zoning act or city planning act, local or general, now in force, except those that are repugnant to or inconsistent herewith. This Part shall be construed to be an enlargement of the duties, powers, and

1971, c. 698, s. 1.)

§ 160A-392. Part applicable to buildings constructed by State and its subdivisions; exception.

All of the provisions of this Part are hereby made applicable to the erection, construction, and use of buildings by the State of North Carolina and its political subdivisions.

Notwithstanding the provisions of any general or local law or ordinance, no land owned by the State of North Carolina may be included within an overlay district or a special use or conditional use district without approval of the Council of State. (1951, c. 1203, s. 1; 1971, c. 698, s. 1; 1985, c. 607, s. 2; 2004-199, s. 41(e); 2005-280, s. 1.)

§ 160A-393. Appeals in the nature of certiorari.

(a)   Applicability. - This section applies to appeals of quasi-judicial decisions of decision-making boards when that appeal is to superior court and in the nature of certiorari as required by this Article.

(b)   For purposes of this section, the following terms mean:

(1)   Decision-making board. - A city council, planning board, board of adjustment, or other board making quasi-judicial decisions appointed by the city council under this Article or under comparable provisions of any local act or any interlocal agreement authorized by law.

(2)   Person. - Any legal entity authorized to bring suit in the legal entity's name.

(3)   Quasi-judicial decision. - A decision involving the finding of facts regarding a specific application of an ordinance and the exercise of discretion when applying the standards of the ordinance. Quasi-judicial decisions include decisions involving variances, special and conditional use permits, and appeals of administrative determinations. Decisions on the approval of site plans are

whether the application complies with one or more generally stated standards requiring a discretionary decision on the findings of fact to be made by the decision-making board.

(c)   Filing the Petition. - An appeal in the nature of certiorari shall be initiated by filing with the superior court a petition for writ of certiorari. The petition shall:

(1)   State the facts that demonstrate that the petitioner has standing to seek review.

(2)   Set forth the grounds upon which the petitioner contends that an error was made.

(3)   Set forth with particularity the allegations and facts, if any, in support of allegations that, as the result of impermissible conflict as described in G.S. 160A-388(e)(2), or locally adopted conflict rules, the decision-making body was not sufficiently impartial to comply with due process principles.

(4)   Set forth the relief the petitioner seeks.

(d)   Standing. - A petition may be filed under this section only by a petitioner who has standing to challenge the decision being appealed. The following persons shall have standing to file a petition under this section:

(1)   Any person meeting any of the following criteria:

a.   Has an ownership interest in the property that is the subject of the decision being appealed, a leasehold interest in the property that is the subject of the decision being appealed, or an interest created by easement, restriction, or covenant in the property that is the subject of the decision being appealed.

b.   Has an option or contract to purchase the property that is the subject of the decision being appealed.

c.   Was an applicant before the decision-making board whose decision is being appealed.

(3) An incorporated or unincorporated association to which owners or lessees of property in a designated area belong by virtue of their owning or leasing property in that area, or an association otherwise organized to protect and foster the interest of the particular neighborhood or local area, so long as at least one of the members of the association would have standing as an individual to challenge the decision being appealed, and the association was not created in response to the particular development or issue that is the subject of the appeal.

(4) A city whose decision-making board has made a decision that the council believes improperly grants a variance from or is otherwise inconsistent with the proper interpretation of an ordinance adopted by that council.

(e) Respondent. - The respondent named in the petition shall be the city whose decision-making board made the decision that is being appealed, except that if the petitioner is a city that has filed a petition pursuant to subdivision (4) of subsection (d) of this section, then the respondent shall be the decision-making board. If the petitioner is not the applicant before the decision-making board whose decision is being appealed, the petitioner shall also name that applicant as a respondent. Any petitioner may name as a respondent any person with an ownership or leasehold interest in the property that is the subject of the decision being appealed who participated in the hearing, or was an applicant, before the decision-making board.

(f) Writ of Certiorari. - Upon filing the petition, the petitioner shall present the petition and a proposed writ of certiorari to the clerk of superior court of the county in which the matter arose. The writ shall direct the respondent city, or the respondent decision-making board if the petitioner is a city that has filed a petition pursuant to subdivision (4) of subsection (d) of this section, to prepare and certify to the court the record of proceedings below within a specified date. The writ shall also direct that the petitioner shall serve the petition and the writ upon each respondent named therein in the manner provided for service of a complaint under Rule 4(j) of the Rules of Civil Procedure, except that, if the respondent is a decision-making board, the petition and the writ shall be served upon the chair of that decision-making board. Rule 4(j)(5)d. of the Rules of Civil Procedure shall apply in the event the chair of a decision-making board cannot be found. No summons shall be issued. The clerk shall issue the writ without notice to the respondent or respondents if the petition has been properly filed

(g) Answer to the Petition. - The respondent may, but need not, file an answer to the petition, except that, if the respondent contends that any petitioner lacks standing to bring the appeal, that contention must be set forth in an answer served on all petitioners at least 30 days prior to the hearing on the petition.

(h) Intervention. - Rule 24 of the Rules of Civil Procedure shall govern motions to intervene as a petitioner or respondent in an action initiated under this section with the following exceptions:

(1) Any person described in subdivision (1) of subsection (d) of this section shall have standing to intervene and shall be allowed to intervene as a matter of right.

(2) Any person, other than one described in subdivision (1) of subsection (d) of this section, who seeks to intervene as a petitioner must demonstrate that the person would have had standing to challenge the decision being appealed in accordance with subdivisions (2) through (4) of subsection (d) of this section.

(3) Any person, other than one described in subdivision (d)(1) of this section, who seeks to intervene as a respondent must demonstrate that the person would have had standing to file a petition in accordance with subdivisions (2) through (4) of subsection (d) of this section if the decision-making board had made a decision that is consistent with the relief sought by the petitioner.

(i) The Record. - The record shall consist of all documents and exhibits submitted to the decision-making board whose decision is being appealed, together with the minutes of the meeting or meetings at which the decision being appealed was considered. Upon request of any party, the record shall also contain an audio or videotape of the meeting or meetings at which the decision being appealed was considered if such a recording was made. Any party may also include in the record a transcript of the proceedings, which shall be prepared at the cost of the party choosing to include it. The parties may agree, or the court may direct, that matters unnecessary to the court's decision be deleted from the record or that matters other than those specified herein be included. The record shall be bound and paginated or otherwise organized for the convenience of the parties and the court. A copy of the record shall be

(j) Hearing on the Record. - The court shall hear and decide all issues raised by the petition by reviewing the record submitted in accordance with subsection (h) of this section. Except that the court may, in its discretion, allow the record to be supplemented with affidavits, testimony of witnesses, or documentary or other evidence if, and to the extent that, the record is not adequate to allow an appropriate determination of the following issues:

(1) Whether a petitioner or intervenor has standing.

(2) Whether, as a result of impermissible conflict as described in G.S. 160A-388(e)(2), or locally adopted conflict rules, the decision-making body was not sufficiently impartial to comply with due process principles.

(3) Whether the decision-making body erred for the reasons set forth in sub-subdivisions a. and b. of subdivision (1) of subsection (k) of this section.

(k) Scope of Review. -

(1) When reviewing the decision of a decision-making board under the provisions of this section, the court shall ensure that the rights of petitioners have not been prejudiced because the decision-making body's findings, inferences, conclusions, or decisions were:

a. In violation of constitutional provisions, including those protecting procedural due process rights.

b. In excess of the statutory authority conferred upon the city or the authority conferred upon the decision-making board by ordinance.

c. Inconsistent with applicable procedures specified by statute or ordinance.

d. Affected by other error of law.

e. Unsupported by substantial competent evidence in view of the entire record.

f. Arbitrary or capricious.

bound by that interpretation, and may freely substitute its judgment as appropriate.

(3) The term "competent evidence," as used in this subsection, shall not preclude reliance by the decision-making board on evidence that would not be admissible under the rules of evidence as applied in the trial division of the General Court of Justice if (i) the evidence was admitted without objection or (ii) the evidence appears to be sufficiently trustworthy and was admitted under such circumstances that it was reasonable for the decision-making board to rely upon it. The term "competent evidence," as used in this subsection, shall not be deemed to include the opinion testimony of lay witnesses as to any of the following:

a. The use of property in a particular way would affect the value of other property.

b. The increase in vehicular traffic resulting from a proposed development would pose a danger to the public safety.

c. Matters about which only expert testimony would generally be admissible under the rules of evidence.

(l) Decision of the Court. - Following its review of the decision-making board in accordance with subsection (k) of this section, the court may affirm the decision, reverse the decision and remand the case with appropriate instructions, or remand the case for further proceedings. If the court does not affirm the decision below in its entirety, then the court shall be guided by the following in determining what relief should be granted to the petitioners:

(1) If the court concludes that the error committed by the decision-making board is procedural only, the court may remand the case for further proceedings to correct the procedural error.

(2) If the court concludes that the decision-making board has erred by failing to make findings of fact such that the court cannot properly perform its function, then the court may remand the case with appropriate instructions so long as the record contains substantial competent evidence that could support the decision below with appropriate findings of fact. However, findings of fact

(3) If the court concludes that the decision by the decision-making board is not supported by substantial competent evidence in the record or is based upon an error of law, then the court may remand the case with an order that directs the decision-making board to take whatever action should have been taken had the error not been committed or to take such other action as is necessary to correct the error. Specifically:

a. If the court concludes that a permit was wrongfully denied because the denial was not based on substantial competent evidence or was otherwise based on an error of law, the court may remand with instructions that the permit be issued, subject to reasonable and appropriate conditions.

b. If the court concludes that a permit was wrongfully issued because the issuance was not based on substantial competent evidence or was otherwise based on an error of law, the court may remand with instructions that the permit be revoked.

(m) Ancillary Injunctive Relief. - Upon motion of a party to a proceeding under this section, and under appropriate circumstances, the court may issue an injunctive order requiring any other party to that proceeding to take certain action or refrain from taking action that is consistent with the court's decision on the merits of the appeal. (2009-421, s. 1(a); 2013-126, ss. 13, 14.)

§ 160A-394. Reserved for future codification purposes.

Part 3A. Historic Districts.

§§ 160A-395 through 160A-399: Repealed by Session Laws 1989, c. 706, s. 1.

Part 3B. Historic Properties Commissions.

§§ 160A-399.1 through 160A-400: Repealed by Session Laws 1989, c. 706.

The historical heritage of our State is one of our most valued and important assets. The conservation and preservation of historic districts and landmarks stabilize and increase property values in their areas and strengthen the overall economy of the State. This Part authorizes cities and counties of the State within their respective zoning jurisdictions and by means of listing, regulation, and acquisition:

(1)   To safeguard the heritage of the city or county by preserving any district or landmark therein that embodies important elements of its culture, history, architectural history, or prehistory; and

(2)   To promote the use and conservation of such district or landmark for the education, pleasure and enrichment of the residents of the city or county and the State as a whole. (1989, c. 706, s. 2.)

§ 160A-400.2. Exercise of powers by counties as well as cities.

The term "municipality" or "municipal" as used in G.S. 160A-400.1 through 160A-400.14 shall be deemed to include the governing board or legislative board of a county, to the end that counties may exercise the same powers as cities with respect to the establishment of historic districts and designation of landmarks. (1989, c. 706, s. 2; 1989 (Reg. Sess., 1990), c. 1024, s. 40.)

§ 160A-400.3. Character of historic district defined.

Historic districts established pursuant to this Part shall consist of areas which are deemed to be of special significance in terms of their history, prehistory, architecture, and/or culture, and to possess integrity of design, setting, materials, feeling, and association. (1989, c. 706, s. 2.)

§ 160A-400.4. Designation of historic districts.

(a)   Any municipal governing board may, as part of a zoning or other ordinance enacted or amended pursuant to this Article, designate and from time

historic districts are designated as separate use districts, the zoning ordinance may include as uses by right or as conditional uses those uses found by the Preservation Commission to have existed during the period sought to be restored or preserved, or to be compatible with the restoration or preservation of the district.

(b)   No historic district or districts shall be designated under subsection (a) of this section until:

(1)   An investigation and report describing the significance of the buildings, structures, features, sites or surroundings included in any such proposed district, and a description of the boundaries of such district has been prepared, and

(2)   The Department of Cultural Resources, acting through the State Historic Preservation Officer or his or her designee, shall have made an analysis of and recommendations concerning such report and description of proposed boundaries. Failure of the department to submit its written analysis and recommendations to the municipal governing board within 30 calendar days after a written request for such analysis has been received by the Department of Cultural Resources shall relieve the municipality of any responsibility for awaiting such analysis, and said board may at any time thereafter take any necessary action to adopt or amend its zoning ordinance.

(c)   The municipal governing board may also, in its discretion, refer the report and proposed boundaries under subsection (b) of this section to any local preservation commission or other interested body for its recommendations prior to taking action to amend the zoning ordinance. With respect to any changes in the boundaries of such district subsequent to its initial establishment, or the creation of additional districts within the jurisdiction, the investigative studies and reports required by subdivision (1) of subsection (b) of this section shall be prepared by the preservation commission, and shall be referred to the local planning agency for its review and comment according to procedures set forth in the zoning ordinance. Changes in the boundaries of an initial district or proposal for additional districts shall also be submitted to the Department of Cultural Resources in accordance with the provisions of subdivision (2) of subsection (b) of this section.

(d) The provisions of G.S. 160A-201 apply to zoning or other ordinances pertaining to historic districts, and the authority under G.S. 160A-201(b) for the ordinance to regulate the location or screening of solar collectors may encompass requiring the use of plantings or other measures to ensure that the use of solar collectors is not incongruous with the special character of the district. (1989, c. 706, s. 2; 2009-553, s. 4.)

§ 160A-400.5. Designation of landmarks; adoption of an ordinance; criteria for designation.

Upon complying with G.S. 160A-400.6, the governing board may adopt and from time to time amend or repeal an ordinance designating one or more historic landmarks. No property shall be recommended for designation as a historic landmark unless it is deemed and found by the preservation commission to be of special significance in terms of its historical, prehistorical, architectural, or cultural importance, and to possess integrity of design, setting, workmanship, materials, feeling and/or association.

The ordinance shall describe each property designated in the ordinance, the name or names of the owner or owners of the property, those elements of the property that are integral to its historical, architectural, or prehistorical value, including the land area of the property so designated, and any other information the governing board deems necessary. For each building, structure, site, area, or object so designated as a historic landmark, the ordinance shall require that the waiting period set forth in this Part be observed prior to its demolition. For each designated landmark, the ordinance may also provide for a suitable sign on the property indicating that the property has been so designated. If the owner consents, the sign shall be placed upon the property. If the owner objects, the sign shall be placed on a nearby public right-of-way. (1989, c. 706, s. 2.)

§ 160A-400.6. Required landmark designation procedures.

As a guide for the identification and evaluation of landmarks, the commission shall undertake, at the earliest possible time and consistent with the resources

the Office of Archives and History. No ordinance designating a historic building, structure, site, area or object as a landmark nor any amendment thereto may be adopted, nor may any property be accepted or acquired by a preservation commission or the governing board of a municipality, until all of the following procedural steps have been taken:

(1) The preservation commission shall (i) prepare and adopt rules of procedure, and (ii) prepare and adopt principles and guidelines, not inconsistent with this Part, for altering, restoring, moving, or demolishing properties designated as landmarks.

(2) The preservation commission shall make or cause to be made an investigation and report on the historic, architectural, prehistorical, educational or cultural significance of each building, structure, site, area or object proposed for designation or acquisition. Such investigation or report shall be forwarded to the Office of Archives and History, North Carolina Department of Cultural Resources.

(3) The Department of Cultural Resources, acting through the State Historic Preservation Officer shall either upon request of the department or at the initiative of the preservation commission be given an opportunity to review and comment upon the substance and effect of the designation of any landmark pursuant to this Part. Any comments shall be provided in writing. If the Department does not submit its comments or recommendation in connection with any designation within 30 days following receipt by the Department of the investigation and report of the commission, the commission and any city or county governing board shall be relieved of any responsibility to consider such comments.

(4) The preservation commission and the governing board shall hold a joint public hearing or separate public hearings on the proposed ordinance. Reasonable notice of the time and place thereof shall be given. All meetings of the commission shall be open to the public, in accordance with the North Carolina Open Meetings Law, Chapter 143, Article 33C.

(5) Following the joint public hearing or separate public hearings, the governing board may adopt the ordinance as proposed, adopt the ordinance with any amendments it deems necessary, or reject the proposed ordinance.

amendments thereto shall be filed by the preservation commission in the office of the register of deeds of the county in which the landmark or landmarks are located. In the case of any landmark property lying within the zoning jurisdiction of a city, a second copy of the ordinance and all amendments thereto shall be kept on file in the office of the city or town clerk and be made available for public inspection at any reasonable time. A third copy of the ordinance and all amendments thereto shall be given to the city or county building inspector. The fact that a building, structure, site, area or object has been designated a landmark shall be clearly indicated on all tax maps maintained by the county or city for such period as the designation remains in effect.

(7) Upon the adoption of the landmarks ordinance or any amendment thereto, it shall be the duty of the preservation commission to give notice thereof to the tax supervisor of the county in which the property is located. The designation and any recorded restrictions upon the property limiting its use for preservation purposes shall be considered by the tax supervisor in appraising it for tax purposes. (1989, c. 706, s. 2; 2002-159, s. 35(m); 2012-18, s. 1.24.)

§ 160A-400.7. Historic Preservation Commission.

Before it may designate one or more landmarks or historic districts, a municipality shall establish or designate a historic preservation commission. The municipal governing board shall determine the number of the members of the commission, which shall be at least three, and the length of their terms, which shall be no greater than four years. A majority of the members of such a commission shall have demonstrated special interest, experience, or education in history, architecture, archaeology, or related fields. All the members shall reside within the territorial jurisdiction of the municipality as established pursuant to G.S. 160A-360. The commission may appoint advisory bodies and committees as appropriate.

In lieu of establishing a historic preservation commission, a municipality may designate as its historic preservation commission, (i) a separate historic districts commission or a separate historic landmarks commission established pursuant to this Part to deal only with historic districts or landmarks respectively, (ii) a planning board established pursuant to this Article, or (iii) a community appearance commission established pursuant to Part 7 of this Article. In order

discretion of the municipality the ordinance may also provide that the preservation commission may exercise within a historic district any or all of the powers of a planning board or a community appearance commission.

A county and one or more cities in the county may establish or designate a joint preservation commission. If a joint commission is established or designated, the county and cities involved shall determine the residence requirements of members of the joint preservation commission. (1989, c. 706, s. 2; 2005-418, s. 12.)

§ 160A-400.8. Powers of the Historic Preservation Commission.

A preservation commission established pursuant to this Part may, within the zoning jurisdiction of the municipality:

(1) Undertake an inventory of properties of historical, prehistorical, architectural, and/or cultural significance;

(2) Recommend to the municipal governing board areas to be designated by ordinance as "Historic Districts"; and individual structures, buildings, sites, areas, or objects to be designated by ordinance as "Landmarks";

(3) Acquire by any lawful means the fee or any lesser included interest, including options to purchase, to properties within established districts or to any such properties designated as landmarks, to hold, manage, preserve, restore and improve the same, and to exchange or dispose of the property by public or private sale, lease or otherwise, subject to covenants or other legally binding restrictions which will secure appropriate rights of public access and promote the preservation of the property;

(4) Restore, preserve and operate historic properties;

(5) Recommend to the governing board that designation of any area as a historic district or part thereof, or designation of any building, structure, site, area, or object as a landmark, be revoked or removed for cause;

(7) Cooperate with the State, federal, and local governments in pursuance of the purposes of this Part. The governing board or the commission when authorized by the governing board may contract with the State, or the United States of America, or any agency of either, or with any other organization provided the terms are not inconsistent with State or federal law;

(8) Enter, solely in performance of its official duties and only at reasonable times, upon private lands for examination or survey thereof. However, no member, employee or agent of the commission may enter any private building or structure without the express consent of the owner or occupant thereof;

(9) Prepare and recommend the official adoption of a preservation element as part of the municipality's comprehensive plan;

(10) Review and act upon proposals for alterations, demolitions, or new construction within historic districts, or for the alteration or demolition of designated landmarks, pursuant to this Part; and

(11) Negotiate at any time with the owner of a building, structure, site, area, or object for its acquisition or its preservation, when such action is reasonably necessary or appropriate. (1989, c. 706, s. 2.)

§ 160A-400.9. Certificate of appropriateness required.

(a) From and after the designation of a landmark or a historic district, no exterior portion of any building or other structure (including masonry walls, fences, light fixtures, steps and pavement, or other appurtenant features), nor above-ground utility structure nor any type of outdoor advertising sign shall be erected, altered, restored, moved, or demolished on such landmark or within such district until after an application for a certificate of appropriateness as to exterior features has been submitted to and approved by the preservation commission. The municipality shall require such a certificate to be issued by the commission prior to the issuance of a building permit or other permit granted for the purposes of constructing, altering, moving, or demolishing structures, which certificate may be issued subject to reasonable conditions necessary to carry out the purposes of this Part. A certificate of appropriateness shall be required whether or not a building or other permit is required.

structure, including the kind and texture of the building material, the size and scale of the building, and the type and style of all windows, doors, light fixtures, signs, and other appurtenant fixtures. In the case of outdoor advertising signs, "exterior features" shall be construed to mean the style, material, size, and location of all such signs. Such "exterior features" may, in the discretion of the local governing board, include historic signs, color, and significant landscape, archaeological, and natural features of the area.

Except as provided in (b) below, the commission shall have no jurisdiction over interior arrangement and shall take no action under this section except to prevent the construction, reconstruction, alteration, restoration, moving, or demolition of buildings, structures, appurtenant fixtures, outdoor advertising signs, or other significant features in the district which would be incongruous with the special character of the landmark or district.

(b)   Notwithstanding subsection (a) of this section, jurisdiction of the commission over interior spaces shall be limited to specific interior features of architectural, artistic or historical significance in publicly owned landmarks; and of privately owned historic landmarks for which consent for interior review has been given by the owner. Said consent of an owner for interior review shall bind future owners and/or successors in title, provided such consent has been filed in the office of the register of deeds of the county in which the property is located and indexed according to the name of the owner of the property in the grantee and grantor indexes. The landmark designation shall specify the interior features to be reviewed and the specific nature of the commission's jurisdiction over the interior.

(c)   Prior to any action to enforce a landmark or historic district ordinance, the commission shall (i) prepare and adopt rules of procedure, and (ii) prepare and adopt principles and guidelines not inconsistent with this Part for new construction, alterations, additions, moving and demolition. The ordinance may provide, subject to prior adoption by the preservation commission of detailed standards, for the review and approval by an administrative official of applications for a certificate of appropriateness or of minor works as defined by ordinance; provided, however, that no application for a certificate of appropriateness may be denied without formal action by the preservation commission.

affected by the application, and shall give the applicant and such owners an opportunity to be heard. In cases where the commission deems it necessary, it may hold a public hearing concerning the application. All meetings of the commission shall be open to the public, in accordance with the North Carolina Open Meetings Law, Chapter 143, Article 33C.

(d)   All applications for certificates of appropriateness shall be reviewed and acted upon within a reasonable time, not to exceed 180 days from the date the application for a certificate of appropriateness is filed, as defined by the ordinance or the commission's rules of procedure. As part of its review procedure, the commission may view the premises and seek the advice of the Division of Archives and History or such other expert advice as it may deem necessary under the circumstances.

(e)   An appeal may be taken to the Board of Adjustment from the commission's action in granting or denying any certificate, which appeals (i) may be taken by any aggrieved party, (ii) shall be taken within times prescribed by the preservation commission by general rule, and (iii) shall be in the nature of certiorari. Any appeal from the Board of Adjustment's decision in any such case shall be heard by the superior court of the county in which the municipality is located.

(f)   All of the provisions of this Part are hereby made applicable to construction, alteration, moving and demolition by the State of North Carolina, its political subdivisions, agencies and instrumentalities, provided however they shall not apply to interiors of buildings or structures owned by the State of North Carolina. The State and its agencies shall have a right of appeal to the North Carolina Historical Commission or any successor agency assuming its responsibilities under G.S. 121-12(a) from any decision of a local preservation commission. The commission shall render its decision within 30 days from the date that the notice of appeal by the State is received by it. The current edition of the Secretary of the Interior's Standards for Rehabilitation and Guidelines for Rehabilitating Historic Buildings shall be the sole principles and guidelines used in reviewing applications of the State for certificates of appropriateness. The decision of the commission shall be final and binding upon both the State and the preservation commission. (1989, c. 706, s. 2.)

period or imposes other higher standards with respect to a designated historic landmark or district than are established under any other statute, charter provision, or regulation, this Part shall govern. Whenever the provisions of any other statute, charter provision, ordinance or regulation require a longer waiting period or impose other higher standards than are established under this Part, such other statute, charter provision, ordinance or regulation shall govern. (1989, c. 706, s. 2.)

§ 160A-400.11. Remedies.

In case any building, structure, site, area or object designated as a historic landmark or located within a historic district designated pursuant to this Part is about to be demolished whether as the result of deliberate neglect or otherwise, materially altered, remodeled, removed or destroyed, except in compliance with the ordinance or other provisions of this Part, the city or county, the historic preservation commission, or other party aggrieved by such action may institute any appropriate action or proceedings to prevent such unlawful demolition, destruction, material alteration, remodeling or removal, to restrain, correct or abate such violation, or to prevent any illegal act or conduct with respect to such building, structure, site, area or object. Such remedies shall be in addition to any others authorized by this Chapter for violation of a municipal ordinance. (1989, c. 706, s. 2.)

§ 160A-400.12. Appropriations.

A city or county governing board is authorized to make appropriations to a historic preservation commission established pursuant to this Part in any amount that it may determine necessary for the expenses of the operation of the commission, and may make available any additional amounts necessary for the acquisition, restoration, preservation, operation, and management of historic buildings, structures, sites, areas or objects designated as historic landmarks or within designated historic districts, or of land on which such buildings or structures are located, or to which they may be removed. (1989, c. 706, s. 2.)

repair of any exterior architectural feature in a historic district or of a landmark which does not involve a change in design, material or appearance thereof, nor to prevent the construction, reconstruction, alteration, restoration, moving or demolition of any such feature which the building inspector or similar official shall certify is required by the public safety because of an unsafe or dangerous condition. Nothing in this Part shall be construed to prevent a property owner from making any use of his property that is not prohibited by other law. Nothing in this Part shall be construed to prevent a) the maintenance, or b) in the event of an emergency the immediate restoration, of any existing above-ground utility structure without approval by the preservation commission. (1989, c. 706, s. 2.)

§ 160A-400.14. Delay in demolition of landmarks and buildings within historic district.

(a) An application for a certificate of appropriateness authorizing the relocation, demolition or destruction of a designated landmark or a building, structure or site within the district may not be denied except as provided in subsection (c). However, the effective date of such a certificate may be delayed for a period of up to 365 days from the date of approval. The maximum period of delay authorized by this section shall be reduced by the commission where it finds that the owner would suffer extreme hardship or be permanently deprived of all beneficial use of or return from such property by virtue of the delay. During such period the preservation commission shall negotiate with the owner and with any other parties in an effort to find a means of preserving the building or site. If the preservation commission finds that a building or site within a district has no special significance or value toward maintaining the character of the district, it shall waive all or part of such period and authorize earlier demolition, or removal.

If the commission or planning board has voted to recommend designation of a property as a landmark or designation of an area as a district, and final designation has not been made by the local governing board, the demolition or destruction of any building, site, or structure located on the property of the proposed landmark or in the proposed district may be delayed by the commission or planning board for a period of up to 180 days or until the local governing board takes final action on the designation, whichever occurs first.

appropriate safeguards to protect property owners from undue economic hardship.

(c) An application for a certificate of appropriateness authorizing the demolition or destruction of a building, site, or structure determined by the State Historic Preservation Officer as having statewide significance as defined in the criteria of the National Register of Historic Places may be denied except where the commission finds that the owner would suffer extreme hardship or be permanently deprived of all beneficial use or return by virtue of the denial. (1989, c. 706, s. 2; 1991, c. 514, s. 1; 2005-418, s. 13.)

§ 160A-400.15. Demolition by neglect to contributing structures outside local historic districts.

Notwithstanding G.S. 160A-400.14 or any other provision of law, the governing board of any municipality may apply its demolition by neglect ordinances to contributing structures located outside the local historic district within an adjacent central business district. The governing board may modify and revise its demolition by neglect ordinances as necessary to implement this section and to further its intent. This section is applicable to any municipality with a population in excess of 100,000, provided such municipality (i) has designated portions of the central business district and its adjacent historic district as an Urban Progress Zone as defined in G.S. 143B-437.09 and (ii) is recognized by the State Historic Preservation Office and the U.S. Department of the Interior as a Certified Local Government in accordance with the National Historic Preservation Act of 1966, as amended (16 U.S.C. § 470, et seq.), and the applicable federal regulations (36 C.F.R. Part 61), but is located in a county that has not received the same certification. (2011-367, s. 1.)

§ 160A-400.16. Reserved for future codification purposes.

§ 160A-400.17. Reserved for future codification purposes.

§ 160A-400.18. Reserved for future codification purposes.

§ 160A-400.19. Reserved for future codification purposes.

(a) The General Assembly finds:

(1) Large-scale development projects often occur in multiple phases extending over a period of years, requiring a long-term commitment of both public and private resources.

(2) Such large-scale developments often create potential community impacts and potential opportunities that are difficult or impossible to accommodate within traditional zoning processes.

(3) Because of their scale and duration, such large-scale projects often require careful integration between public capital facilities planning, financing, and construction schedules and the phasing of the private development.

(4) Because of their scale and duration, such large-scale projects involve substantial commitments of private capital by developers, which developers are usually unwilling to risk without sufficient assurances that development standards will remain stable through the extended period of the development.

(5) Because of their size and duration, such developments often permit communities and developers to experiment with different or nontraditional types of development concepts and standards, while still managing impacts on the surrounding areas.

(6) To better structure and manage development approvals for such large-scale developments and ensure their proper integration into local capital facilities programs, local governments need the flexibility in negotiating such developments.

(b) Local governments and agencies may enter into development agreements with developers, subject to the procedures and requirements of this Part. In entering into such agreements, a local government may not exercise any authority or make any commitment not authorized by general or local act and may not impose any tax or fee not authorized by otherwise applicable law.

(c) This Part is supplemental to the powers conferred upon local governments and does not preclude or supersede rights and obligations

§ 160A-400.21. Definitions.

The following definitions apply in this Part:

(1) Comprehensive plan. - The comprehensive plan, land-use plan, small area plans, neighborhood plans, transportation plan, capital improvement plan, official map, and any other plans regarding land use and development that have been officially adopted by the governing board.

(2) Developer. - A person, including a governmental agency or redevelopment authority, who intends to undertake any development and who has a legal or equitable interest in the property to be developed.

(3) Development. - The planning for or carrying out of a building activity, the making of a material change in the use or appearance of any structure or property, or the dividing of land into two or more parcels. "Development", as designated in a law or development permit, includes the planning for and all other activity customarily associated with it unless otherwise specified. When appropriate to the context, "development" refers to the planning for or the act of developing or to the result of development. Reference to a specific operation is not intended to mean that the operation or activity, when part of other operations or activities, is not development. Reference to particular operations is not intended to limit the generality of this item.

(4) Development permit. - A building permit, zoning permit, subdivision approval, special or conditional use permit, variance, or any other official action of local government having the effect of permitting the development of property.

(5) Governing body. - The city council of a municipality.

(6) Land development regulations. - Ordinances and regulations enacted by the appropriate governing body for the regulation of any aspect of development and includes zoning, subdivision, or any other land development ordinances.

(7) Laws. - All ordinances, resolutions, regulations, comprehensive plans, land development regulations, policies, and rules adopted by a local

(8) Local government. - Any municipality that exercises regulatory authority over and grants development permits for land development or which provides public facilities.

(9) Local planning board. - Any planning board established pursuant to G.S. 160A-361.

(10) Person. - An individual, corporation, business or land trust, estate, trust, partnership, association, two or more persons having a joint or common interest, State agency, or any legal entity.

(11) Property. - All real property subject to land-use regulation by a local government and includes any improvements or structures customarily regarded as a part of real property.

(12) Public facilities. - Major capital improvements, including, but not limited to, transportation, sanitary sewer, solid waste, drainage, potable water, educational, parks and recreational, and health systems and facilities. (2005-426, s. 9(a).)

§ 160A-400.22. Local governments authorized to enter into development agreements; approval of governing body required.

A local government may establish procedures and requirements, as provided in this Part, to consider and enter into development agreements with developers. A development agreement must be approved by the governing body of a local government by ordinance. (2005-426, s. 9(a).)

§ 160A-400.23. Developed property must contain certain number of acres; permissible durations of agreements.

(a) A local government may enter into a development agreement with a developer for the development of property as provided in this Part, provided the property contains 25 acres or more of developable property (exclusive of wetlands, mandatory buffers, unbuildable slopes, and other portions of the property which may be precluded from development at the time of application).

(b) Notwithstanding the acreage requirements of subsection (a) of this section, a local government may enter into a development agreement with a developer for the development of property as provided in this Part for developable property of any size (exclusive of wetlands, mandatory buffers, unbuildable slopes, and other portions of the property which may be precluded from development at the time of application), if the developable property that would be subject to the development agreement is subject to an executed brownfields agreement pursuant to Part 5 of Article 9 of Chapter 130A of the General Statutes. Development agreements shall be of a term specified in the agreement, provided they may not be for a term exceeding 20 years. (2005-426, s. 9(a); 2013-413, s. 44(b).)

§ 160A-400.24. Public hearing.

Before entering into a development agreement, a local government shall conduct a public hearing on the proposed agreement following the procedures set forth in G.S. 160A-364 regarding zoning ordinance adoption or amendment. The notice for the public hearing must specify the location of the property subject to the development agreement, the development uses proposed on the property, and must specify a place where a copy of the proposed development agreement can be obtained. In the event that the development agreement provides that the local government shall provide certain public facilities, the development agreement shall provide that the delivery date of such public facilities will be tied to successful performance by the developer in implementing the proposed development (such as meeting defined completion percentages or other performance standards). (2005-426, s. 9(a).)

§ 160A-400.25. What development agreement must provide; what it may provide; major modification requires public notice and hearing.

(a) A development agreement shall at a minimum include all of the following:

(1) A legal description of the property subject to the agreement and the names of its legal and equitable property owners.

(3) The development uses permitted on the property, including population densities and building types, intensities, placement on the site, and design.

(4) A description of public facilities that will service the development, including who provides the facilities, the date any new public facilities, if needed, will be constructed, and a schedule to assure public facilities are available concurrent with the impacts of the development.

(5) A description, where appropriate, of any reservation or dedication of land for public purposes and any provisions to protect environmentally sensitive property.

(6) A description of all local development permits approved or needed to be approved for the development of the property together with a statement indicating that the failure of the agreement to address a particular permit, condition, term, or restriction does not relieve the developer of the necessity of complying with the law governing their permitting requirements, conditions, terms, or restrictions.

(7) A description of any conditions, terms, restrictions, or other requirements determined to be necessary by the local government for the public health, safety, or welfare of its citizens.

(8) A description, where appropriate, of any provisions for the preservation and restoration of historic structures.

(b) A development agreement may provide that the entire development or any phase of it be commenced or completed within a specified period of time. The development agreement must provide a development schedule, including commencement dates and interim completion dates at no greater than five-year intervals; provided, however, the failure to meet a commencement or completion date shall not, in and of itself, constitute a material breach of the development agreement pursuant to G.S. 160A-400.27 but must be judged based upon the totality of the circumstances. The development agreement may include other defined performance standards to be met by the developer. The developer may request a modification in the dates as set forth in the agreement. Consideration

(c) If more than one local government is made party to an agreement, the agreement must specify which local government is responsible for the overall administration of the development agreement.

(d) The development agreement also may cover any other matter not inconsistent with this Part. (2005-426, s. 9(a).)

§ 160A-400.26. Law in effect at time of agreement governs development; exceptions.

(a) Unless the development agreement specifically provides for the application of subsequently enacted laws, the laws applicable to development of the property subject to a development agreement are those in force at the time of execution of the agreement.

(b) Except for grounds specified in G.S. 160A-385.1(e), a local government may not apply subsequently adopted ordinances or development policies to a development that is subject to a development agreement.

(c) In the event State or federal law is changed after a development agreement has been entered into and the change prevents or precludes compliance with one or more provisions of the development agreement, the local government may modify the affected provisions, upon a finding that the change in State or federal law has a fundamental effect on the development agreement, by ordinance after notice and a hearing.

(d) This section does not abrogate any rights preserved by G.S. 160A-385 or G.S. 160A-385.1, or that may vest pursuant to common law or otherwise in the absence of a development agreement. (2005-426, s. 9(a).)

§ 160A-400.27. Periodic review to assess compliance with agreement; material breach by developer; notice of breach; cure of breach or modification or termination of agreement.

(a) Procedures established pursuant to G.S. 160A-400.22 must include a provision for requiring periodic review by the zoning administrator or other

(b) If, as a result of a periodic review, the local government finds and determines that the developer has committed a material breach of the terms or conditions of the agreement, the local government shall serve notice in writing, within a reasonable time after the periodic review, upon the developer setting forth with reasonable particularity the nature of the breach and the evidence supporting the finding and determination, and providing the developer a reasonable time in which to cure the material breach.

(c) If the developer fails to cure the material breach within the time given, then the local government unilaterally may terminate or modify the development agreement; provided, the notice of termination or modification may be appealed to the board of adjustment in the manner provided by G.S. 160A-388(b). (2005-426, s. 9(a).)

§ 160A-400.28. Amendment or cancellation of development agreement by mutual consent of parties or successors in interest.

A development agreement may be amended or canceled by mutual consent of the parties to the agreement or by their successors in interest. (2005-426, s. 9(a).)

§ 160A-400.29. Validity and duration of agreement entered into prior to change of jurisdiction; subsequent modification or suspension.

(a) Except as otherwise provided by this Part, any development agreement entered into by a local government before the effective date of a change of jurisdiction shall be valid for the duration of the agreement, or eight years from the effective date of the change in jurisdiction, whichever is earlier. The parties to the development agreement and the local government assuming jurisdiction have the same rights and obligations with respect to each other regarding matters addressed in the development agreement as if the property had remained in the previous jurisdiction.

(b) A local government assuming jurisdiction may modify or suspend the provisions of the development agreement if the local government determines

(2005-426, s. 9(a).)

§ 160A-400.30. Developer to record agreement within 14 days; burdens and benefits inure to successors in interest.

Within 14 days after a local government enters into a development agreement, the developer shall record the agreement with the register of deeds in the county where the property is located. The burdens of the development agreement are binding upon, and the benefits of the agreement shall inure to, all successors in interest to the parties to the agreement. (2005-426, s. 9(a).)

§ 160A-400.31. Applicability to local government of constitutional and statutory procedures for approval of debt.

In the event that any of the obligations of the local government in the development agreement constitute debt, the local government shall comply, at the time of the obligation to incur the debt and before the debt becomes enforceable against the local government, with any applicable constitutional and statutory procedures for the approval of this debt. (2005-426, s. 9(a).)

§ 160A-400.32. Relationship of agreement to building or housing code.

A development agreement adopted pursuant to this Chapter shall not exempt the property owner or developer from compliance with the State Building Code or State or local housing codes that are not part of the local government's planning, zoning, or subdivision regulations. (2005-426, s. 9(a).)

Part 3E. Wireless Telecommunications Facilities.

§ 160A-400.50. Purpose and compliance with federal law.

(a) The purpose of this section is to ensure the safe and efficient integration of facilities necessary for the provision of advanced mobile broadband and wireless telecommunications services throughout the community and to ensure

(a1) The deployment of wireless infrastructure is critical to ensuring first responders can provide for the health and safety of all residents of North Carolina and that, consistent with section 6409 of the federal Middle Class Tax Relief and Job Creation Act of 2012, 47 U.S.C. § 1455(a), which creates a national wireless emergency communications network for use by first responders that in large measure will be dependent on facilities placed on existing wireless communications support structures, it is the policy of this State to facilitate the placement of wireless communications support structures in all areas of North Carolina. The following standards shall apply to a city's actions, as a regulatory body, in the regulation of the placement, construction, or modification of a wireless communications facility.

(b) The placement, construction, or modification of wireless communications facilities shall be in conformity with the Federal Communications Act, 47 U.S.C. § 332 as amended, section 6409 of the federal Middle Class Tax Relief and Job Creation Act of 2012, 47 U.S.C. § 1455(a), and in accordance with the rules promulgated by the Federal Communications Commission. (2007-526, s. 1; 2013-185, s. 1.)

§ 160A-400.51. Definitions.

The following definitions apply in this Part.

(1) Antenna. - Communications equipment that transmits, receives, or transmits and receives electromagnetic radio signals used in the provision of all types of wireless communications services.

(2) Application. - A formal request submitted to the city to construct or modify a wireless support structure or a wireless facility.

(2a) Base station. - A station at a specific site authorized to communicate with mobile stations, generally consisting of radio receivers, antennas, coaxial cables, power supplies, and other associated electronics.

(4) Collocation. - The placement or installation of wireless facilities on existing structures, including electrical transmission towers, water towers, buildings, and other structures capable of structurally supporting the attachment of wireless facilities in compliance with applicable codes.

(4a) Eligible facilities request. - A request for modification of an existing wireless tower or base station that involves collocation of new transmission equipment or replacement of transmission equipment but does not include a substantial modification.

(5) Equipment compound. - An area surrounding or near the base of a wireless support structure within which a wireless facility is located.

(5a) Fall zone. - The area in which a wireless support structure may be expected to fall in the event of a structural failure, as measured by engineering standards.

(6) Land development regulation. - Any ordinance enacted pursuant to this Part.

(7) Search ring. - The area within which a wireless support facility or wireless facility must be located in order to meet service objectives of the wireless service provider using the wireless facility or wireless support structure.

(7a) Substantial modification. - The mounting of a proposed wireless facility on a wireless support structure that substantially changes the physical dimensions of the support structure. A mounting is presumed to be a substantial modification if it meets any one or more of the criteria listed below. The burden is on the local government to demonstrate that a mounting that does not meet the listed criteria constitutes a substantial change to the physical dimensions of the wireless support structure.

a. Increasing the existing vertical height of the structure by the greater of (i) more than ten percent (10%) or (ii) the height of one additional antenna array with separation from the nearest existing antenna not to exceed 20 feet.

the wireless support structure the greater of (i) more than 20 feet or (ii) more than the width of the wireless support structure at the level of the appurtenance.

c.   Increasing the square footage of the existing equipment compound by more than 2,500 square feet.

(8)   Utility pole. - A structure that is designed for and used to carry lines, cables, or wires for telephone, cable television, or electricity, or to provide lighting.

(8a)   Water tower. - A water storage tank, a standpipe, or an elevated tank situated on a support structure originally constructed for use as a reservoir or facility to store or deliver water.

(9)   Wireless facility. - The set of equipment and network components, exclusive of the underlying wireless support structure or tower, including antennas, transmitters, receivers, base stations, power supplies, cabling, and associated equipment necessary to provide wireless data and wireless telecommunications services to a discrete geographic area.

(10)   Wireless support structure. - A new or existing structure, such as a monopole, lattice tower, or guyed tower that is designed to support or capable of supporting wireless facilities. A utility pole is not a wireless support structure. (2007-526, s. 1; 2013-185, s. 1.)

§ 160A-400.51A. Local authority.

A city may plan for and regulate the siting or modification of wireless support structures and wireless facilities in accordance with land development regulations and in conformity with this Part. Except as expressly stated, nothing in this Part shall limit a city from regulating applications to construct, modify, or maintain wireless support structures, or construct, modify, maintain, or collocate wireless facilities on a wireless support structure based on consideration of land use, public safety, and zoning considerations, including aesthetics, landscaping, structural design, setbacks, and fall zones, or State and local building code requirements, consistent with the provisions of federal law provided in G.S. 160A-400.50. For purposes of this Part, public safety includes, without limitation,

§ 160A-400.52. Construction of new wireless support structures or substantial modifications of wireless support structures.

(a)   Repealed by Session Laws 2013-185, s. 1, effective October 1, 2013, and applicable to applications received on or after that date.

(b)   Any person that proposes to construct a new wireless support structure or substantially modify a wireless support structure within the planning and land-use jurisdiction of a city must do both of the following:

(1)   Submit a completed application with the necessary copies and attachments to the appropriate planning authority.

(2)   Comply with any local ordinances concerning land use and any applicable permitting processes.

(c)   A city's review of an application for the placement or construction of a new wireless support structure or substantial modification of a wireless support structure shall only address public safety, land development, or zoning issues. In reviewing an application, the city may not require information on or evaluate an applicant's business decisions about its designed service, customer demand for its service, or quality of its service to or from a particular area or site. A city may not require information that concerns the specific need for the wireless support structure, including if the service to be provided from the wireless support structure is to add additional wireless coverage or additional wireless capacity. A city may not require proprietary, confidential, or other business information to justify the need for the new wireless support structure, including propagation maps and telecommunication traffic studies. In reviewing an application, the city may review the following:

(1)   Applicable public safety, land use, or zoning issues addressed in its adopted regulations, including aesthetics, landscaping, land-use based location priorities, structural design, setbacks, and fall zones.

(2)   Information or materials directly related to an identified public safety, land development, or zoning issue including evidence that no existing or previously approved wireless support structure can reasonably be used for the

support structure or initial wireless facility placement or a proposed height increase of a substantially modified wireless support structure, or replacement wireless support structure is necessary to provide the applicant's designed service.

(3)   A city may require applicants for new wireless facilities to evaluate the reasonable feasibility of collocating new antennas and equipment on an existing wireless support structure or structures within the applicant's search ring. Collocation on an existing wireless support structure is not reasonably feasible if collocation is technically or commercially impractical or the owner of the existing wireless support structure is unwilling to enter into a contract for such use at fair market value. Cities may require information necessary to determine whether collocation on existing wireless support structures is reasonably feasible.

(d)   Repealed by Session Laws 2013-185, s. 1, effective October 1, 2013, and applicable to applications received on or after that date.

(e)   The city shall issue a written decision approving or denying an application under this section within a reasonable period of time consistent with the issuance of other land-use permits in the case of other applications, each as measured from the time the application is deemed complete.

(f)   A city may fix and charge an application fee, consulting fee, or other fee associated with the submission, review, processing, and approval of an application to site new wireless support structures or to substantially modify wireless support structures or wireless facilities that is based on the costs of the services provided and does not exceed what is usual and customary for such services. Any charges or fees assessed by a city on account of an outside consultant shall be fixed in advance and incorporated into a permit or application fee and shall be based on the reasonable costs to be incurred by the city in connection with the regulatory review authorized under this section. The foregoing does not prohibit a city from imposing additional reasonable and cost based fees for costs incurred should an applicant amend its application. On request, the amount of the consultant charges incorporated into the permit or application fee shall be separately identified and disclosed to the applicant. The fee imposed by a city for review of the application may not be used for either of the following:

(2)   Reimbursements for a consultant or other third party based on a contingent fee basis or a results-based arrangement.

(g)   The city may condition approval of an application for a new wireless support structure on the provision of documentation prior to the issuance of a building permit establishing the existence of one or more parties, including the owner of the wireless support structure, who intend to locate wireless facilities on the wireless support structure. A city shall not deny an initial land-use or zoning permit based on such documentation. A city may condition a permit on a requirement to construct facilities within a reasonable period of time, which shall be no less than 24 months.

(h)   The city may not require the placement of wireless support structures or wireless facilities on city owned or leased property, but may develop a process to encourage the placement of wireless support structures or facilities on city owned or leased property, including an expedited approval process.

(i)   This section shall not be construed to limit the provisions or requirements of any historic district or landmark regulation adopted pursuant to Part 3C of this Article. (2007-526, s. 1; 2013-185, s. 1.)

§ 160A-400.53. Collocation and eligible facilities requests of wireless support structures.

(a)   Pursuant to section 6409 of the federal Middle Class Tax Relief and Job Creation Act of 2012, 47 U.S.C. § 1455(a), a city may not deny and shall approve any eligible facilities request as provided in this section. Nothing in this Part requires an application and approval for routine maintenance or limits the performance of routine maintenance on wireless support structures and facilities, including in-kind replacement of wireless facilities. Routine maintenance includes activities associated with regular and general upkeep of transmission equipment, including the replacement of existing wireless facilities with facilities of the same size. A city may require an application for collocation or an eligible facilities request.

(a1)   A collocation or eligible facilities request application is deemed complete unless the city provides notice that the application is incomplete in writing to the

application incomplete if there is insufficient evidence provided to show that the proposed collocation or eligible facilities request will comply with federal, State, and local safety requirements. A city may not deem an application incomplete for any issue not directly related to the actual content of the application and subject matter of the collocation or eligible facilities request. An application is deemed complete on resubmission if the additional materials cure the deficiencies indicated.

(a2) The city shall issue a written decision approving an eligible facilities request application within 45 days of such application being deemed complete. For a collocation application that is not an eligible facilities request, the city shall issue its written decision to approve or deny the application within 45 days of the application being deemed complete.

(a3) A city may impose a fee not to exceed one thousand dollars ($1,000) for technical consultation and the review of a collocation or eligible facilities request application. The fee must be based on the actual, direct, and reasonable administrative costs incurred for the review, processing, and approval of a collocation application. A city may engage a third-party consultant for technical consultation and the review of a collocation application. The fee imposed by a city for the review of the application may not be used for either of the following:

(1) Travel expenses incurred in a third-party's review of a collocation application.

(2) Reimbursement for a consultant or other third party based on a contingent fee basis or results-based arrangement.

(b), (c) Repealed by Session Laws 2013-185, s. 1, effective October 1, 2013, and applicable to applications received on or after that date. (2007-526, s. 1; 2013-185, s. 1.)

§ 160A-400.54. Reserved for future codification purposes.

§ 160A-400.55. Reserved for future codification purposes.

§ 160A-400.56. Reserved for future codification purposes.

Part 4. Acquisition of Open Space.

§ 160A-401. Legislative intent.

It is the intent of the General Assembly in enacting this Part to provide a means whereby any county or city may acquire, by purchase, gift, grant, devise, lease, or otherwise, and through the expenditure of public funds, the fee or any lesser interest or right in real property in order to preserve, through limitation of their future use, open spaces and areas for public use and enjoyment. (1963, c. 1129, s. 1; 1971, c. 698, s. 1; 2011-284, s. 116.)

§ 160A-402. Finding of necessity.

The General Assembly finds that the rapid growth and spread of urban development in the State is encroaching upon, or eliminating, many open areas and spaces of varied size and character, including many having significant scenic or esthetic values, which areas and spaces if preserved and maintained in their present open state would constitute important physical, social, esthetic, or economic assets to existing and impending urban development. The General Assembly declares that it is necessary for sound and proper urban development and in the public interest of the people of this State for any county or city to expend or advance public funds for, or to accept by purchase, gift, grant, devise, lease, or otherwise, the fee or any lesser interest or right in real property so as to acquire, maintain, improve, protect, limit the future use of, or otherwise conserve open spaces and areas within their respective jurisdictions as defined by this Article.

The General Assembly declares that the acquisition of interests or rights in real property for the preservation of open spaces and areas constitutes a public purpose for which public funds may be expended or advanced. (1963, c. 1129, s. 2; 1971, c. 698, s. 1; 2011-284, s. 117.)

Any county or city in the State may acquire by purchase, gift, grant, devise, lease, or otherwise, the fee or any lesser interest, development right, easement, covenant, or other contractual right of or to real property within its respective jurisdiction, when it finds that the acquisition is necessary to achieve the purposes of this Part. Any county or city may also acquire the fee to any property for the purpose of conveying or leasing the property back to its original owner or other person under covenants or other contractual arrangements that will limit the future use of the property in accordance with the purposes of this Part, but when this is done, the property may be conveyed back to its original owner but to no other person by private sale. (1963, c. 1129, s. 3; 1971, c. 698, s. 1; 2011-284, s. 118.)

§ 160A-404. Joint action by governing bodies.

Any county or city may enter into any agreement with any other county or city for the purpose of jointly exercising the authority granted by this Part. (1963, c. 1129, s. 4; 1971, c. 698, s. 1.)

§ 160A-405. Powers of governing bodies.

Any county or city, in order to exercise the authority granted by this Part, may:

(1) Enter into and carry out contracts with the State or federal government or any agencies thereof under which grants or other assistance are made to the county or city;

(2) Accept any assistance or funds that may be granted by the State or federal government with or without a contract;

(3) Agree to and comply with any reasonable conditions imposed upon grants;

(4) Make expenditures from any funds so granted. (1963, c. 1129, s. 5; 1971, c. 698, s. 1.)

not otherwise limited as to use by law. (1963, c. 1129, s. 6; 1971, c. 698, s. 1; 1973, c. 426, s. 60; 1975, c. 664, s. 14.)

§ 160A-407. Definitions.

(a) For the purpose of this Part an "open space" or "open area" is any space or area (i) characterized by great natural scenic beauty or (ii) whose existing openness, natural condition, or present state of use, if retained, would enhance the present or potential value of abutting or surrounding urban development, or would maintain or enhance the conservation of natural or scenic resources.

(b) For the purposes of this Part "open space" or "open area" and the "public use and enjoyment" of interests or rights in real property shall also include open space land and open space uses. The term "open space land" means any undeveloped or predominantly undeveloped land in an urban area that has value for one or more of the following purposes: (i) park and recreational purposes, (ii) conservation of land and other natural resources, or (iii) historic or scenic purposes. The term "open space uses" means any use of open space land for (i) park and recreational purposes, (ii) conservation of land and other natural resources, or (iii) historic or scenic purposes. (1963, c. 1129, s. 7; 1969, c. 35, s. 1; 1971, c. 698, s. 1.)

§§ 160A-408 through 160A-410. Reserved for future codification purposes.

Part 5. Building Inspection.

§ 160A-411. Inspection department.

Every city in the State is hereby authorized to create an inspection department, and may appoint one or more inspectors who may be given the titles of building inspector, electrical inspector, plumbing inspector, housing inspector, zoning inspector, heating and air-conditioning inspector, fire prevention inspector, or deputy or assistant inspector, or such other titles as may be generally descriptive of the duties assigned. The department may be headed by a

with one or more other units of local government, pursuant to G.S. 160A-413 or Part 1 of Article 20 of this Chapter; (iii) contracting with another unit of local government for the provision of inspection services pursuant to Part 1 of Article 20 of this Chapter; or (iv) arranging for the county in which it is located to perform inspection services within the city's jurisdiction as authorized by G.S. 160A-413 and G.S. 160A-360. Such action shall be taken no later than the applicable date in the schedule below, according to the city's population as published in the 1970 United States Census:

Cities over 75,000 population - July 1, 1979

Cities between 50,001 and 75,000 - July 1, 1981

Cities between 25,001 and 50,000 - July 1, 1983

Cities 25,000 and under - July 1, 1985.

In the event that any city shall fail to provide inspection services by the date specified above or shall cease to provide such services at any time thereafter, the Commissioner of Insurance shall arrange for the provision of such services, either through personnel employed by his department or through an arrangement with other units of government. In either event, the Commissioner shall have and may exercise within the city's jurisdiction all powers made available to the city council with respect to building inspection under Part 5 of Article 19, and Part 1 of Article 20 of this Chapter. Whenever the Commissioner has intervened in this manner, the city may assume provision of inspection services only after giving the Commissioner two years' written notice of its intention to do so; provided, however, that the Commissioner may waive this requirement or permit assumption at an earlier date if he finds that such earlier assumption will not unduly interfere with arrangements he has made for the provision of those services. (1969, c. 1065, s. 1; 1971, c. 698, s. 1; 1977, c. 531, s. 5.)

§ 160A-411.1. Qualifications of inspectors.

On and after the applicable date set forth in the schedule in G.S. 160A-411, no city shall employ an inspector to enforce the State Building Code as a member

certificate, valid for one year only; (ii) a standard certificate; or (iii) a limited certificate which shall be valid only as an authorization for him to continue in the position held on the date specified in G.S. 143-151.13(c) and which shall become invalid if he does not successfully complete in-service training specified by the Qualification Board within the period specified in G.S. 143-151.13(c). An inspector holding one of the above certificates can be promoted to a position requiring a higher level certificate only upon issuance by the Board of a standard certificate or probationary certificate appropriate for such new position. (1977, c. 531, s. 6.)

§ 160A-412. Duties and responsibilities.

(a) The duties and responsibilities of an inspection department and of the inspectors therein shall be to enforce within their territorial jurisdiction State and local laws relating to

(1) The construction of buildings and other structures;

(2) The installation of such facilities as plumbing systems, electrical systems, heating systems, refrigeration systems, and air-conditioning systems;

(3) The maintenance of buildings and other structures in a safe, sanitary, and healthful condition;

(4) Other matters that may be specified by the city council.

These duties shall include the receipt of applications for permits and the issuance or denial of permits, the making of any necessary inspections, the issuance or denial of certificates of compliance, the issuance of orders to correct violations, the bringing of judicial actions against actual or threatened violations, the keeping of adequate records, and any other actions that may be required in order adequately to enforce those laws. The city council shall have the authority to enact reasonable and appropriate provisions governing the enforcement of those laws.

(b) Except as provided in G.S. 160A-424, a city may not adopt a local ordinance or resolution or any other policy that requires regular, routine obtaining approval from the North Carolina Building Code Council. The North Carolina Building Code Council shall review all applications for additional inspections requested by a city and shall, in a reasonable manner, approve or disapprove the additional inspections. This subsection does not limit the authority of the city to require inspections upon unforeseen or unique circumstances that require immediate action. (1969, c. 1065, s. 1; 1971, c. 698, s. 1; 2013-118, s. 1(b).)

§ 160A-413. Joint inspection department; other arrangements.

A city council may enter into and carry out contracts with another city, county, or combination thereof under which the parties agree to create and support a joint inspection department for the enforcement of State and local laws specified in the agreement. The governing boards of the contracting parties are authorized to make any necessary appropriations for this purpose.

In lieu of a joint inspection department, a city council may designate an inspector from any other city or county to serve as a member of its inspection department with the approval of the governing body of the other city or county. A city may also contract with an individual who is not a city or county employee but who holds one of the applicable certificates as provided in G.S. 160A-411.1 or G.S. 153A-351.1 or with the employer of an individual who holds one of the applicable certificates as provided in G.S. 160A-411.1 or G.S. 153A-351.1. The inspector, if designated from another city or county under this section, shall, while exercising the duties of the position, be considered a municipal employee. The city shall have the same potential liability, if any, for inspections conducted by an individual who is not an employee of the city as it does for an individual who is an employee of the city. The company or individual with whom the city contracts shall have errors and omissions and other insurance coverage acceptable to the city.

The city council of any city may request the board of county commissioners of the county in which the city is located to direct one or more county building inspectors to exercise their powers within part or all of the city's jurisdiction, and they shall thereupon be empowered to do so until the city council officially withdraws its request in the manner provided in G.S. 160A-360(g). (1969, c.

§ 160A-414. Financial support.

The city council may appropriate for the support of the inspection department any funds that it deems necessary. It may provide for paying inspectors fixed salaries or it may reimburse them for their services by paying over part or all of any fees collected. It shall have power to fix reasonable fees for issuance of permits, inspections, and other services of the inspection department. (1969, c. 1065, s. 1; 1971, c. 698, s. 1.)

§ 160A-415. Conflicts of interest.

No member of an inspection department shall be financially interested or employed by a business that is financially interested in the furnishing of labor, material, or appliances for the construction, alteration, or maintenance of any building within the city's jurisdiction or any part or system thereof, or in the making of plans or specifications therefor, unless he is the owner of the building. No member of an inspection department or other individual or an employee of a company contracting with a city to conduct inspections shall engage in any work that is inconsistent with his or her duties or with the interest of the city, as determined by the city. The city must find a conflict of interest if any of the following is the case:

(1)   If the individual, company, or employee of a company contracting to perform inspections for the city has worked for the owner, developer, contractor, or project manager of the project to be inspected within the last two years.

(2)   If the individual, company, or employee of a company contracting to perform inspections for the city is closely related to the owner, developer, contractor, or project manager of the project to be inspected.

(3)   If the individual, company, or employee of a company contracting to perform inspections for the city has a financial or business interest in the project to be inspected.

The provisions of this section do not apply to a firefighter whose primary duties are fire suppression and rescue, but who engages in some fire inspection

preceding six years. (1969, c. 1065, s. 1; 1971, c. 698, s. 1; 1993, c. 232, s. 4; 1998-122, s. 1; 1999-372, s. 4.)

§ 160A-416. Failure to perform duties.

If any member of an inspection department shall willfully fail to perform the duties required of him by law, or willfully shall improperly issue a permit, or shall give a certificate of compliance without first making the inspections required by law, or willfully shall improperly give a certificate of compliance, he shall be guilty of a Class 1 misdemeanor. (1969, c. 1065, s. 1; 1971, c. 698, s. 1; 1993, c. 539, s. 1089; 1994, Ex. Sess., c. 24, s. 14(c).)

§ 160A-417. Permits.

(a) Except as provided in subsection (a2) of this section, no person shall commence or proceed with any of the following without first securing from the inspection department with jurisdiction over the site of the work any and all permits required by the State Building Code and any other State or local laws applicable to the work:

(1) The construction, reconstruction, alteration, repair, movement to another site, removal, or demolition of any building or structure.

(2) The installation, extension, or general repair of any plumbing system except that in any one- or two-family dwelling unit a permit shall not be required for the connection of a water heater that is being replaced, provided that the work is performed by a person licensed under G.S. 87-21, who personally examines the work at completion and ensures that a leak test has been performed on the gas piping, and provided the energy use rate or thermal input is not greater than that of the water heater which is being replaced, there is no change in fuel, energy source, location, capacity, or routing or sizing of venting and piping, and the replacement is installed in accordance with the current edition of the State Building Code.

(3) The installation, extension, alteration, or general repair of any heating or cooling equipment system.

lighting fixtures or devices, such as receptacles and lighting switches, or for the connection of an existing branch circuit to an electric water heater that is being replaced, provided that all of the following requirements are met:

a. With respect to electric water heaters, the replacement water heater is placed in the same location and is of the same or less capacity and electrical rating as the original.

b. With respect to electrical lighting fixtures and devices, the replacement is with a fixture or device having the same voltage and the same or less amperage.

c. The work is performed by a person licensed under G.S. 87-43.

d. The repair or replacement installation meets the current edition of the State Building Code, including the State Electrical Code.

However, a permit is not required for the installation, maintenance, or replacement of any load control device or equipment by an electric power supplier, as defined in G.S. 62-133.8, or an electrical contractor contracted by the electric power supplier, so long as the work is subject to supervision by an electrical contractor licensed under Article 4 of Chapter 87 of the General Statutes. The electric power supplier shall provide such installation, maintenance, or replacement in accordance with (i) an activity or program ordered, authorized, or approved by the North Carolina Utilities Commission pursuant to G.S. 62-133.8 or G.S. 62-133.9 or (ii) a similar program undertaken by a municipal electric service provider, whether the installation, modification, or replacement is made before or after the point of delivery of electric service to the customer. The exemption under this subdivision applies to all existing installations.

(a1) A permit shall be in writing and shall contain a provision that the work done shall comply with the State Building Code and all other applicable State and local laws. Nothing in this section shall require a city to review and approve residential building plans submitted to the city pursuant to Section R-110 of Volume VII of the North Carolina State Building Code; provided that the city may review and approve such residential building plans as it deems necessary. No permits shall be issued unless the plans and specifications are identified by the

plans and specifications bear the North Carolina seal of a registered architect or of a registered engineer. When any provision of the General Statutes of North Carolina or of any ordinance requires that work be done by a licensed specialty contractor of any kind, no permit for the work shall be issued unless the work is to be performed by such a duly licensed contractor. No permit issued under Articles 9 or 9C of Chapter 143 shall be required for any construction, installation, repair, replacement, or alteration costing five thousand dollars ($5,000) or less in any single family residence or farm building unless the work involves: the addition, repair or replacement of load bearing structures; the addition (excluding replacement of same size and capacity) or change in the design of plumbing; the addition, replacement or change in the design of heating, air conditioning, or electrical wiring, devices, appliances, or equipment; the use of materials not permitted by the North Carolina Uniform Residential Building Code; or the addition (excluding replacement of like grade of fire resistance) of roofing. Violation of this section shall constitute a Class 1 misdemeanor.

(a2)   A city shall not require more than one permit for the complete installation or replacement of any natural gas, propane gas, or electrical appliance on an existing structure when the installation or replacement is performed by a person licensed under G.S. 87-21 or G.S. 87-43. The cost of the permit for such work shall not exceed the cost of any one individual trade permit issued by that city, nor shall the city increase the costs of any fees to offset the loss of revenue caused by this provision.

(b)   No permit shall be issued pursuant to subsection (a) for any land-disturbing activity, as defined in G.S. 113A-52(6), for any activity covered by G.S. 113A-57, unless an erosion and sedimentation control plan has been approved by the Sedimentation Pollution Control Commission pursuant to G.S. 113A-54(d)(4) or by a local government pursuant to G.S. 113A-61 for the site of the activity or a tract of land including the site of the activity.

(c)   No permit shall be issued pursuant to subsection (a) of this section for any land-disturbing activity that is subject to, but does not comply with, the requirements of G.S. 113A-71.

(d)   No permit shall be issued pursuant to subdivision (1) of subsection (a) of this section where the cost of the work is thirty thousand dollars ($30,000) or

defined in the North Carolina Uniform Residential Building Code, the use of which is incidental to that residential dwelling unit, unless the name, physical and mailing address, telephone number, facsimile number, and electronic mail address of the lien agent designated by the owner pursuant to G.S. 44A-11.1(a) is conspicuously set forth in the permit or in an attachment thereto. The building permit may contain the lien agent's electronic mail address. The lien agent information for each permit issued pursuant to this subsection shall be maintained by the inspection department in the same manner and in the same location in which it maintains its record of building permits issued. (1905, c. 506, s. 26; Rev., s. 2986; 1915, c. 192, s. 3; C.S., s. 2748; 1957, c. 817; 1969, c. 1065, s. 1; 1971, c. 698, s. 1; 1973, c. 426, s. 65; 1981, c. 677, s. 1; 1983, c. 377, s. 3; c. 614, s. 1; 1987 (Reg. Sess., 1988), c. 1000, s. 2; 1993, c. 539, s. 1090; 1994, Ex. Sess., c. 24, s. 14(c); 1993 (Reg. Sess., 1994), c. 741, s. 2; 2002-165, s. 2.20; 2008-198, s. 8(d); 2009-532, s. 3; 2012-158, s. 5; 2013-58, s. 3; 2013-117, s. 5; 2013-160, s. 2.)

§ 160A-418. Time limitations on validity of permits.

A permit issued pursuant to G.S. 160A-417 shall expire by limitation six months, or any lesser time fixed by ordinance of the city council, after the date of issuance if the work authorized by the permit has not been commenced. If after commencement the work is discontinued for a period of 12 months, the permit therefor shall immediately expire. No work authorized by any permit that has expired shall thereafter be performed until a new permit has been secured. (1969, c. 1065, s. 1; 1971, c. 698, s. 1.)

§ 160A-419. Changes in work.

After a permit has been issued, no changes or deviations from the terms of the application, plans and specifications, or the permit, except where changes or deviations are clearly permissible under the State Building Code, shall be made until specific written approval of proposed changes or deviations has been obtained from the inspection department. (1969, c. 1065, s. 1; 1971, c. 698, s. 1.)

many inspections thereof as may be necessary to satisfy them that the work is being done according to the provisions of any applicable State and local laws and of the terms of the permit. In exercising this power, members of the inspection department shall have a right to enter on any premises within the jurisdiction of the department at all reasonable hours for the purposes of inspection or other enforcement action, upon presentation of proper credentials. If a permit has been obtained by an owner exempt from licensure under G.S. 87-1(b)(2), no inspection shall be conducted without the owner being personally present, unless the plans for the building were drawn and sealed by an architect licensed pursuant to Chapter 83A of the General Statutes. (1969, c. 1065, s. 1; 1971, c. 698, s. 1; 2011-376, s. 4.)

§ 160A-421. Stop orders.

(a) Whenever any building or structure or part thereof is being demolished, constructed, reconstructed, altered, or repaired in a hazardous manner, or in substantial violation of any State or local building law, or in a manner that endangers life or property, the appropriate inspector may order the specific part of the work that is in violation or presents such a hazard to be immediately stopped. The stop order shall be in writing, directed to the person doing the work, and shall state the specific work to be stopped, the specific reasons therefor, and the conditions under which the work may be resumed.

(b) The owner or builder may appeal from a stop order involving alleged violation of the State Building Code or any approved local modification thereof to the North Carolina Commissioner of Insurance or his designee within a period of five days after the order is issued. Notice of appeal shall be given in writing to the Commissioner of Insurance or his designee, with a copy to the local inspector. The Commissioner of Insurance or his designee shall promptly conduct an investigation and the appellant and the inspector shall be permitted to submit relevant evidence. The Commissioner of Insurance or his designee shall as expeditiously as possible provide a written statement of the decision setting forth the facts found, the decision reached, and the reasons for the decision. Pending the ruling by the Commissioner of Insurance or his designee on an appeal no further work shall take place in violation of a stop order. In the event of dissatisfaction with the decision, the person affected shall have the options of:

(c) The owner or builder may appeal from a stop order involving alleged violation of a local zoning ordinance by giving notice of appeal in writing to the board of adjustment. The appeal shall be heard and decided within the period established by the ordinance, or if none is specified, within a reasonable time. No further work shall take place in violation of a stop order pending a ruling.

(d) Violation of a stop order shall constitute a Class 1 misdemeanor. (1969, c. 1065, s. 1; 1971, c. 698, s. 1; 1983, c. 377, s. 5; 1989, c. 681, s. 6; 1991, c. 512, s. 3; 1993, c. 539, s. 1091; 1994, Ex. Sess., c. 24, s. 14(c).)

§ 160A-422. Revocation of permits.

The appropriate inspector may revoke and require the return of any permit by notifying the permit holder in writing stating the reason for the revocation. Permits shall be revoked for any substantial departure from the approved application, plans, or specifications; for refusal or failure to comply with the requirements of any applicable State or local laws; or for false statements or misrepresentations made in securing the permit. Any permit mistakenly issued in violation of an applicable State or local law may also be revoked. (1969, c. 1065, s. 1; 1971, c. 698, s. 1.)

§ 160A-423. Certificates of compliance.

At the conclusion of all work done under a permit, the appropriate inspector shall make a final inspection, and if he finds that the completed work complies with all applicable State and local laws and with the terms of the permit, he shall issue a certificate of compliance. No new building or part thereof may be occupied, and no addition or enlargement of an existing building may be occupied, and no existing building that has been altered or moved may be occupied, until the inspection department has issued a certificate of compliance. A temporary certificate of compliance may be issued permitting occupancy for a stated period of specified portions of the building that the inspector finds may safely be occupied prior to final completion of the entire building. Violation of this section shall constitute a Class 1 misdemeanor. (1969, c. 1065, s. 1; 1971,

§ 160A-424. Periodic inspections.

(a) The inspection department may make periodic inspections, subject to the council's directions, for unsafe, unsanitary, or otherwise hazardous and unlawful conditions in buildings or structures within its territorial jurisdiction. Except as provided in subsection (b) of this section, the inspection department may make periodic inspections only when there is reasonable cause to believe that unsafe, unsanitary, or otherwise hazardous or unlawful conditions may exist in a residential building or structure. For purposes of this section, the term "reasonable cause" means any of the following: (i) the landlord or owner has a history of more than two verified violations of the housing ordinances or codes within a 12-month period; (ii) there has been a complaint that substandard conditions exist within the building or there has been a request that the building be inspected; (iii) the inspection department has actual knowledge of an unsafe condition within the building; or (iv) violations of the local ordinances or codes are visible from the outside of the property. In conducting inspections authorized under this section, the inspection department shall not discriminate between single-family and multifamily buildings. In exercising this power, members of the department shall have a right to enter on any premises within the jurisdiction of the department at all reasonable hours for the purposes of inspection or other enforcement action, upon presentation of proper credentials. Nothing in this section shall be construed to prohibit periodic inspections in accordance with State fire prevention code or as otherwise required by State law.

(b) A city may require periodic inspections as part of a targeted effort within a geographic area that has been designated by the city council. The municipality shall not discriminate in its selection of areas or housing types to be targeted and shall (i) provide notice to all owners and residents of properties in the affected area about the periodic inspections plan and information regarding a public hearing regarding the plan; (ii) hold a public hearing regarding the plan; and (iii) establish a plan to address the ability of low-income residential property owners to comply with minimum housing code standards.

(c) In no event may a city do any of the following: (i) adopt or enforce any ordinance that would require any owner or manager of rental property to obtain any permit or permission from the city to lease or rent residential real property, except for those properties that have more than three verified violations in a 12-

participate in any governmental program as a condition of obtaining a certificate of occupancy; or (iii) except as provided in subsection (d) of this section, levy a special fee or tax on residential rental property that is not also levied against other commercial and residential properties.

(d) A city may levy a fee for residential rental property registration under subsection (c) of this section for those rental units which have been found with more than two verified violations of local ordinances within the previous 12 months or upon the property being identified within the top 10% of properties with crime or disorder problems as set forth in a local ordinance. The fee shall be an amount that covers the cost of operating a residential registration program and shall not be used to supplant revenue in other areas. Cities using registration programs that charge registration fees for all residential rental properties as of June 1, 2011, may continue levying a fee on all residential rental properties as follows:

(1) For properties with 20 or more residential rental units, the fee shall be no more than fifty dollars ($50.00) per year.

(2) For properties with fewer than 20 but more than three residential rental units, the fee shall be no more than twenty-five dollars ($25.00) per year.

(3) For properties with three or fewer residential rental units, the fee shall be no more than fifteen dollars ($15.00) per year. (1969, c. 1065, s. 1; 1971, c. 698, s. 1; 2011-281, s. 2.)

§ 160A-425. Defects in buildings to be corrected.

When a local inspector finds any defects in a building, or finds that the building has not been constructed in accordance with the applicable State and local laws, or that a building because of its condition is dangerous or contains fire hazardous conditions, it shall be his duty to notify the owner or occupant of the building of its defects, hazardous conditions, or failure to comply with law. The owner or occupant shall each immediately remedy the defects, hazardous conditions, or violations of law in the property he owns. (1905, c. 506, s. 28;

§ 160A-425.1: Repealed by Session Laws 2009-263, s. 1, effective October 1, 2009.

§ 160A-426. Unsafe buildings condemned in localities.

(a) Residential Building and Nonresidential Building or Structure. - Every building that shall appear to the inspector to be especially dangerous to life because of its liability to fire or because of bad condition of walls, overloaded floors, defective construction, decay, unsafe wiring or heating system, inadequate means of egress, or other causes, shall be held to be unsafe, and the inspector shall affix a notice of the dangerous character of the structure to a conspicuous place on the exterior wall of the building.

(b) Nonresidential Building or Structure. - In addition to the authority granted in subsection (a) of this section, an inspector may declare a nonresidential building or structure within a community development target area to be unsafe if it meets both of the following conditions:

(1) It appears to the inspector to be vacant or abandoned.

(2) It appears to the inspector to be in such dilapidated condition as to cause or contribute to blight, disease, vagrancy, fire or safety hazard, to be a danger to children, or to tend to attract persons intent on criminal activities or other activities that would constitute a public nuisance.

(c) If an inspector declares a nonresidential building or structure to be unsafe under subsection (b) of this section, the inspector must affix a notice of the unsafe character of the structure to a conspicuous place on the exterior wall of the building. For the purposes of this section, the term "community development target area" means an area that has characteristics of an urban progress zone under G.S. 143B-437.09, a "nonresidential redevelopment area" under G.S. 160A-503(10), or an area with similar characteristics designated by the city council as being in special need of revitalization for the benefit and welfare of its citizens.

the hearing at least 10 days in advance of the hearing. (1905, c. 50-6, s. 15; Rev., s. 3010; 1915, c. 192, s. 15; C.S., s. 2773; 1929, c. 199, s. 1; 1969, c. 1065, s. 1; 1971, c. 698, s. 1; 2000-164, s. 1; 2001-386, s. 1; 2006-252, s. 2.19; 2009-263, s. 2.)

§ 160A-427. Removing notice from condemned building.

If any person shall remove any notice that has been affixed to any building or structure by a local inspector of any municipality and that states the dangerous character of the building or structure, he shall be guilty of a Class 1 misdemeanor. (1905, c. 506, s. 15; Rev., s. 3799; C.S., s. 2775; 1969, c. 1065, s. 1; 1971, c. 698, s. 1; 1993, c. 539, s. 1093; 1994, Ex. Sess., c. 24, s. 14(c).)

§ 160A-428. Action in event of failure to take corrective action.

If the owner of a building or structure that has been condemned as unsafe pursuant to G.S. 160A-426 shall fail to take prompt corrective action, the local inspector shall give him written notice, by certified or registered mail to his last known address or by personal service:

(1) That the building or structure is in a condition that appears to meet one or more of the following conditions:

a. Constitutes a fire or safety hazard.

b. Is dangerous to life, health, or other property.

c. Is likely to cause or contribute to blight, disease, vagrancy, or danger to children.

d. Has a tendency to attract persons intent on criminal activities or other activities which would constitute a public nuisance.

(2) That a hearing will be held before the inspector at a designated place and time, not later than 10 days after the date of the notice, at which time the

(3) That following the hearing, the inspector may issue such order to repair, close, vacate, or demolish the building or structure as appears appropriate.

If the name or whereabouts of the owner cannot after due diligence be discovered, the notice shall be considered properly and adequately served if a copy thereof is posted on the outside of the building or structure in question at least 10 days prior to the hearing and a notice of the hearing is published in a newspaper having general circulation in the city at least once not later than one week prior to the hearing. (1969, c. 1065, s. 1; 1971, c. 698, s. 1; 2000-164, s. 2; 2009-263, s. 4.)

§ 160A-429. Order to take corrective action.

If, upon a hearing held pursuant to the notice prescribed in G.S. 160A-428, the inspector shall find that the building or structure is in a condition that constitutes a fire or safety hazard or renders it dangerous to life, health, or other property, he shall make an order in writing, directed to the owner of such building or structure, requiring the owner to remedy the defective conditions by repairing, closing, vacating, or demolishing the building or structure or taking other necessary steps, within such period, not less than 60 days, as the inspector may prescribe; provided, that where the inspector finds that there is imminent danger to life or other property, he may order that corrective action be taken in such lesser period as may be feasible. (1969, c. 1065, s. 1; 1971, c. 698, s. 1; 1973, c. 426, s. 68; 1977, c. 912, s. 13.)

§ 160A-430. Appeal; finality of order if not appealed.

Any owner who has received an order under G.S. 160A-429 may appeal from the order to the city council by giving notice of appeal in writing to the inspector and to the city clerk within 10 days following issuance of the order. In the absence of an appeal, the order of the inspector shall be final. The city council shall hear and render a decision in an appeal within a reasonable time. The city council may affirm, modify and affirm, or revoke the order. (1969, c. 1065, s. 1; 1971, c. 698, s. 1; 1973, c. 426, s. 69; 2000-164, s. 4.)

pursuant to G.S. 160A-429 from which no appeal has been taken, or fails to comply with an order of the city council following an appeal, he shall be guilty of a Class 1 misdemeanor. (1905, c. 506, s. 15; Rev., s. 3802; 1915, c. 192, s. 19; C.S., s. 2774; 1929, c. 199, s. 2; 1969, c. 1065, s. 1; 1971, c. 698, s. 1; 1993, c. 539, s. 1094; 1994, Ex. Sess., c. 24, s. 14(c).)

§ 160A-432. Enforcement.

(a) [Action Authorized.] - Whenever any violation is denominated a misdemeanor under the provisions of this Part, the city, either in addition to or in lieu of other remedies, may initiate any appropriate action or proceedings to prevent, restrain, correct, or abate the violation or to prevent the occupancy of the building or structure involved.

(a1) Repealed by Session Laws 2009-263, s. 1, effective October 1, 2009.

(b) Removal of Building. - In the case of a building or structure declared unsafe under G.S. 160A-426 or an ordinance adopted pursuant to G.S. 160A-426, a city may, in lieu of taking action under subsection (a), cause the building or structure to be removed or demolished. The amounts incurred by the city in connection with the removal or demolition shall be a lien against the real property upon which the cost was incurred. The lien shall be filed, have the same priority, and be collected in the same manner as liens for special assessments provided in Article 10 of this Chapter. If the building or structure is removed or demolished by the city, the city shall sell the usable materials of the building and any personal property, fixtures, or appurtenances found in or attached to the building. The city shall credit the proceeds of the sale against the cost of the removal or demolition. Any balance remaining from the sale shall be deposited with the clerk of superior court of the county where the property is located and shall be disbursed by the court to the person found to be entitled thereto by final order or decree of the court.

(b1) Additional Lien. - The amounts incurred by the city in connection with the removal or demolition shall also be a lien against any other real property owned by the owner of the building or structure and located within the city limits or within one mile of the city limits, except for the owner's primary residence. The provisions of subsection (b) of this section apply to this additional lien,

(c) [Nonexclusive Remedy.] - Nothing in this section shall be construed to impair or limit the power of the city to define and declare nuisances and to cause their removal or abatement by summary proceedings, or otherwise. (1969, c. 1065, s. 1; 1971, c. 698, s. 1; 2000-164, s. 3; 2001-386, s. 2; 2001-448, s. 2; 2002-118, s. 2; 2003-23, s. 1; 2003-42, s. 1; 2004-6, s. 1; 2007-216, s. 2; 2008-59, s. 2; 2009-9, s. 2; 2009-263, ss. 1, 3.)

§ 160A-433. Records and reports.

The inspection department shall keep complete and accurate records in convenient form of all applications received, permits issued, inspections and reinspections made, defects found, certificates of compliance granted, and all other work and activities of the department. These records shall be kept in the manner and for the periods prescribed by the North Carolina Department of Cultural Resources. Periodic reports shall be submitted to the city council and to the Commissioner of Insurance as they shall by ordinance, rule, or regulation require. (1905, c. 506, ss. 30, 31; Rev., ss. 3004, 3005; 1915, c. 192, s. 12; C.S., ss. 2766, 2767; 1969, c. 1065, s. 1; 1971, c. 698, s. 1; 1983, c. 377, s. 7.)

§ 160A-434. Appeals in general.

Unless otherwise provided by law, appeals from any order, decision, or determination by a member of a local inspection department pertaining to the State Building Code or other State building laws shall be taken to the Commissioner of Insurance or his designee or other official specified in G.S. 143-139, by filing a written notice with him and with the inspection department within a period of 10 days after the order, decision, or determination. Further appeals may be taken to the State Building Code Council or to the courts as provided by law. (1969, c. 1065, s. 1; 1971, c. 698, s. 1; 1989, c. 681, s. 7A.)

§ 160A-435. Establishment of fire limits.

The city council of every incorporated city shall pass one or more ordinances establishing and defining fire limits, which shall include the principal business portions of the city and which shall be known as primary fire limits. In addition,

s. 1; 1971, c. 698, s. 1.)

§ 160A-436. Restrictions within primary fire limits.

Within the primary fire limits of any city, as established and defined by ordinance, no frame or wooden building or structure or addition thereto shall hereafter be erected, altered, repaired, or moved (either into the limits or from one place to another within the limits), except upon the permit of the local inspection department approved by the city council and by the Commissioner of Insurance or his designee. The city council may make additional regulations for the prevention, extinguishment, or mitigation of fires within the primary fire limits. (1905, c. 506, s. 8; Rev., s. 2988; 1915, c. 192, s. 5; C.S., s. 2750; 1969, c. 1065, s. 1; 1971, c. 698, s. 1; 1989, c. 681, s. 8.)

§ 160A-437. Restriction within secondary fire limits.

Within any secondary fire limits of any city or town, as established and defined by ordinance, no frame or wooden building or structure or addition thereto shall be erected, altered, repaired, or moved except in accordance with any rules and regulations established by ordinance of the areas. (1905, c. 506, s. 8; Rev., s. 2988; 1915, c. 192, s. 5; C.S., s. 2750; 1969, c. 1065, s. 1; 1971, c. 698, s. 1.)

§ 160A-438. Failure to establish primary fire limits.

If the council of any city shall fail or refuse to establish and define the primary fire limits of the city as required by law, after having such failure or refusal called to their attention in writing by the State Commissioner of Insurance, the Commissioner shall have the power to establish the limits upon making a determination that they are necessary and in the public interest. (1905, c. 506, s. 7; Rev., s. 3608; C.S., s. 2747; 1969, c. 1065, s. 1; 1971, c. 698, s. 1.)

§ 160A-439. Ordinance authorized as to repair, closing, and demolition of nonresidential buildings or structures; order of public officer.

governing body. The minimum standards shall address only conditions that are dangerous and injurious to public health, safety, and welfare and identify circumstances under which a public necessity exists for the repair, closing, or demolition of such buildings or structures. The ordinance shall provide for designation or appointment of a public officer to exercise the powers prescribed by the ordinance, in accordance with the procedures specified in this section. Such ordinance shall only be applicable within the corporate limits of the city.

(b) Investigation. - Whenever it appears to the public officer that any nonresidential building or structure has not been properly maintained so that the safety or health of its occupants or members of the general public are jeopardized for failure of the property to meet the minimum standards established by the governing body, the public officer shall undertake a preliminary investigation. If entry upon the premises for purposes of investigation is necessary, such entry shall be made pursuant to a duly issued administrative search warrant in accordance with G.S. 15-27.2 or with permission of the owner, the owner's agent, a tenant, or other person legally in possession of the premises.

(c) Complaint and Hearing. - If the preliminary investigation discloses evidence of a violation of the minimum standards, the public officer shall issue and cause to be served upon the owner of and parties in interest in the nonresidential building or structure a complaint. The complaint shall state the charges and contain a notice that a hearing will be held before the public officer (or his or her designated agent) at a place within the county scheduled not less than 10 days nor more than 30 days after the serving of the complaint; that the owner and parties in interest shall be given the right to answer the complaint and to appear in person, or otherwise, and give testimony at the place and time fixed in the complaint; and that the rules of evidence prevailing in courts of law or equity shall not be controlling in hearings before the public officer.

(d) Order. - If, after notice and hearing, the public officer determines that the nonresidential building or structure has not been properly maintained so that the safety or health of its occupants or members of the general public is jeopardized for failure of the property to meet the minimum standards established by the governing body, the public officer shall state in writing findings of fact in support of that determination and shall issue and cause to be served upon the owner thereof an order. The order may require the owner to take remedial action,

(e) Limitations on Orders. -

(1) An order may require the owner to repair, alter, or improve the nonresidential building or structure in order to bring it into compliance with the minimum standards established by the governing body or to vacate and close the nonresidential building or structure for any use.

(2) An order may require the owner to remove or demolish the nonresidential building or structure if the cost of repair, alteration, or improvement of the building or structure would exceed fifty percent (50%) of its then current value. Notwithstanding any other provision of law, if the nonresidential building or structure is designated as a local historic landmark, listed in the National Register of Historic Places, or located in a locally designated historic district or in a historic district listed in the National Register of Historic Places and the governing body determines, after a public hearing as provided by ordinance, that the nonresidential building or structure is of individual significance or contributes to maintaining the character of the district, and the nonresidential building or structure has not been condemned as unsafe, the order may require that the nonresidential building or structure be vacated and closed until it is brought into compliance with the minimum standards established by the governing body.

(3) An order may not require repairs, alterations, or improvements to be made to vacant manufacturing facilities or vacant industrial warehouse facilities to preserve the original use. The order may require such building or structure to be vacated and closed, but repairs may be required only when necessary to maintain structural integrity or to abate a health or safety hazard that cannot be remedied by ordering the building or structure closed for any use.

(f) Action by Governing Body Upon Failure to Comply With Order. -

(1) If the owner fails to comply with an order to repair, alter, or improve or to vacate and close the nonresidential building or structure, the governing body may adopt an ordinance ordering the public officer to proceed to effectuate the purpose of this section with respect to the particular property or properties that the public officer found to be jeopardizing the health or safety of its occupants or members of the general public. The property or properties shall be described in the ordinance. The ordinance shall be recorded in the office of the register of

and closed. The public officer may cause to be posted on the main entrance of any nonresidential building or structure so closed a placard with the following words: "This building is unfit for any use; the use or occupation of this building for any purpose is prohibited and unlawful." Any person who occupies or knowingly allows the occupancy of a building or structure so posted shall be guilty of a Class 3 misdemeanor.

(2)   If the owner fails to comply with an order to remove or demolish the nonresidential building or structure, the governing body may adopt an ordinance ordering the public officer to proceed to effectuate the purpose of this section with respect to the particular property or properties that the public officer found to be jeopardizing the health or safety of its occupants or members of the general public. No ordinance shall be adopted to require demolition of a nonresidential building or structure until the owner has first been given a reasonable opportunity to bring it into conformity with the minimum standards established by the governing body. The property or properties shall be described in the ordinance. The ordinance shall be recorded in the office of the register of deeds and shall be indexed in the name of the property owner or owners in the grantor index. Following adoption of an ordinance, the public officer may cause the building or structure to be removed or demolished.

(g)   Action by Governing Body Upon Abandonment of Intent to Repair. - If the governing body has adopted an ordinance or the public officer has issued an order requiring the building or structure to be repaired or vacated and closed and the building or structure has been vacated and closed for a period of two years pursuant to the ordinance or order, the governing body may make findings that the owner has abandoned the intent and purpose to repair, alter, or improve the building or structure and that the continuation of the building or structure in its vacated and closed status would be inimical to the health, safety, and welfare of the municipality in that it would continue to deteriorate, would create a fire or safety hazard, would be a threat to children and vagrants, would attract persons intent on criminal activities, or would cause or contribute to blight and the deterioration of property values in the area. Upon such findings, the governing body may, after the expiration of the two-year period, enact an ordinance and serve such ordinance on the owner, setting forth the following:

(1)   If the cost to repair the nonresidential building or structure to bring it into compliance with the minimum standards is less than or equal to fifty percent

(2) If the cost to repair the nonresidential building or structure to bring it into compliance with the minimum standards exceeds fifty percent (50%) of its then current value, the ordinance shall require the owner to demolish and remove the building or structure within 90 days.

In the case of vacant manufacturing facilities or vacant industrial warehouse facilities, the building or structure must have been vacated and closed pursuant to an order or ordinance for a period of five years before the governing body may take action under this subsection. The ordinance shall be recorded in the office of the register of deeds in the county wherein the property or properties are located and shall be indexed in the name of the property owner in the grantor index. If the owner fails to comply with the ordinance, the public officer shall effectuate the purpose of the ordinance.

(h) Service of Complaints and Orders. - Complaints or orders issued by a public officer pursuant to an ordinance adopted under this section shall be served upon persons either personally or by registered or certified mail so long as the means used are reasonably designed to achieve actual notice. When service is made by registered or certified mail, a copy of the complaint or order may also be sent by regular mail. Service shall be deemed sufficient if the registered or certified mail is refused, but the regular mail is not returned by the post office within 10 days after the mailing. If regular mail is used, a notice of the pending proceedings shall be posted in a conspicuous place on the premises affected. If the identities of any owners or the whereabouts of persons are unknown and cannot be ascertained by the public officer in the exercise of reasonable diligence, and the public officer makes an affidavit to that effect, the serving of the complaint or order upon the owners or other persons may be made by publication in a newspaper having general circulation in the city at least once no later than the time that personal service would be required under this section. When service is made by publication, a notice of the pending proceedings shall be posted in a conspicuous place on the premises affected.

(i) Liens. -

(1) The amount of the cost of repairs, alterations, or improvements, or vacating and closing, or removal or demolition by the public officer shall be a lien against the real property upon which the cost was incurred, which lien shall

(2) If the real property upon which the cost was incurred is located in an incorporated city, the amount of the costs is also a lien on any other real property of the owner located within the city limits except for the owner's primary residence. The additional lien provided in this subdivision is inferior to all prior liens and shall be collected as a money judgment.

(3) If the nonresidential building or structure is removed or demolished by the public officer, he or she shall offer for sale the recoverable materials of the building or structure and any personal property, fixtures, or appurtenances found in or attached to the building or structure and shall credit the proceeds of the sale, if any, against the cost of the removal or demolition, and any balance remaining shall be deposited in the superior court by the public officer, shall be secured in a manner directed by the court, and shall be disbursed by the court to the persons found to be entitled thereto by final order or decree of the court. Nothing in this section shall be construed to impair or limit in any way the power of the governing body to define and declare nuisances and to cause their removal or abatement by summary proceedings or otherwise.

(j) Ejectment. - If any occupant fails to comply with an order to vacate a nonresidential building or structure, the public officer may file a civil action in the name of the city to remove the occupant. The action to vacate shall be in the nature of summary ejectment and shall be commenced by filing a complaint naming as parties-defendant any person occupying the nonresidential building or structure. The clerk of superior court shall issue a summons requiring the defendant to appear before a magistrate at a certain time, date, and place not to exceed 10 days from the issuance of the summons to answer the complaint. The summons and complaint shall be served as provided in G.S. 42-29. The summons shall be returned according to its tenor, and if on its return it appears to have been duly served and if at the hearing the public officer produces a certified copy of an ordinance adopted by the governing body pursuant to subsection (f) of this section to vacate the occupied nonresidential building or structure, the magistrate shall enter judgment ordering that the premises be vacated and all persons be removed. The judgment ordering that the nonresidential building or structure be vacated shall be enforced in the same manner as the judgment for summary ejectment entered under G.S. 42-30. An appeal from any judgment entered under this subsection by the magistrate may be taken as provided in G.S. 7A-228, and the execution of the judgment may be stayed as provided in G.S. 7A-227. An action to remove an occupant of a

the summary ejectment proceeding, that the governing body has ordered the public officer to proceed to exercise his duties under subsection (f) of this section to vacate and close or remove and demolish the nonresidential building or structure.

(k) Civil Penalty. - The governing body may impose civil penalties against any person or entity that fails to comply with an order entered pursuant to this section. However, the imposition of civil penalties shall not limit the use of any other lawful remedies available to the governing body for the enforcement of any ordinances adopted pursuant to this section.

(l) Powers Supplemental. - The powers conferred by this section are supplemental to the powers conferred by any other law. An ordinance adopted by the governing body may authorize the public officer to exercise any powers necessary or convenient to carry out and effectuate the purpose and provisions of this section, including the following powers in addition to others herein granted:

(1) To investigate nonresidential buildings and structures in the city to determine whether they have been properly maintained in compliance with the minimum standards so that the safety or health of the occupants or members of the general public are not jeopardized.

(2) To administer oaths, affirmations, examine witnesses, and receive evidence.

(3) To enter upon premises pursuant to subsection (b) of this section for the purpose of making examinations in a manner that will do the least possible inconvenience to the persons in possession.

(4) To appoint and fix the duties of officers, agents, and employees necessary to carry out the purposes of the ordinances adopted by the governing body.

(5) To delegate any of his or her functions and powers under the ordinance to other officers and agents.

order of the public officer shall have the remedies provided in G.S. 160A-446.

(n) Funding. - The governing body is authorized to make appropriations from its revenues necessary to carry out the purposes of this section and may accept and apply grants or donations to assist in carrying out the provisions of the ordinances adopted by the governing body.

(o) No Effect on Just Compensation for Taking by Eminent Domain. - Nothing in this section shall be construed as preventing the owner or owners of any property from receiving just compensation for the taking of property by the power of eminent domain under the laws of this State, nor as permitting any property to be condemned or destroyed except in accordance with the police power of the State.

(p) Definitions. -

(1) "Parties in interest" means all individuals, associations, and corporations who have interests of record in a nonresidential building or structure and any who are in possession thereof.

(2) "Vacant industrial warehouse" means any building or structure designed for the storage of goods or equipment in connection with manufacturing processes, which has not been used for that purpose for at least one year and has not been converted to another use.

(3) "Vacant manufacturing facility" means any building or structure previously used for the lawful production or manufacturing of goods, which has not been used for that purpose for at least one year and has not been converted to another use. (2007-414, s. 1.)

§160A-440. Reserved for future codification purposes.

Part 6. Minimum Housing Standards.

this State that are unfit for human habitation are inimical to the welfare and dangerous and injurious to the health, safety and morals of the people of this State, and that a public necessity exists for the repair, closing or demolition of such dwellings. Whenever any city or county of this State finds that there exists in the city or county dwellings that are unfit for human habitation due to dilapidation, defects increasing the hazards of fire, accidents or other calamities, lack of ventilation, light or sanitary facilities, or due to other conditions rendering the dwellings unsafe or unsanitary, or dangerous or detrimental to the health, safety, morals, or otherwise inimical to the welfare of the residents of the city or county, power is hereby conferred upon the city or county to exercise its police powers to repair, close or demolish the dwellings in the manner herein provided. No ordinance enacted by the governing body of a county pursuant to this Part shall be applicable within the corporate limits of any city unless the city council of the city has by resolution expressly given its approval thereto.

In addition to the exercise of police power authorized herein, any city may by ordinance provide for the repair, closing or demolition of any abandoned structure which the city council finds to be a health or safety hazard as a result of the attraction of insects or rodents, conditions creating a fire hazard, dangerous conditions constituting a threat to children or frequent use by vagrants as living quarters in the absence of sanitary facilities. Such ordinance, if adopted, may provide for the repair, closing or demolition of such structure pursuant to the same provisions and procedures as are prescribed herein for the repair, closing or demolition of dwellings found to be unfit for human habitation. (1939, c. 287, s. 1; 1969, c. 913, s. 1; 1971, c. 698, s. 1; 1973, c. 426, s. 60; 1975, c. 664, s. 15.)

§ 160A-442. Definitions.

The following terms shall have the meanings whenever used or referred to as indicated when used in this Part unless a different meaning clearly appears from the context:

(1) "City" means any incorporated city or any county.

(2) "Dwelling" means any building, structure, manufactured home or mobile home, or part thereof, used and occupied for human habitation or intended to be

(3) "Governing body" means the council, board of commissioners, or other legislative body, charged with governing a city or county.

(3a) "Manufactured home" or "mobile home" means a structure as defined in G.S. 143-145(7).

(4) "Owner" means the holder of the title in fee simple and every mortgagee of record.

(5) "Parties in interest" means all individuals, associations and corporations who have interests of record in a dwelling and any who are in possession thereof.

(6) "Public authority" means any housing authority or any officer who is in charge of any department or branch of the government of the city, county, or State relating to health, fire, building regulations, or other activities concerning dwellings in the city.

(7) "Public officer" means the officer or officers who are authorized by ordinances adopted hereunder to exercise the powers prescribed by the ordinances and by this Part. (1939, c. 287, s. 2; 1941, c. 140; 1953, c. 675, s. 29; 1961, c. 398, s. 1; 1969, c. 913, s. 2; 1971, c. 698, s. 1; 1973, c. 426, s. 60; 1983, c. 401, ss. 1, 2.)

§ 160A-443. Ordinance authorized as to repair, closing, and demolition; order of public officer.

Upon the adoption of an ordinance finding that dwelling conditions of the character described in G.S. 160A-441 exist within a city, the governing body of the city is hereby authorized to adopt and enforce ordinances relating to dwellings within the city's territorial jurisdiction that are unfit for human habitation. These ordinances shall include the following provisions:

(1) That a public officer be designated or appointed to exercise the powers prescribed by the ordinance.

own motion) that any dwelling is unfit for human habitation, the public officer shall, if his preliminary investigation discloses a basis for such charges, issue and cause to be served upon the owner of and parties in interest in such dwellings a complaint stating the charges in that respect and containing a notice that a hearing will be held before the public officer (or his designated agent) at a place within the county in which the property is located fixed not less than 10 days nor more than 30 days after the serving of the complaint; that the owner and parties in interest shall be given the right to file an answer to the complaint and to appear in person, or otherwise, and give testimony at the place and time fixed in the complaint; and that the rules of evidence prevailing in courts of law or equity shall not be controlling in hearings before the public officer.

(3) That if, after notice and hearing, the public officer determines that the dwelling under consideration is unfit for human habitation, he shall state in writing his findings of fact in support of that determination and shall issue and cause to be served upon the owner thereof an order,

    a. If the repair, alteration or improvement of the dwelling can be made at a reasonable cost in relation to the value of the dwelling (the ordinance of the city may fix a certain percentage of this value as being reasonable), requiring the owner, within the time specified, to repair, alter or improve the dwelling in order to render it fit for human habitation. The order may require that the property be vacated and closed only if continued occupancy during the time allowed for repair will present a significant threat of bodily harm, taking into account the nature of the necessary repairs, alterations, or improvements; the current state of the property; and any additional risks due to the presence and capacity of minors under the age of 18 or occupants with physical or mental disabilities. The order shall state that the failure to make timely repairs as directed in the order shall make the dwelling subject to the issuance of an unfit order under subdivision (4) of this section; or

    b. If the repair, alteration or improvement of the dwelling cannot be made at a reasonable cost in relation to the value of the dwelling (the ordinance of the city may fix a certain percentage of this value as being reasonable), requiring the owner, within the time specified in the order, to remove or demolish such dwelling. However, notwithstanding any other provision of law, if the dwelling is located in a historic district of the city and the Historic District Commission determines, after a public hearing as provided by ordinance, that the dwelling is

400.14(a).

(4)   That, if the owner fails to comply with an order to repair, alter or improve or to vacate and close the dwelling, the public officer may cause the dwelling to be repaired, altered or improved or to be vacated and closed; that the public officer may cause to be posted on the main entrance of any dwelling so closed, a placard with the following words: "This building is unfit for human habitation; the use or occupation of this building for human habitation is prohibited and unlawful." Occupation of a building so posted shall constitute a Class 1 misdemeanor. The duties of the public officer set forth in this subdivision shall not be exercised until the governing body shall have by ordinance ordered the public officer to proceed to effectuate the purpose of this Article with respect to the particular property or properties which the public officer shall have found to be unfit for human habitation and which property or properties shall be described in the ordinance. This ordinance shall be recorded in the office of the register of deeds in the county wherein the property or properties are located and shall be indexed in the name of the property owner in the grantor index.

(5)   That, if the owner fails to comply with an order to remove or demolish the dwelling, the public officer may cause such dwelling to be removed or demolished. The duties of the public officer set forth in this subdivision shall not be exercised until the governing body shall have by ordinance ordered the public officer to proceed to effectuate the purpose of this Article with respect to the particular property or properties which the public officer shall have found to be unfit for human habitation and which property or properties shall be described in the ordinance. No such ordinance shall be adopted to require demolition of a dwelling until the owner has first been given a reasonable opportunity to bring it into conformity with the housing code. This ordinance shall be recorded in the office of the register of deeds in the county wherein the property or properties are located and shall be indexed in the name of the property owner in the grantor index.

(5a)   If the governing body shall have adopted an ordinance as provided in subdivision (4) of this section, or the public officer shall have:

a.   In a municipality located in counties which have a population in excess of 71,000 by the last federal census (including the entirety of any municipality located in more than one county at least one county of which has a population in

dwelling has been vacated and closed for a period of one year pursuant to the ordinance or order;

b. In a municipality with a population in excess of 190,000 by the last federal census, commenced proceedings under the substandard housing regulations regarding a dwelling to be repaired or vacated and closed, as provided in subdivision (3)a., and if the dwelling has been vacated and closed for a period of one year pursuant to the ordinance or after such proceedings have commenced,

then if the governing body shall find that the owner has abandoned the intent and purpose to repair, alter or improve the dwelling in order to render it fit for human habitation and that the continuation of the dwelling in its vacated and closed status would be inimical to the health, safety, morals and welfare of the municipality in that the dwelling would continue to deteriorate, would create a fire and safety hazard, would be a threat to children and vagrants, would attract persons intent on criminal activities, would cause or contribute to blight and the deterioration of property values in the area, and would render unavailable property and a dwelling which might otherwise have been made available to ease the persistent shortage of decent and affordable housing in this State, then in such circumstances, the governing body may, after the expiration of such one year period, enact an ordinance and serve such ordinance on the owner, setting forth the following:

a. If it is determined that the repair of the dwelling to render it fit for human habitation can be made at a cost not exceeding fifty percent (50%) of the then current value of the dwelling, the ordinance shall require that the owner either repair or demolish and remove the dwelling within 90 days; or

b. If it is determined that the repair of the dwelling to render it fit for human habitation cannot be made at a cost not exceeding fifty percent (50%) of the then current value of the dwelling, the ordinance shall require the owner to demolish and remove the dwelling within 90 days.

This ordinance shall be recorded in the Office of the Register of Deeds in the county wherein the property or properties are located and shall be indexed in the name of the property owner in the grantor index. If the owner fails to comply

This subdivision only applies to municipalities located in counties which have a population in excess of 71,000 by the last federal census (including the entirety of any municipality located in more than one county at least one county of which has a population in excess of 71,000).

[This subdivision does not apply to the local government units listed in subdivision (5b) of this section.]

(5b) If the governing body shall have adopted an ordinance as provided in subdivision (4) of this section, or the public officer shall have:

a. In a municipality other than municipalities with a population in excess of 190,000 by the last federal census, issued an order, ordering a dwelling to be repaired or vacated and closed, as provided in subdivision (3)a, and if the dwelling has been vacated and closed for a period of one year pursuant to the ordinance or order;

b. In a municipality with a population in excess of 190,000 by the last federal census, commenced proceedings under the substandard housing regulations regarding a dwelling to be repaired or vacated and closed, as provided in subdivision (3)a., and if the dwelling has been vacated and closed for a period of one year pursuant to the ordinance or after such proceedings have commenced,

then if the governing body shall find that the owner has abandoned the intent and purpose to repair, alter or improve the dwelling in order to render it fit for human habitation and that the continuation of the dwelling in its vacated and closed status would be inimical to the health, safety, morals and welfare of the municipality in that the dwelling would continue to deteriorate, would create a fire and safety hazard, would be a threat to children and vagrants, would attract persons intent on criminal activities, would cause or contribute to blight and the deterioration of property values in the area, and would render unavailable property and a dwelling which might otherwise have been made available to ease the persistent shortage of decent and affordable housing in this State, then in such circumstances, the governing body may, after the expiration of such one year period, enact an ordinance and serve such ordinance on the owner, setting forth the following:

repair or demolish and remove the dwelling within 90 days; or

b.   If it is determined that the repair of the dwelling to render it fit for human habitation cannot be made at a cost not exceeding fifty percent (50%) of the then current value of the dwelling, the ordinance shall require the owner to demolish and remove the dwelling within 90 days.

This ordinance shall be recorded in the Office of the Register of Deeds in the county wherein the property or properties are located and shall be indexed in the name of the property owner in the grantor index. If the owner fails to comply with this ordinance, the public officer shall effectuate the purpose of the ordinance.

This subdivision applies to the Cities of Eden, Lumberton, Roanoke Rapids, and Whiteville, to the municipalities in Lee County, and the Towns of Bethel, Farmville, Newport, and Waynesville only.

(6)   Liens. -

a.   That the amount of the cost of repairs, alterations or improvements, or vacating and closing, or removal or demolition by the public officer shall be a lien against the real property upon which the cost was incurred, which lien shall be filed, have the same priority, and be collected as the lien for special assessment provided in Article 10 of this Chapter.

b.   If the real property upon which the cost was incurred is located in an incorporated city, then the amount of the cost is also a lien on any other real property of the owner located within the city limits or within one mile thereof except for the owner's primary residence. The additional lien provided in this sub-subdivision is inferior to all prior liens and shall be collected as a money judgment.

c.   If the dwelling is removed or demolished by the public officer, he shall sell the materials of the dwelling, and any personal property, fixtures or appurtenances found in or attached to the dwelling, and shall credit the proceeds of the sale against the cost of the removal or demolition and any balance remaining shall be deposited in the superior court by the public officer, shall be secured in a manner directed by the court, and shall be disbursed by

or abatement by summary proceedings, or otherwise.

(7) If any occupant fails to comply with an order to vacate a dwelling, the public officer may file a civil action in the name of the city to remove such occupant. The action to vacate the dwelling shall be in the nature of summary ejectment and shall be commenced by filing a complaint naming as parties-defendant any person occupying such dwelling. The clerk of superior court shall issue a summons requiring the defendant to appear before a magistrate at a certain time, date and place not to exceed 10 days from the issuance of the summons to answer the complaint. The summons and complaint shall be served as provided in G.S. 42-29. The summons shall be returned according to its tenor, and if on its return it appears to have been duly served, and if at the hearing the public officer produces a certified copy of an ordinance adopted by the governing body pursuant to subdivision (5) authorizing the officer to proceed to vacate the occupied dwelling, the magistrate shall enter judgment ordering that the premises be vacated and that all persons be removed. The judgment ordering that the dwelling be vacated shall be enforced in the same manner as the judgment for summary ejectment entered under G.S. 42-30. An appeal from any judgment entered hereunder by the magistrate may be taken as provided in G.S. 7A-228, and the execution of such judgment may be stayed as provided in G.S. 7A-227. An action to remove an occupant of a dwelling who is a tenant of the owner may not be in the nature of a summary ejectment proceeding pursuant to this paragraph unless such occupant was served with notice at least 30 days before the filing of the summary ejectment proceeding that the governing body has ordered the public officer to proceed to exercise his duties under subdivisions (4) and (5) of this section to vacate and close or remove and demolish the dwelling.

(8) That whenever a determination is made pursuant to subdivision (3) of this section that a dwelling must be vacated and closed, or removed or demolished, under the provisions of this section, notice of the order shall be given by first-class mail to any organization involved in providing or restoring dwellings for affordable housing that has filed a written request for such notices. A minimum period of 45 days from the mailing of such notice shall be given before removal or demolition by action of the public officer, to allow the opportunity for any organization to negotiate with the owner to make repairs, lease, or purchase the property for the purpose of providing affordable housing. The public officer or clerk shall certify the mailing of the notices, and the

officer to wait 45 days before causing removal or demolition. (1939, c. 287, s. 3; 1969, c. 868, ss. 1, 2; c. 1065, s. 2; 1971, c. 698, s. 1; 1973, c. 426, s. 70; 1983, c. 698; 1987, c. 542; 1989, c. 562; 1991, c. 208, s. 1; c. 315, s. 1; c. 581, s. 1; 1993, c. 539, s. 1095; c. 553, ss. 58, 59; 1994, Ex. Sess., c. 24, s. 14(c); 1995, c. 347, s. 1; c. 509, s. 112; c. 733, ss. 1, 2; 1997-101, ss. 1, 2; 1997-414, s. 1; 1997-449, s. 1; 1998-26, s. 1; 1998-87, s. 1; 2000-186, s. 1; 2001-283, s. 1; 2001-448, s. 3; 2002-118, s. 3; 2005-200, s. 3; 2009-279, s. 7.)

§ 160A-443.1. Heat source required.

(a) A city shall, by ordinance, require that by January 1, 2000, every dwelling unit leased as rental property within the city shall have, at a minimum, a central or electric heating system or sufficient chimneys, flues, or gas vents, with heating appliances connected, so as to heat at least one habitable room, excluding the kitchen, to a minimum temperature of 68 degrees Fahrenheit measured three feet above the floor with an outside temperature of 20 degrees Fahrenheit.

(b) If a dwelling unit contains a heating system or heating appliances that meet the requirements of subsection (a) of this section, the owner of the dwelling unit shall not be required to install a new heating system or heating appliances, but the owner shall be required to maintain the existing heating system or heating appliances in a good and safe working condition. Otherwise, the owner of the dwelling unit shall install a heating system or heating appliances that meet the requirements of subsection (a) of this section and shall maintain the heating system or heating appliances in a good and safe working condition.

(c) Portable kerosene heaters are not acceptable as a permanent source of heat as required by subsection (a) of this section but may be used as a supplementary source in single family dwellings and duplex units. An owner who has complied with subsection (a) shall not be held in violation of this section where an occupant of a dwelling unit uses a kerosene heater as a primary source of heat.

(d) This section applies only to cities with a population of 200,000 or over, according to the most recent decennial federal census.

lease agreement, statute, or at common law; or

(2)   Prohibiting a city from adopting an ordinance with more stringent heating requirements than provided for by this section. (1999-14, s. 1.)

§ 160A-444. Standards.

An ordinance adopted by a city under this Part shall provide that the public officer may determine that a dwelling is unfit for human habitation if he finds that conditions exist in the dwelling that render it dangerous or injurious to the health, safety or morals of the occupants of the dwelling, the occupants of neighboring dwellings, or other residents of the city. Defective conditions may include the following (without limiting the generality of the foregoing): defects therein increasing the hazards of fire, accident, or other calamities; lack of adequate ventilation, light, or sanitary facilities; dilapidation; disrepair; structural defects; uncleanliness. The ordinances may provide additional standards to guide the public officers, or his agents, in determining the fitness of a dwelling for human habitation. (1939, c. 287, s. 4; 1971, c. 698, s. 1; 1973, c. 426, s. 60.)

§ 160A-445. Service of complaints and orders.

(a)   Complaints or orders issued by a public officer pursuant to an ordinance adopted under this Part shall be served upon persons either personally or by registered or certified mail. When service is made by registered or certified mail, a copy of the complaint or order may also be sent by regular mail. Service shall be deemed sufficient if the registered or certified mail is unclaimed or refused, but the regular mail is not returned by the post office within 10 days after the mailing. If regular mail is used, a notice of the pending proceedings shall be posted in a conspicuous place on the premises affected.

(a1)   If the identities of any owners or the whereabouts of persons are unknown and cannot be ascertained by the public officer in the exercise of reasonable diligence, or, if the owners are known but have refused to accept service by registered or certified mail, and the public officer makes an affidavit to that effect, then the serving of the complaint or order upon the owners or other persons may be made by publication in a newspaper having general circulation

conspicuous place on the premises thereby affected.

(b)   Repealed by Session Laws 1997, c. 201, s. 1. (1939, c. 287, s. 5; 1965, c. 1055; 1969, c. 868, ss. 3, 4; 1971, c. 698, s. 1; 1973, c. 426, s. 60; 1977, c. 912, s. 14; 1979, 2nd Sess., c. 1247, s. 38; 1991, c. 526, s. 1; 1997-201, s. 1.)

§ 160A-446. Remedies.

(a)   The governing body may provide for the creation and organization of a housing appeals board to which appeals may be taken from any decision or order of the public officer, or may provide for such appeals to be heard and determined by its zoning board of adjustment.

(b)   The housing appeals board, if created, shall consist of five members to serve for three-year staggered terms. It shall have the power to elect its own officers, to fix the times and places for its meetings, to adopt necessary rules of procedure, and to adopt other rules and regulations for the proper discharge of its duties. It shall keep an accurate record of all its proceedings.

(c)   An appeal from any decision or order of the public officer may be taken by any person aggrieved thereby or by any officer, board or commission of the city. Any appeal from the public officer shall be taken within 10 days from the rendering of the decision or service of the order by filing with the public officer and with the board a notice of appeal which shall specify the grounds upon which the appeal is based. Upon the filing of any notice of appeal, the public officer shall forthwith transmit to the board all the papers constituting the record upon which the decision appealed from was made. When an appeal is from a decision of the public officer refusing to allow the person aggrieved thereby to do any act, his decision shall remain in force until modified or reversed. When any appeal is from a decision of the public officer requiring the person aggrieved to do any act, the appeal shall have the effect of suspending the requirement until the hearing by the board, unless the public officer certifies to the board, after the notice of appeal is filed with him, that because of facts stated in the certificate (a copy of which shall be furnished the appellant), a suspension of his requirement would cause imminent peril to life or property. In that case the requirement shall not be suspended except by a restraining order, which may be granted for due cause shown upon not less than one day's written notice to the

(d) The appeals board shall fix a reasonable time for hearing appeals, shall give due notice to the parties, and shall render its decision within a reasonable time. Any party may appear in person or by agent or attorney. The board may reverse or affirm, wholly or partly, or may modify the decision or order appealed from, and may make any decision and order that in its opinion ought to be made in the matter, and to that end it shall have all the powers of the public officer, but the concurring vote of four members of the board shall be necessary to reverse or modify any decision or order of the public officer. The board shall have power also in passing upon appeals, when practical difficulties or unnecessary hardships would result from carrying out the strict letter of the ordinance, to adapt the application of the ordinance to the necessities of the case to the end that the spirit of the ordinance shall be observed, public safety and welfare secured, and substantial justice done.

(e) Every decision of the board shall be subject to review by proceedings in the nature of certiorari instituted within 15 days of the decision of the board, but not otherwise.

(f) Any person aggrieved by an order issued by the public officer or a decision rendered by the board may petition the superior court for an injunction restraining the public officer from carrying out the order or decision and the court may, upon such petition, issue a temporary injunction restraining the public officer pending a final disposition of the cause. The petition shall be filed within 30 days after issuance of the order or rendering of the decision. Hearings shall be had by the court on a petition within 20 days, and shall be given preference over other matters on the court's calendar. The court shall hear and determine the issues raised and shall enter such final order or decree as law and justice may require. It shall not be necessary to file bond in any amount before obtaining a temporary injunction under this subsection.

(g) If any dwelling is erected, constructed, altered, repaired, converted, maintained, or used in violation of this Part or of any ordinance or code adopted under authority of this Part or any valid order or decision of the public officer or board made pursuant to any ordinance or code adopted under authority of this Part, the public officer or board may institute any appropriate action or proceedings to prevent the unlawful erection, construction, reconstruction, alteration or use, to restrain, correct or abate the violation, to prevent the occupancy of the dwelling, or to prevent any illegal act, conduct or use in or

§ 160A-447. Compensation to owners of condemned property.

Nothing in this Part shall be construed as preventing the owner or owners of any property from receiving just compensation for the taking of property by the power of eminent domain under the laws of this State, nor as permitting any property to be condemned or destroyed except in accordance with the police power of the State. (1939, c. 386; 1943, c. 196; 1971, c. 698, s. 1.)

§ 160A-448. Additional powers of public officer.

An ordinance adopted by the governing body of the city may authorize the public officer to exercise any powers necessary or convenient to carry out and effectuate the purpose and provisions of this Part, including the following powers in addition to others herein granted:

(1)   To investigate the dwelling conditions in the city in order to determine which dwellings therein are unfit for human habitations;

(2)   To administer oaths, affirmations, examine witnesses and receive evidence;

(3)   To enter upon premises for the purpose of making examinations in a manner that will do the least possible inconvenience to the persons in possession;

(4)   To appoint and fix the duties of officers, agents and employees necessary to carry out the purposes of the ordinances; and

(5)   To delegate any of his functions and powers under the ordinance to other officers and other agents. (1939, c. 287, s. 7; 1971, c. 698, s. 1; 1973, c. 426, s. 60.)

§ 160A-449. Administration of ordinance.

The governing body of any city adopting an ordinance under this Part shall, as soon as possible thereafter, prepare an estimate of the annual expenses or enforcement and administration of its ordinances adopted under this Part. The city is authorized to make appropriations from its revenues necessary for this purpose and may accept and apply grants or donations to assist it in carrying out the provisions of the ordinances. (1939, c. 287, s. 8; 1971, c. 698, s. 1.)

§ 160A-450. Supplemental nature of Part.

Nothing in this Part shall be construed to abrogate or impair the powers of the courts or of any department of any city to enforce any provisions of its charter or its ordinances or regulations, nor to prevent or punish violations thereof; and the powers conferred by this Part shall be in addition and supplemental to the powers conferred by any other law. (1939, c. 287, s. 9; 1971, c. 698, s. 1.)

Part 7. Community Appearance Commissions.

§ 160A-451. Membership and appointment of commission; joint commission.

Each municipality and county in the State may create a special commission, to be known as the official appearance commission for the city or county. The commission shall consist of not less than seven nor more than 15 members, to be appointed by the governing body of the municipality or county for such terms, not to exceed four years, as the governing body may by ordinance provide. All members shall be residents of the municipality's or county's area of planning and zoning jurisdiction at the time of appointment. Where possible, appointments shall be made in such a manner as to maintain on the commission at all times a majority of members who have had special training or experience in a design field, such as architecture, landscape design, horticulture, city planning, or a closely related field. Members of the commission may be reimbursed for actual expenses incidental to the performance of their duties within the limits of any funds available to the commission, but shall serve without pay unless otherwise provided in the ordinance establishing the commission. Membership of the commission is declared to be an office that may be held concurrently with any other elective or appointive office pursuant to Article VI, Sec. 9, of the Constitution.

commission. (1971, c. 896, s. 6; c. 1058; 1973, c. 426, s. 63.)

§ 160A-452. Powers and duties of commission.

The commission, upon its appointment, shall make careful study of the visual problems and needs of the municipality or county within its area of zoning jurisdiction, and shall make any plans and carry out any programs that will, in accordance with the powers herein granted, enhance and improve the visual quality and aesthetic characteristics of the municipality or county. To this end, the governing board may confer upon the appearance commission the following powers and duties:

(1)   To initiate, promote and assist in the implementation of programs of general community beautification in the municipality or county;

(2)   To seek to coordinate the activities of individuals, agencies and organizations, public and private, whose plans, activities and programs bear upon the appearance of the municipality or county;

(3)   To provide leadership and guidance in matters of area or community design and appearance to individuals, and to public and private organizations, and agencies;

(4)   To make studies of the visual characteristics and problems of the municipality or county, including surveys and inventories of an appropriate nature, and to recommend standards and policies of design for the entire area, any portion or neighborhood thereof, or any project to be undertaken;

(5)   To prepare both general and specific plans for the improved appearance of the municipality or county. These plans may include the entire area or any part thereof, and may include private as well as public property. The plans shall set forth desirable standards and goals for the aesthetic enhancement of the municipality or county or any part thereof within its area of planning and zoning jurisdiction, including public ways and areas, open spaces, and public and private buildings and projects;

may include in the ordinance the following powers:

a. To request from the proper officials of any public agency or body, including agencies of the State and its political subdivisions, its plans for public buildings, facilities, or projects to be located within the municipality or its area of planning and zoning jurisdiction of the city or county.

b. To review these plans and to make recommendations regarding their aesthetic suitability to the appropriate agency, or to the municipal or county planning or governing board. All plans shall be reviewed by the commission in a prompt and expeditious manner, and all recommendations of the commission with regard to any public project shall be made in writing. Copies of the recommendations shall be transmitted promptly to the planning or governing body of the city or county, and to the appropriate agency.

c. To formulate and recommend to the appropriate municipal planning or governing board the adoption or amendment of ordinances (including the zoning ordinance, subdivision regulations, and other local ordinances regulating the use of property) that will, in the opinion of the commission, serve to enhance the appearance of the municipality and its surrounding areas.

d. To direct the attention of city or county officials to needed enforcement of any ordinance that may in any way affect the appearance of the city or county.

e. To seek voluntary adherence to the standards and policies of its plans.

f. To enter, in the performance of its official duties and at reasonable times, upon private lands and make examinations or surveys.

g. To promote public interest in and an understanding of its recommendations, studies, and plans, and to that end to prepare, publish and distribute to the public such studies and reports as will, in the opinion of the commission, advance the cause of improved municipal or county appearance.

h. To conduct public meetings and hearings, giving reasonable notice to the public thereof. (1971, c. 896, s. 6; c. 1058.)

suitable arrangements for the procurement or provision of staff or technical services for the commission, and the governing board may appropriate such amount as it deems necessary to carry out the purposes for which it was created. The commission may establish an advisory council or other committees. (1971, c. 896, s. 6; c. 1058.)

§ 160A-454. Annual report.

The commission shall, no later than April 15 of each year, submit to the municipal or county governing body a written report of its activities, a statement of its expenditures to date for the current fiscal year, and its requested budget for the next fiscal year. All accounts and funds of the commission shall be administered substantially in accordance with the requirements of the Municipal Fiscal Control Act or the County Fiscal Control Act. (1971, c. 896, s. 6; c. 1058.)

§ 160A-455. Receipt and expenditure of funds.

The commission may receive contributions from private agencies, foundations, organizations, individuals, the State or federal government, or any other source, in addition to any sums appropriated for its use by the city or county governing body. It may accept and disburse these funds for any purpose within the scope of its authority as herein specified. All sums appropriated by the city or county to further the work and purposes of the commission are deemed to be for a public purpose. (1971, c. 896, s. 6; c. 1058; 1975, c. 664, s. 16.)

Part 8. Miscellaneous Powers.

§ 160A-456. Community development programs and activities.

(a)   Any city is authorized to engage in, to accept federal and State grants and loans for, and to appropriate and expend funds for community development programs and activities. In undertaking community development programs and activities, in addition to other authority granted by law, a city may engage in the following activities:

direct repair, the making of grants or loans, the subsidization of interest payments on loans, and the guaranty of loans;

(2)   Programs concerned with employment, economic development, crime prevention, child care, health, drug abuse, education, and welfare needs of persons of low and moderate income.

(b)   Any city council may exercise directly those powers granted by law to municipal redevelopment commissions and those powers granted by law to municipal housing authorities, and may do so whether or not a redevelopment commission or housing authority is in existence in such city. Any city council desiring to do so may delegate to any redevelopment commission or to any housing authority the responsibility of undertaking or carrying out any specified community development activities. Any city council and any board of county commissioners may by agreement undertake or carry out for each other any specified community development activities. Any city council may contract with any person, association, or corporation in undertaking any specified community development activities. Any county or city board of health, county board of social services, or county or city board of education, may by agreement undertake or carry out for any city council any specified community development activities.

(c)   Any city council undertaking community development programs or activities may create one or more advisory committees to advise it and to make recommendations concerning such programs or activities.

(d)   Any city council proposing to undertake any loan guaranty or similar program for rehabilitation of private buildings is authorized to submit to its voters the question whether such program shall be undertaken, such referendum to be conducted pursuant to the general and local laws applicable to special elections in such city.

(d1)   Any city may receive and dispense funds from the Community Development Block Grant Section 108 Loan Guarantee program, Subpart M, 24 CFR 570.700 et seq., either through application to the North Carolina Department of Commerce or directly from the federal government, in accordance with State and federal laws governing these funds. Any city that receives these funds directly from the federal government may pledge current and future CDBG funds for use as loan guarantees in accordance with State

accordance with applicable laws governing the CDBG program.

Any city that has pledged current or future CDBG funds for use as loan guarantees prior to the enactment of this subsection is authorized to have taken such action. A pledge of future CDBG funds under this subsection is not a debt or liability of the State or any political subdivision of the State or a pledge of the faith and credit of the State or any political subdivision of the State. The pledging of future CDBG funds under this subsection does not directly, indirectly, or contingently obligate the State or any political subdivision of the State to levy or to pledge any taxes.

(e)   Repealed by Session Laws 1985, c. 665, s. 5.

(e1)   All program income from Economic Development Grants from the Small Cities Community Development Block Grant Program may be retained by recipient cities in "economically distressed counties", as defined in G.S. 143B-437.01, for the purposes of creating local economic development revolving loan funds. Such program income derived through the use by cities of Small Cities Community Development Block Grant money includes but is not limited to: (i) payment of principal and interest on loans made by the county using Community Development Block Grant Funds; (ii) proceeds from the lease or disposition of real property acquired with Community Development Block Grant Funds; and (iii) any late fees associated with loan or lease payments in (i) and (ii) above. The local economic development revolving loan fund set up by the city shall fund only those activities eligible under Title I of the federal Housing and Community Development Act of 1974, as amended (P.L. 93-383), and shall meet at least one of the three national objectives of the Housing and Community Development Act. Any expiration of G.S. 143B-437.01 or G.S. 105-129.3 shall not affect this subsection as to designations of economically distressed counties made prior to its expiration. (1975, c. 435, s. 1; c. 689, s. 1; c. 879, s. 46; 1983, c. 908, s. 4; 1985, c. 665, s. 5; 1987, c. 464, s. 10; 1987 (Reg. Sess., 1988), c. 992, s. 2; 1995, c. 310, s. 3; 1995 (Reg. Sess., 1996), c. 13, s. 3.9; c. 575, s. 3; 2006-259, s. 27(b).)

§ 160A-457. Acquisition and disposition of property for redevelopment.

exercise the following powers:

(1)   To acquire, by voluntary purchase from the owner or owners, real property which is either:

a.   Blighted, deteriorated, deteriorating, undeveloped, or inappropriately developed from the standpoint of sound community development and growth;

b.   Appropriate for rehabilitation or conservation activities;

c.   Appropriate for housing construction or the economic development of the community; or

d.   Appropriate for the preservation or restoration of historic sites, the beautification of urban land, the conservation of open space, natural resources, and scenic areas, the provision of recreational opportunities, or the guidance of urban development;

(2)   To clear, demolish, remove, or rehabilitate buildings and improvements on land so acquired; and

(3)   To retain property so acquired for public purposes, or to dispose, through sale, lease, or otherwise, of any property so acquired to any person, firm, corporation, or governmental unit; provided, the disposition of such property shall be undertaken in accordance with the procedures of Article 12 of this Chapter, or the procedures of G.S. 160A-514, or any applicable local act or charter provision modifying such procedures; or subsection (4) of this section.

(4)   To sell, exchange, or otherwise transfer real property or any interest therein in a community development project area to any redeveloper at private sale for residential, recreational, commercial, industrial or other uses or for public use in accordance with the community development plan, subject to such covenants, conditions and restrictions as may be deemed to be in the public interest or to carry out the purposes of this Article; provided that such sale, exchange or other transfer, and any agreement relating thereto, may be made only after approval of the municipal governing body and after a public hearing; a notice of the public hearing shall be given once a week for two successive weeks in a newspaper having general circulation in the municipality, and the

property to be sold, exchanged or transferred shall be disclosed; and the consideration for the conveyance shall not be less than the appraised value. (1977, c. 660, s. 1; 1983, c. 797, ss. 1, 2.)

§ 160A-457.1. Urban Development Action Grants.

In addition to the powers granted by G.S. 160A-456 and G.S. 160A-457, any city is authorized, either as a part of a community development program or independently thereof, to enter into contracts or agreements with any person, association, or corporation to undertake and carry out specified activities in furtherance of the purposes of Urban Development Action Grants authorized by the Housing and Community Development Act of 1977 (P.L. 95-128) or any amendment thereto which is a continuation of such grant programs by whatever designation, including the authority to enter into and carry out contracts or agreements to extend loans, loan subsidies, or grants to persons, associations, or corporations and to dispose of real or personal property by private sale in furtherance of such contracts or agreements.

Any enabling legislation contained in local acts which refers to "Urban Development Action Grants" or the Housing and Community Development Act of 1977 (P.L. 95-128) shall be construed also to refer to any continuation of such grant programs by whatever designation. (1981, c. 865, ss. 1, 2.)

§ 160A-457.2. Urban homesteading programs.

A city may establish a program of urban homesteading, in which residential property of little or no value is conveyed to persons who agree to rehabilitate the property and use it, for a minimum number of years, as their principal place of residence. Residential property is considered of little or no value if the cost of bringing the property into compliance with the city's housing code exceeds sixty percent (60%) of the property's appraised value on the county tax records. In undertaking such a program a city may:

(1) Acquire by purchase, gift or otherwise, but not eminent domain, residential property specifically for the purpose of reconveyance in the urban homesteading program or may transfer to the program residential property

(2) Under procedures and standards established by the city, convey residential property by private sale under G.S. 160A-267 and for nominal monetary consideration to persons who qualify as grantees.

(3) Convey property subject to conditions that:

a. Require the grantee to use the property as his or her principal place of residence for a minimum number of years,

b. Require the grantee to rehabilitate the property so that it meets or exceeds minimum code standards,

c. Require the grantee to maintain insurance on the property,

d. Set out any other specific conditions (including, but not limited to, design standards) or actions that the city may require, and

e. Provide for the termination of the grantee's interest in the property and its reversion to the city upon the grantee's failure to meet any condition so established.

(4) Subordinate the city's interest in the property to any security interest granted by the grantee to a lender of funds to purchase or rehabilitate the property. (1987, c. 464, s. 8; 1997-456, s. 27.)

§ 160A-458. Erosion and sedimentation control.

Any city may enact and enforce erosion and sedimentation control ordinances as authorized by Article 4 of Chapter 113A of the General Statutes, and in such enactment and enforcement shall comply with all applicable provisions of Article 4. (1979, 2nd Sess., c. 1247, s. 39.)

§ 160A-458.1. Floodway regulations.

(1979, 2nd Sess., c. 1247, s. 39.)

§ 160A-458.2. Mountain ridge protection.

Cities may enact and enforce mountain ridge protection ordinances pursuant to Article 14 of Chapter 113A of the General Statutes, and in such enactment and enforcement shall comply with all applicable provisions of Article 14 unless the city has removed itself from the coverage of Article 14 through the procedure provided by law. (1983, c. 676, s. 3.)

§ 160A-458.3. Downtown development projects.

(a) In this section, "downtown development project" means a capital project in the city's central business district, as that district is defined by the city council, comprising one or more buildings and including both public and private facilities. By way of illustration but not limitation, such a project might include a single building comprising a publicly owned parking structure and publicly owned convention center and a privately owned hotel or office building.

(b) If the city council finds that it is likely to have a significant effect on the revitalization of the central business district, the city may acquire, construct, own, and operate or participate in the acquisition, construction, ownership, and operation of a downtown development project or of specific facilities within such a project. The city may enter into binding contracts with one or more private developers with respect to acquiring, constructing, owning, or operating such a project. Such a contract may, among other provisions, specify the following:

(1) The property interests of both the city and the developer or developers in the project, provided that the property interests of the city shall be limited to facilities for a public purpose;

(2) The responsibilities of the city and the developer or developers for construction of the project;

(3) The responsibilities of the city and the developer or developers with respect to financing the project.

(c)   A downtown development project may be constructed on property acquired by the developer or developers, on property directly acquired by the city, or on property acquired by the city while exercising the powers, duties, and responsibilities of a redevelopment commission pursuant to G.S. 160A-505 or G.S. 160A-456.

(d)   In connection with a downtown development project, the city may convey interests in property owned by it, including air rights over public facilities, as follows:

(1)   If the property was acquired while the city was exercising the powers, duties, and responsibilities of a redevelopment commission, the city may convey property interests pursuant to the "Urban Redevelopment Law" or any local modification thereof.

(2)   If the property was acquired by the city directly, the city may convey property interests pursuant to G.S. 160A-457, and Article 12 of Chapter 160A of the General Statutes does not apply to such dispositions.

(3)   In lieu of conveying the fee interest in air rights, the city may convey a leasehold interest for a period not to exceed 99 years, using the procedures of subparagraphs (1) or (2) of this subsection, as applicable.

(e)   The contract between the city and the developer or developers may provide that the developer or developers shall be responsible for construction of the entire downtown development project. If so, the contract shall include such provisions as the city council deems sufficient to assure that the public facility or facilities included in the project meet the needs of the city and are constructed at a reasonable price. A project constructed pursuant to this paragraph is not subject to Article 8 of Chapter 143 of the General Statutes, provided that city funds constitute no more than fifty percent (50%) of the total costs of the downtown development project. Federal funds available for loan to private developers in connection with a downtown development project shall not be considered city funds for purposes of this subsection.

(f)   Operation. - The city may contract for the operation of any public facility or facilities included in a downtown redevelopment project by a person,

(g) Grant funds. - To assist in the financing of its share of a downtown development project, the city may apply for, accept and expend grant funds from the federal or State governments. (1987, c. 619, s. 1.)

§ 160A-458.4. Designation of transportation corridor official maps.

Any city may establish transportation corridor official maps and may enact and enforce ordinances pursuant to Article 2E of Chapter 136 of the General Statutes. (1987, c. 747, s. 23; 1998-184, s. 4.)

§ 160A-458.5. Restriction of certain forestry activities prohibited.

(a) The following definitions apply to this section:

(1) Development. - Any activity, including timber harvesting, that is associated with the conversion of forestland to nonforest use.

(2) Forest management plan. - A document that defines a landowner's forest management objectives and describes specific measures to be taken to achieve those objectives. A forest management plan shall include silvicultural practices that both ensure optimal forest productivity and environmental protection of land by either commercially growing timber through the establishment of forest stands or by ensuring the proper regeneration of forest stands to commercial levels of production after the harvest of timber.

(3) Forestland. - Land that is devoted to growing trees for the production of timber, wood, and other forest products.

(4) Forestry. - The professional practice embracing the science, business, and art of creating, conserving, and managing forests and forestland for the sustained use and enjoyment of their resources, materials, or other forest products.

regulations pertaining to forestry.

(b)   A city shall not adopt or enforce any ordinance, rule, regulation, or resolution that regulates either:

(1)   Forestry activity on forestland that is taxed on the basis of its present-use value as forestland under Article 12 of Chapter 105 of the General Statutes.

(2)   Forestry activity that is conducted in accordance with a forest management plan that is prepared or approved by a forester registered in accordance with Chapter 89B of the General Statutes.

(c)   This section shall not be construed to limit, expand, or otherwise alter the authority of a city to:

(1)   Regulate activity associated with development. A city may deny a building permit or refuse to approve a site or subdivision plan for either a period of up to:

a.   Three years after the completion of a timber harvest if the harvest results in the removal of all or substantially all of the trees that were protected under city regulations governing development from the tract of land for which the permit or approval is sought.

b.   Five years after the completion of a timber harvest if the harvest results in the removal of all or substantially all of the trees that were protected under city regulations governing development from the tract of land for which the permit or approval is sought and the harvest was a willful violation of the city regulations.

(2)   Regulate trees pursuant to any local act of the General Assembly.

(3)   Adopt ordinances that are necessary to comply with any federal or State law, regulation, or rule.

(4)   Exercise its planning or zoning authority under this Article.

§ 160A-459. Stormwater control.

(a)   A city may adopt and enforce a stormwater control ordinance to protect water quality and control water quantity. A city may adopt a stormwater management ordinance pursuant to this Chapter, its charter, other applicable laws, or any combination of these powers.

(b)   A federal, State, or local government project shall comply with the requirements of a city stormwater control ordinance unless the federal, State, or local government agency has a National Pollutant Discharge Elimination System (NPDES) stormwater permit that applies to the project. A city may take enforcement action to compel a State or local government agency to comply with a stormwater control ordinance that implements the National Pollutant Discharge Elimination System (NPDES) stormwater permit issued to the city. To the extent permitted by federal law, including Chapter 26 of Title 33 of the United States Code, a city may take enforcement action to compel a federal government agency to comply with a stormwater control ordinance.

(c)   A city may implement illicit discharge detection and elimination controls, construction site stormwater runoff controls, and post-construction runoff controls through an ordinance or other regulatory mechanism to the extent allowable under State law.

(d)   A city that holds a National Pollutant Discharge Elimination System (NPDES) permit issued pursuant to G.S. 143-214.7 may adopt an ordinance, applicable within its corporate limits and its planning jurisdiction, to establish the stormwater control program necessary for the city to comply with the permit. A city may adopt an ordinance that bans illicit discharges within its corporate limits and its planning jurisdiction. A city may adopt an ordinance, applicable within its corporate limits and its planning jurisdiction, that requires (i) deed restrictions and protective covenants to ensure that each project, including the stormwater management system, will be maintained so as to protect water quality and control water quantity and (ii) financial arrangements to ensure that adequate funds are available for the maintenance and replacement costs of the project.

(e)   Unless the city requests the permit condition in its permit application, the Environmental Management Commission may not require as a condition of a

extraterritorial jurisdiction. (2006-246, s. 17(b).)

§ 160A-459.1. Program to finance energy improvements.

(a) Purpose. - The General Assembly finds it is in the best interest of the citizens of North Carolina to promote and encourage renewable energy and energy efficiency within the State in order to conserve energy, promote economic competitiveness, and expand employment in the State. The General Assembly also finds that a city has an integral role in furthering this purpose by promoting and encouraging renewable energy and energy efficiency within the city's territorial jurisdiction. In furtherance of this purpose, a city may establish a program to finance the purchase and installation of distributed generation renewable energy sources or energy efficiency improvements that are permanently affixed to residential, commercial, or other real property.

(b) Financing Assistance. - A city may establish a revolving loan fund and a loan loss reserve fund for the purpose of financing or assisting in the financing of the purchase and installation of distributed generation renewable energy sources or energy efficiency improvements that are permanently fixed to residential, commercial, or other real property. A city may establish other local government energy efficiency and distributed generation renewable energy source finance programs funded through federal grants. A city may use State and federal grants and loans and its general revenue for this financing. The annual interest rate charged for the use of funds from the revolving fund may not exceed eight percent (8%) per annum, excluding other fees for loan application review and origination. The term of any loan originated under this section may not be greater than 20 years.

(c) Definition. - As used in this Article, "renewable energy source" has the same meaning as "renewable energy resource" in G.S. 62-133.8. (2009-522, s. 1; 2010-167, s. 4(c).)

Article 20.

Interlocal Cooperation.

The words defined in this section shall have the meanings indicated when used in this Part:

(1)   "Undertaking" means the joint exercise by two or more units of local government, or the contractual exercise by one unit for one or more other units, of any power, function, public enterprise, right, privilege, or immunity of local government.

(2)   "Unit," or "unit of local government" means a county, city, consolidated city-county, local board of education, sanitary district, facility authority created under Part 4 of this Article, special district created under Article 43 of Chapter 105 of the General Statutes, or other local political subdivision, authority, or agency of local government. (1971, c. 698, s. 1; 1975, c. 821, s. 4; 1979, c. 774, s. 1; 1981, c. 641; 1995, c. 458, s. 3; 2009-527, s. 2(f).)

§ 160A-461. Interlocal cooperation authorized.

Any unit of local government in this State and any one or more other units of local government in this State or any other state (to the extent permitted by the laws of the other state) may enter into contracts or agreements with each other in order to execute any undertaking. The contracts and agreements shall be of reasonable duration, as determined by the participating units, and shall be ratified by resolution of the governing board of each unit spread upon its minutes. (1971, c. 698, s. 1.)

§ 160A-462. Joint agencies.

(a)   Units agreeing to an undertaking may establish a joint agency charged with any or all of the responsibility for the undertaking. The units may confer on the joint agency any power, duty, right, or function needed for the execution of the undertaking, except that legal title to all real property necessary to the undertaking shall be held by the participating units individually, or jointly as tenants in common, in such manner and proportion as they may determine.

§ 160A-463. Personnel.

(a) The units may agree that any joint agency established under G.S. 160A-462 shall appoint the officers, agents, and employees necessary to execute the undertaking, or that the units jointly shall appoint these personnel, or that one of the units shall appoint the personnel with their services contracted for by the other units or by the joint agency. If the units determine that one unit shall appoint the personnel, the agreement shall provide that the jurisdiction, authority, rights, privileges, and immunities (including coverage under the workers' compensation laws) which the officers, agents, and employees of the appointing unit enjoy within the territory of that unit shall also be enjoyed by them outside its territory when they are acting pursuant to the agreement and within the scope of their authority or the course of their employment.

(b) When the subject of an undertaking is a sovereign function of government, the exercise of which has been delegated to an officer of each participating unit, the agreement may provide that one officer shall exercise the function for all the participating units, with all of the powers, duties, and obligations that an officer exercising the function in a single unit would have. (1971, c. 698, s. 1; 1991, c. 636, s. 3.)

§ 160A-464. Provisions of the agreement.

Any contract or agreement establishing an undertaking shall specify:

(1) The purpose or purposes of the contract or agreement;

(2) The duration of the agreement;

(3) If a joint agency is established, its composition, organization, and nature, together with the powers conferred on it;

(4) The manner of appointing the personnel necessary to the execution of the undertaking;

(6) The formula for ownership of real property involved in the undertaking, and procedures for the disposition of such property when the contract or agreement expires or is terminated;

(7) Methods for amending the contract or agreement;

(8) Methods for terminating the contract or agreement;

(9) Any other necessary or proper matter. (1971, c. 698, s. 1.)

§ 160A-465. Repealed by Session Laws 1979, c. 774, s. 2.

§ 160A-466. Revenue and expenditures for joint undertakings.

When two or more units of local government are engaged in a joint undertaking, they may enter into agreements regarding financing, expenditures, and revenues related to the joint undertaking. Funds collected by any participating unit of government may be transferred to and expended by any other unit of government in a manner consistent with the agreement. An agreement regarding expenses and revenues may be of reasonable duration not to exceed 99 years. (2003-417, s. 1.)

§§ 160A-467 through 160A-469. Reserved for future codification purposes.

Part 2. Regional Councils of Governments.

§ 160A-470. Creation of regional councils; definition of "unit of local government".

(a) Any two or more units of local government may create a regional council of governments by adopting identical concurrent resolutions to that effect in accordance with the provisions and procedures of this Part. To the extent permitted by the laws of its state, a local government in a state adjoining North Carolina may participate in regional councils of governments organized under this Part to the same extent as if it were located in this State. The concurrent

(b) For the purposes of this Part, "unit of local government" means a county, city, or consolidated city-county. (1971, c. 698, s. 1; 1973, c. 426, s. 71.)

§ 160A-471. Membership.

Each unit of local government initially adopting a concurrent resolution under G.S. 160A-470 shall become a member of the regional council. Thereafter, any local government may join the regional council by ratifying its charter and by being admitted by a majority vote of the existing members. All of the rights and privileges of membership in a regional council of governments shall be exercised on behalf of its member governments by their delegates to the council. (1971, c. 698, s. 1; 1973, c. 426, s. 72.)

§ 160A-472. Contents of charter.

The charter of a regional council of governments shall:

(1) Specify the name of the council;

(2) Establish the powers, duties, and functions that it may exercise and perform;

(3) Establish the number of delegates to represent the member governments, fix their terms of office, provide methods for filling vacancies, and prescribe the compensation and allowances, if any, to be paid to delegates;

(4) Set out the method of determining the financial support that will be given to the council by each member government;

(5) Establish a method for amending the charter, and for dissolving the council and liquidating its assets and liabilities.

In addition, the charter may, but need not, contain rules and regulations for the conduct of council business and any other matter pertaining to the organization, powers, and functioning of the council that the member governments deem appropriate. (1971, c. 698, s. 1.)

by its member governments and shall organize by electing a chairman and any other officers that the charter may specify or the delegates may deem advisable. The council shall then adopt bylaws for the conduct of its business. All meetings of the council shall be open to the public. (1971, c. 698, s. 1.)

§ 160A-474. Withdrawal from council.

Any member government may withdraw from a regional council at the end of any fiscal year by giving at least 60 days' written notice to each of the other members. Withdrawal of a member government shall not dissolve the council if at least two members remain. (1971, c. 698, s. 1.)

§ 160A-475. Specific powers of council.

The charter may confer on the regional council any of the following powers:

(1) To apply for, accept, receive, and dispense funds and grants made available to it by the State of North Carolina or any agency thereof, the United States of America or any agency thereof, any unit of local government (whether or not a member of the council), and any private or civic agency.

(2) To employ personnel.

(3) To contract with consultants.

(4) To contract with the State of North Carolina, any other state, the United States of America, or any agency thereof, for services.

(5) To study regional governmental problems, including matters affecting health, safety, welfare, education, recreation, economic conditions, regional planning, and regional development.

(6) To promote cooperative arrangements and coordinated action among its member governments.

(7a) For the purpose of meeting the regional council's office space and program needs, to acquire real property by purchase, gift, or otherwise, and to improve that property. The regional council may pledge real property as security for indebtedness used to finance acquisition of that property or for improvements to that real property, subject to approval by the Local Government Commission as required under G.S. 159-153. A regional council may not exercise the power of eminent domain.

(8) Any other powers that are exercised or capable of exercise by its member governments and desirable for dealing with problems of mutual concern to the extent such powers are specifically delegated to it from time to time by resolution of the governing board of each of its member governments which are affected thereby, provided, that no regional council of governments shall have the authority to construct or purchase buildings, or acquire title to real property, except for the purposes permitted under subdivision (7a) of this section or in order to exercise the authority granted by Chapter 260 of the Session Laws of 1979. (1971, c. 698, s. 1; 1975, c. 517, ss. 1, 2; 1979, c. 902; 2005-290, s. 1; 2006-211, s. 1.)

§ 160A-476. Fiscal affairs.

Each unit of local government having membership in a regional council may appropriate funds to the council from any legally available revenues. Services of personnel, use of equipment and office space, and other services may be made available to the council by its member governments as a part of their financial support. (1971, c. 698, s. 1; 1973, c. 426, s. 73.)

§ 160A-477. Reports.

Each regional council shall prepare and distribute to its member governments and to the public an annual report of its activities including a financial statement. (1971, c. 698, s. 1.)

any powers heretofore or hereafter granted by any other general law, local act, or city charter for the same or similar purposes. (1971, c. 698, s. 1.)

Part 3. Regional Sports Authorities.

§ 160A-479. Creation of authority; definition.

(a) Any two or more units of local government may create a regional sports authority by adopting identical concurrent resolutions to that effect in accordance with the provisions of this Part. The concurrent resolutions creating a regional sports authority, and any amendments thereto will be referred to in this Part as the "charter" of the regional sports authority. For the purposes of this Part, "unit of local government" means a county, city or consolidated city-county.

(b) Any regional sports authority created pursuant to this Part shall be a body corporate and politic. (1989, c. 780, s. 1.)

§ 160A-479.1. Purpose of the authority.

The purpose of a regional sports authority shall be to research, design, construct, provide, finance, operate, improve, and maintain facilities for public participation and enjoyment of sports, fitness, health and recreational activities of as many different types and kinds as possible. The primary purpose of any and all such facilities shall be the conduct of sports events but use of these facilities need not be limited to such. (1989, c. 780, s. 1.)

§ 160A-479.2. Jurisdiction of the authority.

(a) The territorial jurisdiction of any authority created pursuant to this Part shall be coterminous with the boundaries of the respective units of local government creating and participating in the authority.

(b) The jurisdiction of any authority created pursuant to this Part shall include any and all currently existing public sports facilities operating within its

(c) The jurisdiction of an authority shall also include any and all new public sports facilities within the regional authority's territorial jurisdiction developed specifically for operation and maintenance by an authority with the agreement of an authority. (1989, c. 780, s. 1.)

§ 160A-479.3. Membership.

Each unit of local government initially adopting a concurrent resolution under G.S. 160A-479 shall become a member of the regional authority. Thereafter, any local government may join the regional authority by ratifying its charter and by being admitted by a majority vote of the existing members. All of the rights and privileges of membership in a regional sports authority shall be exercised on behalf of its member governments by their delegates to the authority. (1989, c. 780, s. 1.)

§ 160A-479.4. Contents of charter.

The charter of a regional sports authority shall:

(1) Specify the name of the authority;

(2) Establish the powers, duties, and functions that it may exercise and perform;

(3) Establish the number of delegates to represent the member governments, fix their terms of office, provide methods for filling vacancies, and prescribe the compensation and allowances, if any, to be paid to delegates;

(4) Set out the method of determining the financial support that will be given to the authority by each member government;

(5) Establish a method for amending the charter, and for dissolving the authority and liquidating its assets and liabilities.

governments deem appropriate. (1989, c. 780, s. 1.)

§ 160A-479.5. Organization of authority.

Upon its creation, a regional sports authority shall meet at a time and place agreed upon by its member governments and shall organize by electing a chairman and any other officers that the charter may specify or the delegates may deem advisable. The authority shall then adopt bylaws for the conduct of its business. All meetings of the authority shall be open to the public. (1989, c. 780, s. 1.)

§ 160A-479.6. Withdrawal from authority.

Any member government may withdraw from a regional sports authority at the end of any fiscal year by giving at least 60 days' written notice to each of the other members. A withdrawal does not affect the validity of any revenue bonds or notes, and any revenue from sports facilities in the area of the member government that was pledged in payment of bonds or notes issued before the date of notice of withdrawal remains pledged for that purpose until the bonds and notes and interest on the bonds and notes have been paid. Withdrawal of a member government shall not dissolve the authority if at least two members remain. (1989, c. 780, s. 1.)

§ 160A-479.7. Powers of authority.

(a) The charter may confer on the regional sports authority any or all of the following powers:

(1) To apply for, accept, receive, and dispense funds and grants made available to it by the State of North Carolina or any agency thereof, the United States of America or any agency thereof, any unit of local government (whether or not a member of the authority), and any private or civic agency;

(2) To employ personnel;

States of America, or any agency thereof, for services;

(5) To adopt bylaws for the regulation of the affairs and the conduct of its business, and to prescribe rules, regulations and policies in connection with the performance of its functions and duties, not inconsistent with this Part;

(6) To adopt an official seal and alter the same at pleasure;

(7) To acquire and maintain an administrative building or office at such place or places as it may determine, which building or office may be used or owned alone or together with any municipalities, corporations, associations or persons under such terms and provisions for sharing costs and otherwise as may be determined;

(8) To sue and be sued in its own name, and to plead and be impleaded;

(9) To receive, administer, and comply with the conditions and requirements respecting any gift, grant, or donation of any property or money;

(10) To acquire by purchase, lease, gift, or otherwise, or to obtain options for the acquisition of, any property, real or personal, improved or unimproved, including an interest in land less than the fee thereof;

(11) To sell, lease, exchange, transfer, or otherwise dispose of, or to grant options for any such purposes with respect to, any real or personal property or interest therein;

(12) To pledge, assign, mortgage, or otherwise grant a security interest in any real or personal property or interest therein, including the right and power to pledge, assign, or otherwise grant a security interest in any money, rents, charges, or other revenues and any proceeds derived by an authority from any and all sources;

(13) To issue revenue bonds of the authority to finance regional sports and recreational facilities, including support facilities, to refund any revenue bonds or notes issued by the authority, whether or not in advance of their maturity or earliest redemption date, or to provide funds for other corporate purposes of the authority;

agreeable;

(15) To develop and make data, plans, information, surveys, and studies of public sports and recreation facilities within the territorial jurisdiction of an authority, to prepare and make recommendations in regard thereto;

(16) To study and plan for new and improved major regional sports and recreational facilities including but not limited to arenas, stadia, gymnasia, natatoria, pitches, fields, watercourses, and other areas for the conduct of sports and recreational activities. These facilities should be of such sizes and in such locations that they will be adequate to serve the population of the entire jurisdiction of the authority (and beyond) to the extent possible;

(17) To design any new such facilities so they include such equipment and design that efficiency, cost, accessibility, utility, and usability of such facilities will be maximized;

(18) To have sports facilities grouped into complexes or separated as an authority may see fit, and such facilities may include ancillary support facilities including but not limited to those for administration, sports science, sports medicine, training, museums, meeting rooms and conference centers, accommodations, food services, retail shops, theatres, video services, schools, and educational services.

(19) To operate the facilities in such a way as to make them as accessible as possible for rental and use by the public while balancing the need for as many of the facilities as possible (particularly any arenas and stadia) to operate annually without a deficit (exclusive of any debt service);

(20) To operate such facilities together with the State, any entity of the State, or local government as appropriate to maintain a high profile and promotional value for North Carolina and the region encompassed by an authority and to attract as many major regional, national, and international tournaments, events, championships training centers, training camps, and headquarters for the governance of various sports, associations, and events as reasonable and possible;

(22) To set and collect such fees and charges for use of such facilities as is reasonable to offset operating costs of said facilities and yet enable said facilities to be affordable to and used by as much of the regional and State population as possible;

(23) To apply to the appropriate agencies of the State, the United States or any state thereof, and to any other proper agency for such permits, licenses, certificates or approvals as may be necessary, and to construct, maintain and operate projects in accordance with such licenses, permits, certificates or approvals in the same manner as any other person or operating unit of any other person;

(24) To employ engineers, architects, attorneys, real estate counselors, appraisers, financial advisors and such other consultants and employees as may be required in the judgment of an authority and to fix and pay their compensation from funds available to an authority therefor and to select and retain subject to approval of the Local Government Commission, the financial consultants, underwriters and bond attorneys to be associated with the issuance of any revenue bonds and to pay for services rendered by underwriters, financial consultants, or bond attorneys out of the proceeds of any such issue with regard to which the services were performed; and

(25) To do all acts and things necessary, convenient, or desirable to carry out the purposes, and to exercise the powers granted to an authority herein.

(b) The charter may not confer the following powers on the regional sports authority:

(1) To issue general obligation bonds or otherwise incur a debt that is secured by the full faith and/or credit of the authority, a member government of the authority, or the State.

(2) To levy a property tax or other tax.

(3) To acquire property by eminent domain. (1989, c. 780, s. 1; 2007-495, s. 19.)

Chapter 159 of the General Statutes of North Carolina. (1989, c. 780, s. 1.)

§ 160A-479.9. Funds.

(a) The establishment and operation of an authority as herein authorized are governmental functions and constitute a public purpose, and the State of North Carolina and any unit of local government may appropriate funds to support the establishment and operation of an authority.

(b) The State of North Carolina and any unit of local government may also dedicate, sell, convey, donate or lease any of their interests in any property to an authority. (1989, c. 780, s. 1.)

§ 160A-479.10. Controlling provisions.

Insofar as the provisions of this Part are not consistent with the provisions of any other law, public or private, the provisions of this Part shall be controlling. (1989, c. 780, s. 1.)

§ 160A-479.11. Conflicts of interest of public officials.

Members, officers, and employees of any authority created under this Part shall be subject to the provisions of G.S. 14-234. (1989, c. 780, s. 1.)

§ 160A-479.12. Issuance of revenue bonds and notes.

The Local Government Revenue Bond Act, G.S. Chapter 159, Article 5, governs the issuance of revenue bonds by an authority. G.S. Chapter 159, Article 9, governs the issuance of notes in anticipation of the sale of revenue bonds. (1989, c. 780, s. 1.)

§ 160A-479.13. Acquisition of property.

the fee or any lesser interest in real or personal property for use by an authority. (1989, c. 780, s. 1; 2011-284, s. 119.)

§ 160A-479.14. Tax exemption.

(a) The property of an authority, both real and personal, its acts, activities and income shall be exempt from any tax or tax obligation; in the event of any lease of authority property, or other arrangement which amounts to a leasehold interest, to a private party, this exemption shall not apply to the value of such leasehold interest nor shall it apply to the income of the lessee.

(b) Otherwise, however, for the purpose of taxation, when property of an authority is leased to private parties solely for the purpose of an authority, the acts and activities of an authority for the purpose of exemption of the lessee shall be considered as the acts and activities of the private parties.

(c) The interest on revenue bonds or notes issued by an authority shall be exempt from State taxes. (1989, c. 780, s. 1.)

§ 160A-479.15. Removal and relocation of utility structures.

(a) An authority may require any public utility, railroad, or other public service corporation owning or operating any installations, structures, equipment, apparatus, appliances or facilities in, upon, under, over, across or along any land or facility where an authority has the right to own, construct, operate or maintain its facilities to remove or relocate such installation, structures, equipment, apparatus, appliances or facilities from their location.

(b) If the owner or operator thereof fails or refuses to remove or relocate them, an authority may proceed to do so.

(c) An authority may provide the necessary new locations or an authority may also acquire the necessary new locations by purchase or otherwise, but not by eminent domain.

cost of any increase in the service capacity of the new installations, structures, equipment, apparatus, appliances or facilities and any salvage value derived from the old installations, structures, equipment, apparatus or appliances. (1989, c. 780, s. 1.)

§ 160A-479.16. Advances.

Any member government unit may make advances, from any moneys that may be available for such purpose, in connection with the creation of the authority and to provide for the preliminary expenses of such authority. Any such advances may be repaid to such participating units of local government from the proceeds of the revenue bonds issued by such authority, if capital in nature, or from other available funds of the authority. (1989, c. 780, s. 1.)

§ 160A-479.17. Annexation.

The annexation by a member government which is a city of areas lying outside of the territorial jurisdiction of the authority shall make such annexed area a part of the territorial jurisdiction of the authority, and such area shall be subject to all debts and all obligations thereof. (1989, c. 780, s. 1.)

§ 160A-480. Reserved for future codification purposes.

Part 4. Facility Authorities.

§ 160A-480.1. Short title.

This Part is the "Facility Authority Act" and may be cited by that name. (1995, c. 458, s. 1.)

§ 160A-480.2. Definitions.

The following definitions apply in this Part:

institution, an investment institution, or other financial institution located inside or outside the United States of America that provides for prompt payment, whether at maturity, presentment, or tender for purchase, redemption, or acceleration, of part or all of the principal or purchase price, redemption premium, if any, and interest on a bond or note issued by the Authority and for repayment of the institution.

(3) Member. - A person appointed to a facility authority.

(4) Par formula. - A provision or formula to make periodic adjustments in the interest rate of a bond or note, including:

a. A provision for an adjustment to keep the purchase price of the bond or note in the open market as close to par as possible.

b. A provision for an adjustment based on one or more percentages of a prime rate or base rate that may vary or apply for specified periods of time.

c. Any other provision that does not materially and adversely affect the financial position of the Authority and the marketing of the bonds or notes at a reasonable interest cost to the Authority.

(5) Regional facility. - A facility consisting of an arena, coliseum, or other buildings or both, or areas where sports, fitness, health, recreational, entertainment, or cultural activities can be conducted. The facility may be composed of buildings grouped into complexes or separated from each other and may include ancillary support facilities, such as those for administration, sports science, sports medicine, training, museums, meeting rooms and conference centers, accommodations, parking, and food services. The facility should be designed to attract to the State as many major regional, national, and international tournaments, events, championships, training centers, training camps, and headquarters for the governance of various sports, associations, and events as possible. The regional facility shall be constructed on land owned by the State. (1995, c. 458, s. 1.)

§ 160A-480.3. Creation of Authority; additional membership.

General Assembly to levy a room occupancy tax and a prepared food and beverage tax, and where both those taxes have been levied.

(b) Membership. - An authority shall have 10 or 21 members. Members shall be chosen for terms as follows:

(1) Five shall be appointed by the General Assembly upon the recommendation of the Speaker of the House of Representatives in accordance with G.S. 120-121, at least one of whom shall be a resident of the territorial jurisdiction of the authority, and at least one other of whom shall have been recommended by the board of trustees of the constituent institution of The University of North Carolina whose main campus is located within the county;

(2) Five shall be appointed by the General Assembly upon the recommendation of the President Pro Tempore of the Senate in accordance with G.S. 120-121, at least one of whom shall be a resident of the territorial jurisdiction of the authority, and at least one other of whom shall have been recommended by the Board of Trustees of the constituent institution of The University of North Carolina whose main campus is located within the county; and

(3) If the territorial jurisdiction of the authority is a county where the main campus of a constituent institution of The University of North Carolina is located, then:

a. Four members shall be appointed by the board of commissioners of that county, one of whom at the time of appointment is a resident of the municipality with the second largest population in the county, according to the most recent decennial federal census;

b. Four members shall be appointed by the city council of the city with the largest population in the county, according to the most recent decennial federal census;

c. Two members shall be appointed jointly by the mayors of all the cities in that county.

Beginning January 1, 1999, a majority of any executive committee, or other committee however termed having supervisory or management authority over the facility to be constructed by the authority, shall consist of authority members appointed under this subsection.

Neither the board of commissioners nor the city council may appoint a member of its board to serve on the authority.

Two of the initial appointments under subdivision (1) of this subsection, two of the initial appointments under subdivision (2) of this subsection, one of the initial appointments under subdivision (3)a. of this subsection, and one of the initial appointments under subdivision (3)b. of this section shall be for terms expiring July 1 of the second year after the year in which the authority is created. The remaining initial appointments shall be for terms expiring July 1 of the fourth year after the year in which the authority is created. The third member appointed by the board of commissioners shall serve a term beginning January 1, 1999, and expiring July 1, 2001, and the fourth member appointed by the board of commissioners shall serve a term beginning January 1, 1999, and expiring July 1, 2003. The third member appointed by the city council shall serve a term beginning January 1, 1999, and expiring July 1, 2001, and the fourth member appointed by the city council shall serve a term beginning January 1, 1999, and expiring July 1, 2003. Of the two appointments made by the General Assembly in 1999 and quadrennially thereafter upon the recommendation of the Speaker of the House of Representatives, one shall be the person recommended by the board of trustees of the constituent institution of The University of North Carolina whose main campus is located within the county. Of the two appointments made by the General Assembly in 1999 and quadrennially thereafter upon the recommendation of the President Pro Tempore of the Senate, one shall be the person recommended by the board of trustees of the constituent institution of The University of North Carolina whose main campus is located within the county. The second member appointed under sub-subdivision (3)c. of this section shall serve an initial term expiring July 1, 2003. Successors shall be appointed in the same manner for four-year terms. A member may be removed by the appointing authority for cause. Vacancies occurring in the membership of the authority shall be filled by the remaining members.

(c)   Purpose. - The purpose of an authority is to study, design, plan, construct, own, promote, finance, and operate a regional facility.

that conflicts with the declared public policy of the State as expressed by law is void and unenforceable. The bylaws may do any one or more of the following:

(1)   Limit the powers, duties, and functions that the Authority may exercise and perform.

(2)   Prescribe the compensation and allowances not to exceed those provided by G.S. 93B-5, if any, to be paid to the members of the Authority.

(3)   Contain rules for the conduct of Authority business and any other matter pertaining to the organization, powers, and functioning of the Authority that the members consider appropriate.

(e)   Meetings. - An authority shall meet at a time and place agreed upon by its members. The initial meeting may be called by any four members. At its first meeting, the members shall elect a chairperson and any other officers that the charter may specify or the members may consider advisable. The Authority shall then adopt bylaws for the conduct of its business.

(f)   Fiscal Accountability. - An authority is a public authority subject to the provisions of Article 3 of Chapter 159 of the General Statutes.

(g)   Conflicts. - If any member, officer, or employee of an Authority shall be:

(1)   Interested either directly or indirectly; or

(2)   An officer or employee of or have an ownership interest in any firm or corporation, not including units of local government or the Chancellor of the main campus of a constituent institution of The University of North Carolina within the county, or the Chancellor's designee, interested directly or indirectly in any contract with that Authority, the interest shall be disclosed to the Authority and shall be set forth in the minutes of the Authority. The member, officer, or employee having an interest shall not participate on behalf of the Authority in the authorization of such contract. Other provisions of law notwithstanding, failure to take any or all actions necessary to carry out the purposes of this subsection do not affect the validity of any bonds or notes issued under this Chapter.

matter, including but not limited to the execution of any contract by the Authority, where the matter relates to the interest of a constituent institution of The University of North Carolina within the county.

(h) Any authority created under this Part shall be treated as a board for purposes of Chapter 138A of the General Statutes. (1995, c. 458, s. 1; 1997-68, s. 1; 2000-181, s. 2.5; 2001-311, ss. 1, 2; 2004-158, ss. 3.1, 3.2, 3.3; 2007-348, s. 43.)

§ 160A-480.4. Powers of an Authority.

An Authority shall have all of the powers necessary or convenient to carry out and effectuate the purposes and provisions of this Part. These powers may include any one or more of the following:

(1) To apply for, accept, receive, and dispense funds and grants made available to it by the State or any of its agencies or political subdivisions, the United States, any member unit, or any private entity.

(2) To study, design, plan, construct, own, and operate a regional facility.

(3) To employ consultants and employees as may be required in the judgment of the Authority, to fix and pay their compensation from funds available to the Authority. In employing consultants, the Authority shall promote participation by minority businesses.

(4) To contract with any public or private entity, and The University of North Carolina or any constituent institution of The University of North Carolina may enter into any such contract if the function is one The University of North Carolina or any constituent institution of The University of North Carolina could undertake separately.

(5) To adopt bylaws for the regulation of its affairs and the conduct of its business, and to adopt rules in connection with the performance of its functions and duties.

(6) To adopt an official seal.

(9) To receive, administer, and comply with the conditions and requirements respecting any gift, grant, or donation of any property or money.

(10) To acquire by purchase, lease, gift, or otherwise, or to obtain options for the acquisition of, any real or personal property or interest therein.

(11) To sell, lease, exchange, transfer, or otherwise dispose of, or to grant options for any of these purposes with respect to, any real or personal property or interest therein.

(12) Subject to the provisions of this Part, to pledge, assign, mortgage, or otherwise grant a security interest in any real or personal property or interest therein, including a leasehold interest, including the right and power to pledge, assign, or otherwise grant a security interest in any money, rents, charges, or other revenues and any proceeds derived by the Authority from any and all sources.

(13) Subject to the provisions of this Part, to borrow money to finance part or all of a regional facility, to issue revenue bonds or notes, to refund any revenue bonds or notes issued by the Authority, or to provide funds for other corporate purposes of the Authority.

(14) To use officers, employees, agents, and facilities of units of local government or constituent institutions of The University of North Carolina for purposes and upon the terms that are mutually agreeable between the Authority and the unit or institution.

(15) To develop and make data, plans, information, surveys, and studies of public facilities within the area where constituent institutions of The University of North Carolina are located, and to prepare and make recommendations in regard thereto.

(16) To set and collect fees and charges for the use of the regional facility.

(17) To pay for services rendered by underwriters, financial consultants, or bond attorneys in connection with the issuance of revenue bonds or notes of the Authority out of the proceeds of the bonds or notes. In employing consultants,

(18) To purchase or finance real or personal property in the manner provided for cities and counties under G.S. 160A-20. (1995, c. 458, s. 1.)

§ 160A-480.5. Dissolution of Authority.

The General Assembly may dissolve an authority if all bonds or notes issued by the Authority and all other obligations incurred by the Authority have been fully paid or satisfied. In such event any assets of the Authority shall become the property of the county authorized to levy a room occupancy and prepared food and beverage tax to be distributed to the Authority. (1995, c. 458, s. 1.)

§ 160A-480.6. Construction contracts.

Article 8 of Chapter 143 of the General Statutes applies to a construction contract of an Authority. An Authority may solicit bids on the basis of separate specifications for the branches or work described in G.S. 143-128(a) and on a single-prime contract basis and accept the lowest bid. (1995, c. 458, s. 1.)

§ 160A-480.7. Seating at regional facility arena.

The Authority shall ensure that at least fifty percent (50%) of the seats for an athletic event that is sponsored by a constituent institution of The University of North Carolina whose principal campus is in the territorial jurisdiction of the authority and is held at the arena of the regional facility are made available to students at that constituent institution and members of the general public. (1995, c. 458, s. 1.)

§ 160A-480.8. Bonds.

(a) Terms. - An Authority may provide for the issuance, at one time or from time to time, of bonds or notes to carry out its corporate purposes. The principal of, the interest on, and any premium payable upon the redemption of the bonds or notes shall be payable from the proceeds of bonds or renewal notes, or, in the event bond or renewal note proceeds are not available, from any available

dates, and upon the terms and conditions set by the Authority. The bonds or notes may also be made payable from time to time on demand or tender for purchase by the owner upon terms and conditions set by the Authority. Notes and bonds shall mature at times determined by the Authority, not exceeding 40 years from the date of issue. The Authority shall determine the form and the manner of execution of the bonds or notes, and shall fix the denomination of the bonds or notes and the place of payment of principal and interest. In case an officer whose signature or a facsimile of whose signature appears on any bonds or notes ceases to be an officer before the delivery of the bond or note, the signature or facsimile shall nevertheless be valid and sufficient for all purposes the same as if the officer had remained in office until delivery. The Authority may also provide for the authentication of the bonds or notes by a trustee or fiscal agent.

Bonds or notes may be issued under this Part without obtaining, except as otherwise expressly provided in this Part, the consent of any department, division, commission, board, body, bureau, or other agency of the State or of a political subdivision of the State, and without any other proceedings or conditions except as specifically required by this Part or the provisions of the resolution authorizing the issuance of, or any trust agreement securing, the bonds or notes.

Prior to the preparation of definitive bonds, the Authority may issue interim receipts or temporary bonds exchangeable for definitive bonds when the bonds have been executed and are available for delivery. The Authority may also provide for the replacement of any bonds or notes which have been mutilated, destroyed, or lost.

(b) Use of Proceeds. - The proceeds of a bond or note shall be used solely for the purposes for which the bond or note was issued and shall be disbursed in accordance with the resolution authorizing the issuance of a bond or note and with any trust agreement securing the bond or note. If the proceeds of a bond or note of any issue, by reason of increased construction costs or error in estimates or otherwise, is less than the cost, additional bonds or notes may in like manner be issued to provide the amount of the deficiency.

(c) Security. - Bonds or notes issued by an Authority may be secured in one or more of the following ways:

including a leasehold interest, acquired with the proceeds of the bonds or notes or improved with the proceeds of the bonds or notes as described in subsection (e) of this section.

(3)   With the approval of the county levying the tax, by receipts, if any, from a room occupancy and prepared food and beverage tax levied by a county and distributed to the Authority; provided, however, that any agreement or undertaking by a county to distribute receipts, if any, from the tax to the Authority may not obligate the county to exercise any power of taxation, or restrict the ability of the county to repeal the tax. However, no action by a county to discontinue, decrease, or repeal a room occupancy tax shall become effective while previously issued bonds or notes secured by receipts from such a tax allocated to an authority by the county remain outstanding.

The security for the bonds or notes shall be specified in the resolution or trust instrument authorizing the bonds or notes.

(d)   Revenues. - The Authority may pledge to the payment of its revenue bonds or notes the revenues from the regional facility, including revenues from improvements, betterments, or extensions to the facility. The Authority may establish, maintain, revise, charge, and collect such rates, fees, rentals, or other charges for the use, services, and facilities of or furnished by a regional facility and provide methods of collection of and penalties for nonpayment of these rates, fees, rentals, or other charges. Except as otherwise permitted, the rates, fees, rentals, and charges fixed and charged shall be in an amount that will produce sufficient revenues, with any other available funds, to meet the maintenance and operation expenses of the regional facility as well as any improvements and renewals and replacements to the facility, including reserves to pay the principal, interest, and redemption premium due, if any, on any bonds or notes secured by the facility, and to fulfill the terms of any agreements made by the Authority with the holders of bonds or notes secured by revenues of the facility.

(e)   Security Interests. - Bonds or notes may be secured by security interests in any real or personal property or interest therein, including a leasehold interest, either acquired with the proceeds of bonds or notes, or upon which improvements are provided from the proceeds of bonds or notes. The security interest may cover all real and personal property acquired or improved

agreements, and similar instruments as shall be necessary to carry out the powers in this subsection. Bonds or notes may also be secured by security interests in any real or personal property conveyed to the Authority.

In the event the Authority fails to perform its obligations with respect to the bonds or notes and foreclosure or similar sale of property subject to a security interest occurs, a deficiency judgment may not be rendered against the Authority except to the extent that the deficiency is payable from either revenues from the regional facility or from any revenues dedicated by act of the General Assembly to the Authority.

(f) Issuance. - The issuance of bonds or notes of the Authority is subject to the approval of the Local Government Commission. Upon the filing with the Local Government Commission of a resolution of the Authority requesting that its bonds or notes be sold, the Commission shall determine the manner in which the bonds or notes will be sold and the price or prices at which the bonds or notes will be sold. In determining whether to approve a proposed bond or note issue of the Authority, the Local Government Commission shall consider the criteria for approval of revenue bonds under G.S. 159-86. The Local Government Commission shall approve the proposed issue if it determines the bond or note issue will meet such criteria and will effect the purposes of this Part. With the approval of the Authority, the Local Government Commission shall sell the bonds or notes either at public or private sale in the manner and at the prices determined to be in the best interests of the Authority and to effect the purposes of this Part.

(g) Certification of Approval. - Each bond or note that is represented by an instrument shall contain a statement signed by the Secretary of the Local Government Commission, or an assistant designated by the Secretary, certifying that the issuance of the bond or note has been approved under this Part. The signature may be a manual signature or a facsimile signature, as determined by the Local Government Commission. Each bond or note that is not represented by an instrument shall be evidenced by a writing relating to the obligation that identifies the obligation or the issue of which it is a part, contains the signed statement certifying approval of the Local Government Commission that is required on an instrument, and is filed with the Local Government Commission. A certification of approval by the Local Government Commission is conclusive evidence that a bond or note complies with this Part.

was issued in a way that impairs the ability of the Authority to produce revenues sufficient with other available funds to do all of the following:

(1)   Maintain and operate the facility for which the bond or note was issued.

(2)   Pay the principal of, interest on, and redemption premium, if any, of the bond or note.

(3)   Fulfill the terms of an agreement with the holder.

The State further pledges to the holder of a bond or note issued under this Part that the State will not impair the rights and remedies of the holder concerning the bond or note.

(i)   Investment Securities. - All bonds and notes and interest coupons, if any, issued under this Part are made investment securities within the meaning of and for all the purposes of Article 8 of the Uniform Commercial Code, as enacted in Chapter 25 of the General Statutes.

(j)   Details of Bonds or Notes. - In fixing the details of bonds or notes, the Authority may provide that the bonds or notes may:

(1)   Be payable from time to time on demand or tender for purchase by the owner of the bond or note if a credit facility supports the bond or note, unless the Local Government Commission specifically determines that a credit facility is not required because the absence of a credit facility will not materially and adversely affect the financial position of the Authority and the marketing of the bonds or notes at a reasonable interest cost to the Authority.

(2)   Be additionally supported by a credit facility.

(3)   Be made subject to redemption or a mandatory tender for purchase prior to maturity.

(4)   Be capital appreciation bonds.

(5)   Bear interest at a rate or rates that may vary, including variations permitted pursuant to a par formula.

(k) Basis of Investment. - In connection with or incidental to the acquisition or carrying of any investment relating to bonds, program of investment relating to bonds, or carrying of bonds, the Authority may, with the approval of the Local Government Commission, enter into a contract to place the investment or obligation of the Authority, as represented by the bonds, investment, or program of investment and the contract or contracts, in whole or in part, on an interest rate, currency, cash flow, or other basis, including the following:

(1) Interest rate swap agreements, currency swap agreements, insurance agreements, forward payment conversion agreements, and futures.

(2) Contracts providing for payments based on levels of, or changes in, interest rates, currency exchange rates, or stock or other indices.

(3) Contracts to exchange cash flows or a series of payments.

(4) Contracts to hedge payment, currency, rate, spread, or similar exposure, including interest rate floors or caps, options, puts, and calls.

The Authority may enter a contract of this type in connection with, or incidental to, entering into or maintaining any agreement that secures bonds. A contract shall contain the payment, security, term, default, remedy, and other terms and conditions the Board considers appropriate. The Authority may enter a contract of this type with any person after giving due consideration, where applicable, of the person's creditworthiness as determined by a rating by a nationally recognized rating agency or any other criteria the Board considers appropriate. In connection with, or incidental to, the issuance or carrying of bonds, or the entering of any contract described in this subsection, the Authority may enter into credit enhancement or liquidity agreements, with payment, interest rate, termination date, currency, security, default, remedy, and other terms and conditions as the Authority determines. Proceeds of bonds and any moneys set aside and pledged to secure payment of bonds or any of the contracts entered into under this subsection may be pledged to and used to service any of the contracts entered into under this section. (1995, c. 458, s. 1; 1997-68, s. 2.)

be secured by a trust instrument between the Authority and a bank or trust company or individual within the State, or a bank or a trust company outside the State, as trustee. The trust instrument or the resolution of the Authority authorizing the issuance of bonds or notes may pledge and assign all or any part of the revenues, funds, and other property provided for the security of the bonds, including proceeds from the sale of any project, or part thereof, insurance proceeds, and condemnation awards, and may convey or mortgage property to secure a bond issue as provided in this Part.

The revenues and other funds derived from the project, except any part thereof that may be necessary to provide reserves therefor, if any, shall be set aside at regular intervals as may be provided in the resolution or trust instrument in a sinking fund which may be thereby pledged to, and charged with, the payment of the principal of and the interest on the bonds or notes as they become due and of the redemption price or the purchase price of bonds retired by call or purchase as therein provided. This pledge shall be valid and binding from the time the pledge is made. The revenues so pledged and thereafter received by the Authority shall immediately be subject to the lien of the pledge without any physical delivery thereof or further act, and the lien of the pledge shall be valid and binding as against all parties having claims of any kind in tort, contract, or otherwise against the Authority, irrespective of whether the parties have notice of the pledge. The use and disposition of money to the credit of such sinking fund shall be subject to the provisions of the resolution or trust instrument. The resolution or trust instrument may contain provisions for protecting and enforcing the rights and remedies of the bondholders as may be reasonable and proper and not in violation of law, including, without limitation, any one or more of the following:

(1)   Acceleration of all amounts payable under the resolution or trust instrument.

(2)   Appointment of a receiver to manage the project and any other property mortgaged or assigned as security for the bonds.

(3)   Foreclosure and sale of the project and any other property mortgaged or assigned as security for the bonds.

It shall be lawful for any bank or trust company incorporated under the laws of this State which may act as depository of the proceeds of bonds, revenues, or other funds provided under this Part to furnish such indemnifying bonds or to pledge such securities as may be required by the Authority. All expenses incurred in carrying out the provisions of the resolution or trust instrument may be treated as a part of the cost of the project in connection with which bonds or notes are issued or as an expense of administration of the project.

The Authority may subordinate bonds or notes to any prior, contemporaneous, or future securities or obligations or lien, mortgage, or other security interest securing bonds or notes.

Any owner of bonds or notes issued under the provisions of this Part or any coupons appertaining thereto, and the trustee under any trust agreement securing or resolution authorizing the issuance of such bonds or notes, except to the extent the rights given may be restricted by the trust agreement or resolution, may either at law or in equity, by suit, action, mandamus, or other proceeding, protect and enforce any and all rights under the laws of the State or granted hereunder or under the trust agreement or resolution, or under any other contract executed by the Authority pursuant to this Chapter; and may enforce and compel the performance of all duties required by this Part or by the trust agreement or resolution by the Authority or by any officer of the Authority. (1995, c. 458, s. 1.)

§ 160A-480.10. Trust funds.

Notwithstanding any other provision of law to the contrary, all money received pursuant to the authority of this Part, whether as proceeds from the sale of bonds or notes or as revenues, shall be deemed to be trust funds to be held and applied solely as provided in this Part. The resolution authorizing the issuance of, or the trust agreement securing, any bonds or notes may provide that any of these moneys may be temporarily invested and reinvested pending their disbursement and shall provide that any officer with whom, or any bank or trust company with which, the moneys shall be deposited shall act as trustee of the moneys and shall hold and apply the moneys for the purpose hereof, subject to any regulations this Part and the resolution or trust agreement may provide. Any

§ 160A-480.11. Faith and credit of State and units of local government not pledged.

Bonds or notes issued under this Part shall not constitute a debt secured by a pledge of the faith and credit of the State or a political subdivision of the State and shall be payable solely from the revenues, property, and other funds pledged for their payment. The bonds or notes issued by an Authority shall contain a statement that the Authority is obligated to pay the bond or note or the interest on the bond or note only from the revenues, property, or other funds pledged for their payment and that neither the faith and credit nor the taxing power of the State or any political subdivision of the State is pledged as security for the payment of the principal of or the interest or premium on the bonds or notes. (1995, c. 458, s. 1.)

§ 160A-480.12. Revenue refunding bonds.

The Authority may issue refunding bonds or notes for one or more of the following purposes:

(1)   Refunding any outstanding bonds or notes issued under this Part, including any redemption premium on the bonds or notes and any interest accrued or to accrue to the date of redemption.

(2)   Constructing improvements, additions, extensions or enlargements of the project, or projects in connection with which the bonds or notes to be refunded have been issued.

(3)   Paying all or any part of the cost of any additional project or projects.

Refunding bonds or notes shall be issued in accordance with the same procedures and requirements as bonds or notes. Refunding bonds issued under this section may be sold or exchanged for outstanding bonds or notes issued under this Part and, if sold, the proceeds of the refunding bonds may be applied, in addition to any authorized purposes, to the purchase, redemption, or payment of outstanding bonds or notes.

or permitted in securing the same, to the payment of any interest on such refunding bonds and any expenses in connection with such refunding, such proceeds may be invested in direct obligations of, or obligations the principal of and the interest on which are unconditionally guaranteed by, the United States of America which shall mature or which shall be subject to redemption by the holder thereof, at the option of such holder, not later than the respective dates when the proceeds, together with the interest accruing thereon, will be required for the purposes intended. (1995, c. 458, s. 1.)

§ 160A-480.13. Bonds eligible for investment.

Bonds and notes issued under this Part are hereby made securities in which all public officers, agencies, and public bodies of the State and its political subdivisions, all insurance companies, trust companies, investment companies, banks, savings banks, building and loan associations, credit unions, pension or retirement funds, other financial institutions engaged in business in the State, executors, administrators, trustees, and other fiduciaries may properly and legally invest funds, including capital in their control or belonging to them. These bonds or notes are hereby made securities that may properly and legally be deposited with and received by any officer or agency of the State or political subdivision of the State for any purpose for which the deposit of bonds, notes, or obligations of the State or any political subdivision of the State is authorized by law. This section does not apply to any State pension or retirement fund or a pension or retirement fund of a political subdivision of the State. (1995, c. 458, s. 1.)

§ 160A-480.14. Taxation of revenue bonds.

Any bonds and notes issued by the Authority under the provisions of this Part shall be exempt from all State, county, and municipal taxation or assessment, direct or indirect, general or special, whether imposed for the purpose of general revenue or otherwise, excluding inheritance and gift taxes, income taxes on the gain from the transfer of bonds and notes, and franchise taxes. The interest on bonds and notes issued by an Authority under the provisions of this Part shall not be subject to taxation as to income. (1995, c. 458, s. 1.)

accountability by reason of the execution of any bonds or notes or the issuance of any bonds or notes. (1995, c. 458, s. 1.)

§§ 160A-481 through 160A-484. Reserved for future codification purposes.

Article 21.

Miscellaneous.

§ 160A-485. Waiver of immunity through insurance purchase.

(a) Any city is authorized to waive its immunity from civil liability in tort by the act of purchasing liability insurance. Participation in a local government risk pool pursuant to Article 23 of General Statute Chapter 58 shall be deemed to be the purchase of insurance for the purposes of this section. Immunity shall be waived only to the extent that the city is indemnified by the insurance contract from tort liability. No formal action other than the purchase of liability insurance shall be required to waive tort immunity, and no city shall be deemed to have waived its tort immunity by any action other than the purchase of liability insurance. If a city uses a funded reserve instead of purchasing insurance against liability for wrongful death, negligence, or intentional damage to personal property, or absolute liability for damage to person or property caused by an act or omission of the city or any of its officers, agents, or employees acting within the scope of their authority and the course of their employment, the city council may adopt a resolution that deems the creation of a funded reserve to be the same as the purchase of insurance under this section. Adoption of such a resolution waives the city's governmental immunity only to the extent specified in the council's resolution, but in no event greater than funds available in the funded reserve for the payment of claims.

(b) An insurance contract purchased pursuant to this section may cover such torts and such officials, employees, and agents of the city as the governing board may determine. The city may purchase one or more insurance contracts, each covering different torts or different officials, employees, or agents of the city. An insurer who issues a contract of insurance to a city pursuant to this section thereby waives any defense based upon the governmental immunity of

(c)   Any plaintiff may maintain a tort claim against a city insured under this section in any court of competent jurisdiction. As to any such claim, to the extent that the city is insured against such claim pursuant to this section, governmental immunity shall be no defense. Except as expressly provided herein, nothing in this section shall be construed to deprive any city of any defense to any tort claim lodged against it, or to restrict, limit, or otherwise affect any defense that the city may have at common law or by virtue of any statute. Nothing in this section shall relieve a plaintiff from any duty to give notice of his claim to the city, or to commence his action within the applicable period of time limited by statute. No judgment may be entered against a city in excess of its insurance policy limits on any tort claim for which it would have been immune but for the purchase of liability insurance pursuant to this section. No judgment may be entered against a city on any tort claim for which it would have been immune but for the purchase of liability insurance pursuant to this section except a claim arising at a time when the city is insured under an insurance contract purchased and issued pursuant to this section. If, in the trial of any tort claim against a city for which it would have been immune but for the purchase of liability insurance pursuant to this section, a verdict is returned awarding damages to the plaintiff in excess of the insurance limits, the presiding judge shall reduce the award to the maximum policy limits before entering judgment.

(d)   Except as otherwise provided in this section, tort claims against a city shall be governed by the North Carolina Rules of Civil Procedure. No document or exhibit which relates to or alleges facts as to the city's insurance against liability shall be read, exhibited, or mentioned in the presence of the trial jury in the trial of any claim brought pursuant to this section, nor shall the plaintiff, his counsel, or anyone testifying in his behalf directly or indirectly convey to the jury any inference that the city's potential liability is covered by insurance. No judgment may be entered against the city unless the plaintiff waives his right to a jury trial on all issues of law or fact relating to insurance coverage. All issues relating to insurance coverage shall be heard and determined by the judge without resort to a jury. The jury shall be absent during all motions, arguments, testimony, or announcement of findings of fact or conclusions of law with respect to insurance coverage. The city may waive its right to have issues concerning insurance coverage determined by the judge without a jury, and may request a jury trial on these issues.

Sess., 1986), c. 1027, s. 27; 2003-175, s. 1.)

§ 160A-485.1: Reserved for future codification purposes.

§ 160A-485.2: Reserved for future codification purposes.

§ 160A-485.3: Reserved for future codification purposes.

§ 160A-485.4: Reserved for future codification purposes.

§ 160A-485.5. Waiver of immunity for large cities through State Tort Claims Act.

(a)   Any city with a population of 500,000 or more according to the most recent decennial federal census is authorized to waive its immunity from civil liability in tort by passage of a resolution expressing the intent of the city to waive its sovereign immunity pursuant to Article 31 of Chapter 143 of the General Statutes, as modified by subsection (b) of this section, and subject to the limitations set forth by subsection (c) of this section. Any resolution passed pursuant to this section shall apply to all claims arising on or after the passage of the resolution, until repealed.

(b)   The following modifications of Article 31 of Chapter 143 of the General Statutes shall apply to the waiver of sovereign immunity described by subsection (a) of this section:

(1)   Jurisdiction for tort claims against the city shall be vested in the Superior Court Division of the General Court of Justice of the county where the city is principally located, and, except as otherwise provided in this section, tort claims against a city shall be governed by the North Carolina Rules of Civil Procedure. The city shall be solely responsible for the expenses of its legal representation in connection with claims asserted against it, and for payment of the amount for which it is found liable under this section. Therefore, G.S. 143-291, 143-291.1, 143-291.2, 143-291.3, 143-292, 143-293, 143-295, 143-295.1, 143-296, 143-297, 143-298, 143-299.4, and 143-300 shall not apply to claims under this section.

(3) The limitation on claims set forth in G.S. 143-299; the burden of proof and defense set forth in G.S. 143-299.1; notwithstanding G.S. 143-299.1A(c), the defense set forth in G.S. 143-299.1A; and the limitation on payments set forth in G.S. 143-299.2 shall apply to claims filed with the Superior Court Division under this section.

(c) If a city waives its immunity pursuant to subsection (a) of this section, G.S. 160A-485 shall not apply to that city. The city may purchase liability insurance or adopt a resolution creating a self-funded reserve to insure liability for negligence of any officer, employee, involuntary servant or agent of the city while acting within the scope of his office, employment, service, agency or authority, under circumstances where the city, if a private person, would be liable to the claimant in accordance with the laws of North Carolina.

(d) No document or exhibit that relates to or alleges facts as to the city's insurance against liability shall be read, exhibited, or mentioned in the presence of the trial jury in the trial of any claim brought pursuant to this section, nor shall the plaintiff, plaintiff's counsel, or anyone testifying on the plaintiff's behalf directly or indirectly convey to the jury any inference that the city's potential liability is covered by insurance. No judgment may be entered against the city unless the plaintiff waives the plaintiff's right to a jury trial on all issues of law or fact relating to insurance coverage. All issues relating to insurance coverage shall be heard and determined by the judge without resort to a jury. The jury shall be absent during all motions, arguments, testimony, or announcement of findings of fact or conclusions of law with respect to insurance coverage. The city may waive its right to have issues concerning insurance coverage determined by the judge without a jury and may request a jury trial on these issues. (2009-519, s. 1.)

§ 160A-486. Estimates of population.

When a newly incorporated municipality is not included in the most recent federal census of population but otherwise qualifies for distribution of State-collected funds allocated wholly or partially on the basis of current population estimates, the municipality shall be entitled to participate in the distribution of these funds by reporting all information designated by the Office of State Budget agencies charged with the responsibility of distributing funds to local governments along with the current population estimates for all other municipalities. (1953, c. 79; 1969, c. 873; 1971, c. 698, s. 1; 1979, 2nd Sess., c. 1137, s. 46; 2000-140, s. 93.1(a); 2001-424, s. 12.2(b).)

§ 160A-487. City and county financial support for rescue squads.

Each city and county is authorized to appropriate funds to rescue squads or teams to enable them to purchase and maintain rescue equipment and to finance the operation of the rescue squad either within or outside the boundaries of the city or county. (1959, c. 989; 1971, c. 698, s. 1.)

§ 160A-488. Museums and arts programs.

(a) Any city or county is authorized to establish and support museums, art galleries, or arts centers, so long as the facility is open to the public.

(b) Any city or county is authorized to establish and support arts programs and facilities. As used in this section, "arts" refers to the performing arts, visual arts, and literary arts and includes dance, drama, music, painting, drawing, sculpture, printmaking, crafts, photography, film, video, architecture, design and literature, when part of a performing, visual or literary arts program.

(c) Any city or county may contract with any other governmental agency, or with any public or nonprofit private association, corporation or organization to establish and support museums, art galleries, arts centers, arts facilities, and arts programs and may appropriate funds to any such governmental agency, or to any such public or nonprofit private association, corporation or organization for the purpose of establishing and supporting such museums, galleries, centers, facilities and programs.

(d) As used in this section, "support" includes, but is not limited to: acquisition, construction, and renovation of buildings, including acquisition of land and other property therefor; purchase of paintings and other works of art; acquisition, lease, or purchase of materials and equipment; compensation of

(e) In the event funds appropriated for the purposes of this section are turned over to any agency or organization other than the city or county for expenditure, no such expenditure shall be made until the city or county has approved it, and all such expenditures shall be accounted for by the agency or organization at the end of the fiscal year for which they were appropriated.

(f) For the purposes set forth in this section, a city or county may appropriate funds not otherwise limited as to use by law. (1955, c. 1338; 1961, c. 309; 1965, c. 1019; 1971, c. 698, s. 1; 1975, c. 664, s. 17; 1979, 2nd Sess., c. 1201.)

§ 160A-489. Auditoriums, coliseums, and convention centers.

Any city is authorized to establish and support public auditoriums, coliseums, and convention centers. As used in this section, "support" includes but is not limited to: acquisition, construction, and renovation of buildings and acquisition of the necessary land and other property therefor; purchase of equipment; compensation of personnel; and all operating and maintenance expenses of the facility. For the purposes set forth in this section, a city may appropriate funds not otherwise limited as to use by law. (1971, c. 698, s. 1; 1975, c. 664, s. 18.)

§ 160A-490. Photographic reproduction of records.

(a) General Statutes 153A-436 shall apply to cities. When a county officer is designated by title in that Article, the designation shall be construed to mean the appropriate city officer, and the city council shall perform powers and duties conferred and imposed on the board of county commissioners.

(b) The provisions of subsection (a) of this section shall apply to records stored on any form of permanent, computer-readable media, such as a CD-ROM, if the medium is not subject to erasure or alteration. Nonerasable, computer-readable storage media may be used for preservation duplicates, as defined in G.S. 132-8.2, or for the preservation of permanently valuable records as provided in G.S. 121-5(d). (1955, c. 451; 1971, c. 698, s. 1; 1979, 2nd Sess., c. 1247, s. 41; 1999-131, s. 5; 1999-456, s. 47(e); 2011-326, s. 13(e).)

funds for the acquisition, construction, reconstruction, extension, maintenance, improvement, or enlargement of groins, jetties, dikes, moles, walls, sand dunes, vegetation, or other types of works or improvements which are designed for the control of beach erosion or for protection from hurricane floods and for the preservation or restoration of facilities or natural features which afford protection to the beaches or other land areas of the municipalities or to the life and property thereon. (1971, c. 896, s. 5; c. 1159, s. 2.)

§ 160A-492. Human relations, community action and manpower development programs.

The governing body of any city, town, or county is hereby authorized to undertake, and to expend tax or nontax funds for, human relations, community action and manpower development programs. In undertaking and engaging in such programs, the governing body may enter into contracts with and accept loans and grants from the State or federal governments. The governing body may appoint such human relations, community action and manpower development committees or boards and citizens' committees, as it may deem necessary in carrying out such programs and activities, and may authorize the employment of personnel by such committees or boards, and may establish their duties, responsibilities, and powers. The cities and counties may jointly undertake any program or activity which they are authorized to undertake by this section. The expenses of undertaking and engaging in the human relations, community action and manpower development programs and activities authorized by this section are necessary expenses for which funds derived from taxation may be expended without the necessity of prior approval of the voters.

For the purposes of this section, a "human relations program" is one devoted to (i) the study of problems in the area of human relations, (ii) the promotion of equality of opportunity for all citizens, (iii) the promotion of understanding, respect and goodwill among all citizens, (iv) the provision of channels of communication among the races, (v) dispute resolution, (vi) encouraging the employment of qualified people without regard to race, or (vii) encouraging youth to become better trained and qualified for employment. (1971, c. 896, s. 11; c. 1207, ss. 1, 2; 1973, c. 641; 1989 (Reg. Sess., 1990), c. 1062, s. 1.)

contribute to the support of an animal shelter, and for these purposes may appropriate funds not otherwise limited as to use by law. The animal shelters shall meet the same standards as animal shelters regulated by the Department of Agriculture pursuant to its authority under Chapter 19A of the General Statutes. (1973, c. 426, s. 73.1; 2004-199, s. 39(b).)

§ 160A-494. Drug abuse programs.

Any city may provide for the prevention and treatment of narcotic, barbituric and other types of drug abuse and addiction through education, medication, medical care, hospitalization, and outpatient housing, and may appropriate the necessary funds therefor. (1973, c. 608.)

§ 160A-495. Appropriations for establishment, etc., of local government center in Raleigh.

Counties, cities and towns are hereby authorized to appropriate money for payment to their respective instrumentalities, the North Carolina Association of County Commissioners and the North Carolina League of Municipalities for the purpose of financing the cost, in whole or in part, of purchasing, constructing, equipping, maintaining and operating a local government center in the City of Raleigh to serve as permanent headquarters for said organizations. (1973, c. 1131.)

§ 160A-496. Incorporation of local acts into charter.

(a) A city may from time to time require the city attorney to present to the council any local acts relating to the property, affairs, and government of the city and not part of the city's charter which the city attorney recommends be incorporated into the charter. In his recommendations, the city attorney may include suggestions for renumbering or rearranging the provisions of the charter and other local acts, for providing catchlines, and for any other modifications in arrangement or form that do not change the provisions themselves of the charter or local acts and that may be necessary to effect an orderly incorporation of local acts into the charter.

State and with the Legislative Library.

(c) For purposes of this section, "charter" means that local act of the General Assembly or action of the Municipal Board of Control incorporating a city or a later local act that includes provisions expressly denominated the city's "charter," plus any other local acts inserted therein pursuant to this section or a comparable provision of a local act. (1975, c. 156; 1985 (Reg. Sess., 1986), c. 935, s. 3; 1989, c. 191, s. 3.)

§ 160A-497. Senior citizens programs.

Any city or county may undertake programs for the assistance and care of its senior citizens including but not limited to programs for in-home services, food service, counseling, recreation and transportation, and may appropriate funds for such programs. Any city council or county may contract with any other governmental agency, or with any public or private association, corporation or organization in undertaking senior citizens programs, and may appropriate funds to any such governmental agency, or to any such public or private association, corporation or organization for the purpose of carrying out such programs. In the event funds appropriated for the purposes of this section are turned over to any agency or organization other than the city or county for expenditure, no such expenditure shall be made until the city or county has approved it, and all such expenditures shall be accounted for by the agency or organization at the end of the fiscal year for which they were appropriated. For purposes of this section, the words "senior citizens" shall mean citizens of a city or county who are at least 60 years of age. (1977, c. 187, s. 1; c. 647, ss. 1, 2; 1979, 2nd Sess., c. 1094, ss. 4, 5.)

§ 160A-498. Railroad corridor preservation.

A city or county may acquire property, by purchase or gift, to preserve a railroad corridor established by the Department of Transportation. A city or county that acquires property to preserve a railroad corridor may lease the property or use the property for interim compatible uses until the property is used for a railroad. (1989, c. 600, s. 9.)

and property owners for the design and construction of municipal infrastructure that is included on the city's Capital Improvement Plan and serves the developer or property owner. For the purpose of this act, municipal infrastructure includes, without limitation, water mains, sanitary sewer lines, lift stations, stormwater lines, streets, curb and gutter, sidewalks, traffic control devices, and other associated facilities.

(b)   A city shall enact ordinances setting forth procedures and terms under which such agreements may be approved.

(c)   A city may provide for such reimbursements to be paid from any lawful source.

(d)   Reimbursement agreements authorized by this section shall not be subject to Article 8 of Chapter 143 of the General Statutes, except as provided by this subsection. A developer or property owner who is party to a reimbursement agreement authorized under this section shall solicit bids in accordance with Article 8 of Chapter 143 of the General Statutes when awarding contracts for work that would have required competitive bidding if the contract had been awarded by the city. (2005-426, s. 8(a).)

§ 160A-499.2. Fair housing ordinances in certain municipalities.

(a)   A municipality shall have the power to adopt ordinances prohibiting discrimination on the basis of race, color, sex, religion, handicap, familial status, or national origin in real estate transactions. The ordinances may regulate or prohibit any act, practice, activity, or procedure related, directly or indirectly, to the sale or rental of public or private housing, which affects or may tend to affect the availability or desirability of housing on an equal basis to all persons; may provide that violations constitute a criminal offense; may subject the offender to civil penalties; and may provide that the municipality may enforce the ordinances by application to the Superior Court Division of the General Court of Justice for appropriate legal and equitable remedies, including mandatory and prohibitory injunctions and orders of abatement, attorneys' fees, and punitive damages, and the court shall have jurisdiction to grant the remedies.

Housing Act (41 U.S.C. §§ 3601, et seq.). Any ordinance enacted pursuant to this section prohibiting discrimination on the basis of familial status shall not apply to housing for older persons, as defined in the federal Fair Housing Act (41 U.S.C. §§ 3601, et seq.).

(c) Any ordinance enacted pursuant to this section may provide for exemption from its coverage:

(1) The rental of a housing accommodation in a building containing accommodations for not more than four families living independently of each other if the lessor or a member of his family resides in one of those accommodations.

(2) The rental of a room or rooms in a housing accommodation by an individual if he or a member of his family resides there.

(3) With respect to discrimination based on sex, the rental or leasing of housing accommodations in single-sex dormitory property.

(4) With respect to discrimination based on religion to housing accommodations owned and operated for other than a commercial purpose by a religious organization, association, or society, or any nonprofit institution or organization operated, supervised, or controlled by or in conjunction with a religious organization, association, or society, the sale, rental, or occupancy of the housing accommodation being limited or preference being given to persons of the same religion, unless membership in the religion is restricted because of race, color, national origin, or sex.

(5) Any person, otherwise subject to its provisions, who adopts and carries out a plan to eliminate present effects of past discriminatory practices or to assure equal opportunity in real estate transactions, if the plan is part of a conciliation agreement entered into by that person under the provisions of the ordinance.

(d) A municipality may create or designate a committee to assume the duty and responsibility of enforcing ordinances adopted pursuant to this section. The committee may be granted any authority deemed necessary by the city council for the proper enforcement of any fair housing ordinance, including the power to:

(2) Require answers to interrogatories, the production of documents and things, and the entry upon land and premises in the possession of a party to a complaint alleging a violation of the ordinance; compel the attendance of witnesses at hearings; administer oaths; and examine witnesses under oath or affirmation.

(3) Apply to the Superior Court Division of the General Court of Justice, upon the failure of any person to respond to or comply with a lawful interrogatory, request for production of documents and things, request to enter upon land and premises, or subpoena, for an order requiring the person to respond or comply.

(4) Upon finding reasonable cause to believe that a violation of the ordinance has occurred, to petition the Superior Court Division of the General Court of Justice for appropriate civil relief on behalf of the aggrieved person or persons.

(e) A municipality may provide that neither complaints filed with any committee pursuant to the ordinance nor the results of the committee's investigations, discovery, or attempts at conciliation, in whatever form prepared and preserved, shall be subject to inspection, examination, or copying under the provisions of what is now Chapter 132 of the General Statutes.

(f) A municipality may provide that the statutory provisions relating to meetings of governmental bodies, presently embodied in Article 33C of Chapter 143 of the General Statutes, shall not apply to the activity of any committee authorized to enforce the ordinance to the extent that the committee is receiving a complaint or conducting an investigation, discovery, or conciliation pertaining to a complaint filed pursuant to the ordinance.

(g) This section applies only to municipalities that have a permanent population of 90,000 or more according to the most recent decennial census and that are the location of a recurring special accommodation event requiring temporary accommodations for at least 50,000 people. For purposes of this section, the term "recurring special accommodation event" means a trade show or other event of less than 11 days' duration that has been held in the municipality at least once a year for at least 10 years. (2007-475, ss. 1, 2.)

election or a particular candidate for elective office. (2010-114, s. 1.5(b).)

Article 22.

Urban Redevelopment Law.

§ 160A-500. Short title.

This Article shall be known and may be cited as the "Urban Redevelopment Law." (1951, c. 1095, s. 1; 1973, c. 426, s. 75.)

§ 160A-501. Findings and declaration of policy.

It is hereby determined and declared as a matter of legislative finding:

(1) That there exist in urban communities in this State blighted areas as defined herein.

(2) That such areas are economic or social liabilities, inimical and injurious to the public health, safety, morals and welfare of the residents of the State, harmful to the social and economic well-being of the entire communities in which they exist, depreciating values therein, reducing tax revenues, and thereby depreciating further the general community-wide values.

(3) That the existence of such areas contributes substantially and increasingly to the spread of disease and crime, necessitating excessive and disproportionate expenditures of public funds for the preservation of the public health and safety, for crime prevention, correction, prosecution, punishment and the treatment of juvenile delinquency and for the maintenance of adequate police, fire and accident protection and other public services and facilities, constitutes an economic and social liability, substantially impairs or arrests the sound growth of communities.

(4) That the foregoing conditions are beyond remedy or control entirely by regulatory processes in the exercise of the police power and cannot be

(5) That the acquisition, preparation, sale, sound replanning, and redevelopment of such areas in accordance with sound and approved plans for their redevelopment will promote the public health, safety, convenience and welfare.

Therefore, it is hereby declared to be the policy of the State of North Carolina to promote the health, safety, and welfare of the inhabitants thereof by the creation of bodies corporate and politic to be known as redevelopment commissions, which shall exist and operate for the public purposes of acquiring and replanning such areas and of holding or disposing of them in such manner that they shall become available for economically and socially sound redevelopment. Such purposes are hereby declared to be public uses for which public money may be spent, and private property may be acquired by the exercise of the power of eminent domain. (1951, c. 1095, s. 2; 1973, c. 426, s. 75.)

§ 160A-502. Additional findings and declaration of policy.

It is further determined and declared as a matter of legislative finding:

(1) That the cities of North Carolina constitute important assessts for the State and its citizens; that the preservation of the cities and of urban life against physical, social, and other hazards is vital to the safety, health, and welfare of the citizens of the State, and sound urban development in the future is essential to the continued economic development of North Carolina, and that the creation, existence, and growth of substandard areas present substantial hazards to the cities of the State, to urban life, and to sound future urban development.

(2) That blight exists in commercial and industrial areas as well as in residential areas, in the form of dilapidated, deteriorated, poorly ventilated, obsolete, overcrowded, unsanitary, or unsafe buildings, inadequate and unsafe streets, inadequate lots, and other conditions detrimental to the sound growth of the community; that the presence of such conditions tends to depress the value of neighboring properties, to impair the tax base of the community, and to inhibit private efforts to rehabilitate or improve other structures in the area; and that the acquisition, preparation, sale, sound replanning and redevelopment of such areas in accordance with sound and approved plans will promote the public health, safety, convenience and welfare.

new blighted areas or the expansion of existing blighted areas; that vigorous enforcement of municipal and State building standards, sound planning of new community facilities, public acquisition of dilapidated, obsolescent buildings, and other municipal action can aid in preventing the creation of new blighted areas or the expansion of existing blighted areas; and that rehabilitation, conservation, and reconditioning of areas in accordance with sound and approved plans, where, in the absence of such action, there is a clear and present danger that the area will become blighted, will protect and promote the public health, safety, convenience and welfare.

Therefore it is hereby declared to be the policy of the State of North Carolina to protect and promote the health, safety, and welfare of the inhabitants of its urban areas by authorizing redevelopment commissions to undertake nonresidential redevelopment in accord with sound and approved plans and to undertake the rehabilitation, conservation, and reconditioning of areas where, in the absence of such action, there is a clear and present danger that the area will become blighted. (1961, c. 837, s. 1; 1973, c. 426, s. 75.)

§ 160A-503. Definitions.

The following terms where used in this Article, shall have the following meanings, except where the context clearly indicates a different meaning:

(1) "Area of operation" - The area within the territorial boundaries of the city or county for which a particular commission is created.

(2) "Blighted area" shall mean an area in which there is a predominance of buildings or improvements (or which is predominantly residential in character), and which, by reason of dilapidation, deterioration, age or obsolescence, inadequate provision for ventilation, light, air, sanitation, or open spaces, high density of population and overcrowding, unsanitary or unsafe conditions, or the existence of conditions which endanger life or property by fire and other causes, or any combination of such factors, substantially impairs the sound growth of the community, is conducive to ill health, transmission of disease, infant mortality, juvenile delinquency and crime, and is detrimental to the public health, safety, morals or welfare; provided, no area shall be considered a blighted area within the meaning of this Article, unless it is determined by the planning commission

eminent domain shall be exercised under the provisions of this Article, it may only be exercised to take a blighted parcel as defined in subdivision (2a) of this section, and the property owner or owners or persons having an interest in property shall be entitled to be represented by counsel of their own selection and their reasonable counsel fees fixed by the court, taxed as a part of the costs and paid by the petitioners.

(2a) "Blighted parcel" shall mean a parcel on which there is a predominance of buildings or improvements (or which is predominantly residential in character), and which, by reason of dilapidation, deterioration, age or obsolescence, inadequate provision for ventilation, light, air, sanitation, or open spaces, high density of population and overcrowding, unsanitary or unsafe conditions, or the existence of conditions which endanger life or property by fire and other causes, or any combination of such factors, substantially impairs the sound growth of the community, is conducive to ill health, transmission of disease, infant mortality, juvenile delinquency and crime, and is detrimental to the public health, safety, morals or welfare; provided, no parcel shall be considered a blighted parcel nor subject to the power of eminent domain, within the meaning of this Article, unless it is determined by the planning commission that the parcel is blighted.

(3) "Bonds" - Any bonds, interim certificates, notes, debentures or other obligations of a commission issued pursuant to this Article.

(4) "City" - Any city or town. "The city" shall mean the particular city for which a particular commission is created.

(5) "Commission" or "redevelopment commission" - A public body and a body corporate and politic created and organized in accordance with the provisions of this Article.

(6) "Field of operation" - The area within the territorial boundaries of the city for which a particular commission is created.

(7) "Governing body" - In the case of a city or town, the city council or other legislative body. The board of county commissioners.

(9)   "Municipality" - Any incorporated city or town, or any county.

(10)   "Nonresidential redevelopment area" shall mean an area in which there is a predominance of buildings or improvements, whose use is predominantly nonresidential, and which, by reason of:

a.   Dilapidation, deterioration, age or obsolescence of buildings and other structures,

b.   Inadequate provisions for ventilation, light, air, sanitation or open spaces,

c.   Defective or inadequate street layout,

d.   Faulty lot layout in relation to size, adequacy, accessibility, or usefulness,

e.   Tax or special assessment delinquency exceeding the fair value of the property,

f.   Unsanitary or unsafe conditions,

g.   The existence of conditions which endanger life or property by fire and other causes, or

h.   Any combination of such factors

1.   Substantially impairs the sound growth of the community,

2.   Has seriously adverse effects on surrounding development, and

3.   Is detrimental to the public health, safety, morals or welfare;

provided, no such area shall be considered a nonresidential redevelopment area nor subject to the power of eminent domain, within the meaning of this Article, unless it is determined by the planning commission that at least one half of the number of buildings within the area are of the character described in this subdivision and substantially contribute to the conditions making such area a

represented by counsel of their own selection and their reasonable counsel fees fixed by the court, taxed as a part of the costs and paid by the petitioners.

(11) "Obligee of the commission" or "obligee" - Any bondholder, trustee or trustees for any bondholders, any lessor demising property to a commission used in connection with a redevelopment project, or any assignees of such lessor's interest, or any part thereof, and the federal government, when it is a party to any contract with a commission.

(12) "Planning commission" - Any planning commission established by ordinance for a municipality of this State. "The planning commission" shall mean the particular planning commission of the city or town in which a particular commission operates.

(13) "Real property" - Lands, lands under water, structures and any and all easements, franchises and incorporeal hereditaments and every estate and right therein, legal and equitable, including terms for years and liens by way of judgment, mortgage or otherwise.

(14) "Redeveloper" - Any individual, partnership or public or private corporation that shall enter or propose to enter into a contract with a commission for the redevelopment of an area under the provisions of this Article.

(15) "Redevelopment" - The acquisition, replanning, clearance, rehabilitation or rebuilding of an area for residential, recreational, commercial, industrial or other purposes, including the provision of streets, utilities, parks, recreational areas and other open spaces; provided, without limiting the generality thereof, the term "redevelopment" may include a program of repair and rehabilitation of buildings and other improvements, and may include the exercise of any powers under this Article with respect to the area for which such program is undertaken.

(16) "Redevelopment area" - Any area which a planning commission may find to be

a. A blighted area because of the conditions enumerated in subdivision (2) of this section;

c. A rehabilitation, conservation, and reconditioning area within the meaning of subdivision (21) of this section;

d. Any combination thereof, so as to require redevelopment under the provisions of this Article.

(17) "Redevelopment contract" - A contract between a commission and a redeveloper for the redevelopment of an area under the provisions of this Article.

(18) "Redevelopment plan" - A plan for the redevelopment of a redevelopment area made by a "commission" in accordance with the provisions of this Article.

(19) "Redevelopment project" shall mean any work or undertaking:

a. To acquire blighted or nonresidential redevelopment areas or portions thereof, or individual tracts in rehabilitation, conservation, and reconditioning areas, including lands, structures, or improvements, the acquisition of which is necessary or incidental to the proper clearance, development, or redevelopment of such areas or to the prevention of the spread or recurrence of conditions of blight;

b. To clear any such areas by demolition or removal of existing buildings, structures, streets, utilities or other improvements thereon and to install, construct, or reconstruct streets, utilities, and site improvements essential to the preparation of sites for uses in accordance with the redevelopment plan;

c. To sell land in such areas for residential, recreational, commercial, industrial or other use or for the public use to the highest bidder as herein set out or to retain such land for public use, in accordance with the redevelopment plan;

d. To carry out plans for a program of voluntary or compulsory repair, rehabilitation, or reconditioning of buildings or other improvements in such areas; including the making of loans therefor; and

redevelopment area.

The term "redevelopment project" may also include the preparation of a redevelopment plan, the planning, survey and other work incident to a redevelopment project, and the preparation of all plans and arrangements for carrying out a redevelopment project.

(20) "Redevelopment proposal" - A proposal, including supporting data and the form of a redevelopment contract for the redevelopment of all or any part of a redevelopment area.

(21) "Rehabilitation, conservation, and reconditioning area" shall mean any area which the planning commission shall find, by reason of factors listed in subdivision (2) or subdivision (10), to be subject to a clear and present danger that, in the absence of municipal action to rehabilitate, conserve, and recondition the area, it will become in the reasonably foreseeable future a blighted area or a nonresidential redevelopment area as defined herein. In such an area, no individual tract, building, or improvement shall be subject to the power of eminent domain, within the meaning of this Article, unless it is of the character described in subdivision (2) or subdivision (10) and substantially contributes to the conditions endangering the area; provided that if the power of eminent domain shall be exercised under the provisions of this Article, the respondent or respondents shall be entitled to be represented by counsel of their own selection and their reasonable counsel fees fixed by the court, taxed as part of the costs and paid by the petitioners. (1951, c. 1095, s. 3; 1957, c. 502, ss. 1-3; 1961, c. 837, ss. 2, 3, 4, 6; 1967, c. 1249; 1969, c. 1208, s. 1; 1973, c. 426, s. 75; 1981, c. 907, ss. 1, 2; 1985, c. 665, s. 6; 2006-224, ss. 2.1, 2.2; 2006-259, s. 47.)

§ 160A-504. Formation of commissions.

(a) Each municipality, as defined herein, is hereby authorized to create separate and distinct bodies corporate and politic to be known as the redevelopment commission of the municipality by the passage by the governing body of such municipality of an ordinance or resolution creating a commission to function within the territorial limits of said municipality. Notice of the intent to

(b)   The governing body of a municipality shall not adopt a resolution pursuant to subsection (a) above unless it finds:

(1)   That blighted areas (as herein defined) exist in such municipality, and

(2)   That the redevelopment of such areas is necessary in the interest of the public health, safety, morals or welfare of the residents of such municipality.

(c)   The governing body shall cause a certified copy of such ordinance or resolution to be filed in the office of the Secretary of State; upon receipt of the said certificate the Secretary of State shall issue a certificate of incorporation.

(d)   In any suit, action or proceeding involving or relating to the validity or enforcement of any contract or act of a commission, a copy of the certificate of incorporation duly certified by the Secretary of State shall be admissible in evidence and shall be conclusive proof of the legal establishment of the commission. (1951, c. 1095, s. 4; 1973, c. 426, s. 75.)

§ 160A-505. Alternative organization.

(a)   (See note) In lieu of creating a redevelopment commission as authorized herein, the governing body of any municipality may, if it deems wise, either designate a housing authority created under the provisions of Chapter 157 of the General Statutes to exercise the powers, duties, and responsibilities of a redevelopment commission as prescribed herein, or undertake to exercise such powers, duties, and responsibilities itself. Any such designation shall be by passage of a resolution adopted in accordance with the procedure and pursuant to the findings specified in G.S. 160A-504(a) and (b). In the event a governing body designates itself to perform the powers, duties, and responsibilities of a redevelopment commission, then where any act or proceeding is required to be done, recommended, or approved both by a redevelopment commission and by the municipal governing body, then the performance, recommendation, or approval thereof once by the municipal governing body shall be sufficient to make such performance, recommendation, or approval valid and legal. In the event a municipal governing body designates itself to exercise the powers, duties, and responsibilities of a redevelopment commission, it may assign the

(a) (For effective date, see note) In lieu of creating a redevelopment commission as authorized herein, the governing body of any municipality may, if it deems wise, either designate a housing authority created under the provisions of Chapter 157 of the General Statutes to exercise the powers, duties, and responsibilities of a redevelopment commission as prescribed herein, or undertake to exercise such powers, duties, and responsibilities itself. Any such designation shall be by passage of a resolution adopted in accordance with the procedure and pursuant to the findings specified in G.S. 160A-504(a) and (b). In the event a governing body designates itself to perform the powers, duties, and responsibilities of a redevelopment commission under this subsection, or exercises those powers, duties, and responsibilities pursuant to G.S. 153A-376 or G.S. 160A-456, then where any act or proceeding is required to be done, recommended, or approved both by a redevelopment commission and by the municipal governing body, then the performance, recommendation, or approval thereof once by the municipal governing body shall be sufficient to make such performance, recommendation, or approval valid and legal. In the event a municipal governing body designates itself to exercise the powers, duties, and responsibilities of a redevelopment commission, it may assign the administration of redevelopment policies, programs and plans to any existing or new department of the municipality.

(b) The governing body of any municipality which has prior to July 1, 1969, created, or which may hereafter create, a redevelopment commission may, in its discretion, by resolution abolish such redevelopment commission, such abolition to be effective on a day set in such resolution not less than 90 days after its adoption. Upon the adoption of such a resolution, the redevelopment commission of the municipality is hereby authorized and directed to take such actions and to execute such documents as will carry into effect the provisions and the intent of the resolution, and as will effectively transfer its authority, responsibilities, obligations, personnel, and property, both real and personal, to the municipality. Any municipality which abolishes a redevelopment commission pursuant to this subsection may, at any time subsequent to such abolition or concurrently therewith, exercise the authority granted by subsection (a) of this section.

On the day set in the resolution of the governing body:

(2) All property, real and personal and mixed, belonging to the redevelopment commission shall vest in, belong to, and be the property of the municipality;

(3) All judgments, liens, rights of liens, and causes of action of any nature in favor of the redevelopment commission shall remain, vest in, and inure to the benefit of the municipality;

(4) All rentals, taxes, assessments, and any other funds, charges or fees, owing to the redevelopment commission shall be owed to and collected by the municipality;

(5) Any actions, suits, and proceedings pending against, or having been instituted by the redevelopment commission shall not be abated by such abolition, but all such actions, suits, and proceedings shall be continued and completed in the same manner as if abolition had not occurred, and the municipality shall be a party to all such actions, suits, and proceedings in the place and stead of the redevelopment commission and shall pay or cause to be paid any judgment rendered against the redevelopment commission in any such actions, suits, or proceedings, and no new process need be served in any such action, suit, or proceeding;

(6) All obligations of the redevelopment commission, including outstanding indebtedness, shall be assumed by the municipality, and all such obligations and outstanding indebtedness shall be constituted obligations and indebtedness of the municipality;

(7) All ordinances, rules, regulations and policies of the redevelopment commission shall continue in full force and effect until repealed or amended by the governing body of the municipality.

(c) Where the governing body of any municipality has in its discretion, by resolution, abolished a redevelopment commission pursuant to subsection (b) above, the governing body of such municipality may, at any time subsequent to the passage of a resolution abolishing a redevelopment commission, or concurrently therewith, by the passage of a resolution adopted in accordance with the procedures and pursuant to the findings specified in G.S. 160A-504(a) and (b), designate an existing housing authority created pursuant to Chapter pursuant to Chapter 157 of the General Statutes to exercise the powers, duties, and responsibilities of a redevelopment commission, on the day set in the resolution of the governing body passed pursuant to subsection (b) of this section, or pursuant to subsection (c) of this section:

(1)   The redevelopment commission shall cease to exist as a body politic and corporate and as a public body;

(2)   All property, real and personal and mixed, belonging to the redevelopment commission or to the municipality as hereinabove provided in subsections (a) or (b), shall vest in, belong to, and be the property of the existing housing authority of the municipality;

(3)   All judgments, liens, rights of liens, and causes of action of any nature in favor of the redevelopment commission or in favor of the municipality as hereinabove provided in subsections (a) or (b), shall remain, vest in, and inure to the benefit of the existing housing authority of the municipality;

(4)   All rentals, taxes, assessments, and any other funds, charges or fees owing to the redevelopment commission, or owing to the municipality as hereinabove provided in subsections (a) or (b), shall be owed to and collected by the existing housing authority of the municipality;

(5)   Any actions, suits, and proceedings pending against or having been instituted by the redevelopment commission, or the municipality, or to which the municipality has become a party, as hereinabove provided in subsections (a) or (b), shall not be abated by such abolition but all such actions, suits, and proceedings shall be continued and completed in the same manner as if abolition had not occurred, and the existing housing authority of the municipality shall be a party to all such actions, suits, and proceedings in the place and stead of the redevelopment commission, or the municipality, and shall pay or cause to be paid any judgments rendered in such actions, suits, or proceedings, and no new processes need be served in such action, suit, or proceeding;

(6)   All obligations of the redevelopment commission, or the municipality as hereinabove provided in subsections (a) or (b), including outstanding indebtedness, shall be assumed by the existing housing authority of the municipality; and all such obligations and outstanding indebtedness shall be

(7) All ordinances, rules, regulations, and policies of the redevelopment commission, or of the municipality as hereinabove provided in subsections (a) or (b), shall continue in full force and effect until repealed and amended by the existing housing authority of the municipality.

(d) A housing authority designated by the governing body of any municipality to exercise the powers, duties and responsibilities of a redevelopment commission shall, when exercising the same, do so in accordance with Article 22 of Chapter 160A of the General Statutes. Otherwise the housing authority shall continue to exercise the powers, duties and responsibilities of a housing authority in accordance with Chapter 157 of the General Statutes. (1969, c. 1217, s. 1; 1971, c. 116, ss. 1, 2; 1973, c. 426, s. 75; 1981 (Reg. Sess., 1982), c. 1276, s. 13; 2003-403, s. 16.)

§ 160A-505.1. Commission budgeting and accounting systems as a part of municipality budgeting and accounting systems.

The governing body of a municipality may by resolution provide that the budgeting and accounting systems of the municipality's redevelopment commission or, if the municipality's housing authority is exercising the powers, duties, and responsibilities of a redevelopment commission, the budgeting and accounting systems of the housing authority, shall be an integral part of the budgeting and accounting systems of the municipality. If such a resolution is adopted:

(1) For purposes of the Local Government Budget and Fiscal Control Act, the commission or authority shall not be considered a "public authority," as that phrase is defined in G.S. 159-7(b), but rather shall be considered a department or agency of the municipality. The operations of the commission or authority shall be budgeted and accounted for as if the operations were those of a public enterprise of the municipality.

(2) The budget of the commission or authority shall be prepared and submitted in the same manner and according to the same procedures as are the budgets of other departments and agencies of the municipality; and the budget ordinance of the municipality shall provide for the operations of the commission or authority.

operations of the commission or authority. (1971, c. 780, s. 37.2; 1973, c. 474, s. 30.)

§ 160A-506. Creation of a county redevelopment commission.

If the board of county commissioners of a county by resolution declares that blighted areas do exist in said county, and the redevelopment of such areas is necessary in the interest of public health, safety, morals, or welfare of the residents of such county, the county commissioners of said county are hereby authorized to create a separate and distinct body corporate and politic to be known as the redevelopment commission of said county by passing a resolution to create such a commission to function in the territorial limits of said county. Provided, however, that notice of the intent to consider passage of such a resolution or ordinance shall be published at least 10 days prior to the meeting of the board of county commissioners for such purposes, and further provided that the redevelopment commission shall not function in an area where such a commission exists or in the corporate limits of a municipality without resolution of agreement by said municipality.

All of the provisions of Article 22, Chapter 160A of the General Statutes, shall be applicable to county redevelopment commissions, including the formation, appointment, tenure, compensation, organization, interest and powers as specified therein. (1969, c. 1208, s. 2; 1973, c. 426, s. 75.)

§ 160A-507. Creation of a regional redevelopment commission.

If the board of county commissioners of two or more contiguous counties by resolution declare that blighted areas do exist in said counties and the redevelopment of such areas is necessary in the interest of public health, morals, or welfare of the residents of such counties, the county commissioners of said counties are hereby authorized to create a separate and distinct body corporate and politic to be known as the regional redevelopment commission by the passage of a resolution by each county to create such a commission to function in the territorial limits of the counties; provided, however, that notice of the intent to consider passage of such a resolution or ordinance shall be published at least 10 days prior to the meeting of the board of county

municipality.

The board of county commissioners of each county included in the regional redevelopment commission shall appoint one person as a commissioner and such a person may be appointed at or after the time of the adoption of the resolution creating the redevelopment commission. The board of county commissioners shall have the authority to appoint successors or to remove persons for misconduct who are appointed by them. Each commissioner to the redevelopment commission shall serve for a five-year term except that initial appointments may be for less time in order to establish a fair donation system of appointments. In the event that a regional redevelopment commission shall have an even number of counties, the Governor of North Carolina shall appoint a member to the commission from the area to be served. The appointed members as commissioners shall constitute the regional redevelopment commission and certification of appointment shall be filed with the Secretary of State as part of the application for charter.

All provisions of the "Urban Redevelopment Law" as defined in Article 22 of Chapter 160A of the General Statutes, shall apply to the creation and operation of a regional redevelopment commission, and where reference is made to municipality, it shall be interpreted to apply to the area served by the regional redevelopment commission. (1969, c. 1208, s. 3; 1973, c. 426, s. 75.)

§ 160A-507.1. Creation of a joint county-city redevelopment commission.

A county and one or more cities within the county are hereby authorized to create a separate and distinct body corporate and politic to be known as the joint redevelopment commission by the passage of a resolution by the board of county commissioners and the governing body of one or more cities within the county creating such a commission to function within the territorial limits of such participating units of government; provided, however, that notice of the intent to consider passage of such a resolution or ordinance shall be published at least 10 days prior to the meeting of the affected governing boards for such purposes, and further provided that a joint redevelopment commission created hereunder shall have authority to operate in an area where there presently exists a redevelopment commission upon the approval of the municipality or county concerned. The governing body of each participating local government shall have the authority to appoint successors or to remove persons for misfeasance, malfeasance or nonfeasance who are appointed by them. Each commissioner shall serve for a term designated by the governing bodies of not less than one nor more than five years. The appointed members as commissioners shall constitute the joint redevelopment commission and certification of appointment shall be filed with the Secretary of State as part of the application for charter.

All provisions of the "Urban Redevelopment Law" as defined in Article 22 of Chapter 160A of the General Statutes shall apply to the creation and operation of a joint redevelopment commission and where reference is made to municipality, it shall be interpreted to apply to the units of government creating a joint redevelopment commission. (1975, c. 407.)

§ 160A-508. Appointment and qualifications of members of commission.

Upon certification of a resolution declaring the need for a commission to operate in a city or town, the mayor and governing board thereof, respectively, shall appoint, as members of the commission, not less than five nor more than nine citizens who shall be residents of the city or town in which the commission is to operate. The governing body may at any time by resolution or ordinance increase or decrease the membership of a commission, within the limitations herein prescribed. (1951, c. 1095, s. 5; 1971, c. 362, ss. 6, 7; 1973, c. 426, s. 75.)

§ 160A-509. Tenure and compensation of members of commission.

The mayor and governing body shall designate overlapping terms of not less than one nor more than five years for the members who are first appointed. Thereafter, the term of office shall be five years. A member shall hold office until his successor has been appointed and qualified. Vacancies for the unexpired terms shall be promptly filled by the mayor and governing body. A member shall receive such compensation, if any, as the municipal governing board may provide for this service, and shall be entitled within the budget appropriation to the necessary expenses, including traveling expenses, incurred in the discharge of his duties. (1951, c. 1095, s. 6; 1967, c. 932, s. 4; 1971, c. 362, s. 8; 1973, c. 426, s. 75.)

a vice-chairman, and such other officers as the commission may determine. A commission may employ a secretary, its own counsel, and such technical experts, and such other agents and employees, permanent or temporary, as it may require, and may determine the qualifications and fix the compensation of such persons. A majority of the members shall constitute a quorum for its meeting. Members shall not be liable personally on the bonds or other obligations of the commission, and the rights of creditors shall be solely against such commission. A commission may delegate to one or more of its members, agents or employees such of its powers as it shall deem necessary to carry out the purposes of this Article, subject always to the supervision and control of the commission. For inefficiency or neglect of duty or misconduct in office, a commissioner of a commission may be removed by the governing body, but a commissioner shall be removed only after a hearing and after he shall have been given a copy of the charges at least 10 days prior to such hearing and have had an opportunity to be heard in person or by counsel. (1951, c. 1095, s. 7; 1971, c. 362, s. 9; 1973, c. 426, s. 75.)

§ 160A-511. Interest of members or employees.

No member or employee of a commission shall acquire any interest, direct or indirect, in any redevelopment project or in any property included or planned to be included in any redevelopment area, or in any area which he may have reason to believe may be certified to be a redevelopment area, nor shall he have any interest, direct or indirect, in any contract or proposed contract for materials or services to be furnished or used by a commission, or in any contract with a redeveloper or prospective redeveloper relating, directly or indirectly, to any redevelopment project, except that a member or employee of a commission may acquire property in a residential redevelopment area from a person or entity other than the commission after the residential redevelopment plan for that area is adopted if:

(1)   The primary purpose of acquisition is to occupy the property as his principal residence;

(2)   The redevelopment plan does not provide for acquisition of such property by the commission; and

residence.

Except as authorized herein, the acquisition of any such interest in a redevelopment project or in any such property or contract shall constitute misconduct in office. If any member or employee of a commission shall have already owned or controlled within the preceding two years any interest, direct or indirect, in any property later included or planned to be included in any redevelopment project, under the jurisdiction of the commission, or has any such interest in any contract for material or services to be furnished or used in connection with any redevelopment project, he shall disclose the same in writing to the commission and to the local governing body. Any disclosure required herein shall be entered in writing upon the minute books of the commission. Failure to make disclosure shall constitute misconduct in office. (1951, c. 1095, s. 8; 1973, c. 426, s. 75; 1977, 2nd Sess., c. 1139.)

§ 160A-512. Powers of commission.

A commission shall constitute a public body, corporate and politic, exercising public and essential governmental powers, which powers shall include all powers necessary or appropriate to carry out and effectuate the purposes and provisions of this Article, including the following powers in addition to those herein otherwise granted:

(1)   To procure from the planning commission the designation of areas in need of redevelopment and its recommendation for such redevelopment;

(2)   To cooperate with any government or municipality as herein defined;

(3)   To act as agent of the State or federal government or any of its instrumentalities or agencies for the public purposes set out in this Article;

(4)   To prepare or cause to be prepared and recommend redevelopment plans to the governing body of the municipality and to undertake and carry out "redevelopment projects" within its area of operation;

(5)   Subject to the provisions of G.S. 160A-514(b) to arrange or contract for the furnishing or repair, by any person or agency, public or private, of services,

conditions that it may deem reasonable and appropriate attached to federal financial assistance and imposed pursuant to federal law relating to the determination of prevailing salaries or wages or compliance with labor standards, in the undertaking or carrying out of a redevelopment project, and to include in any contract let in connection with such a project, provisions to fulfill such of said conditions as it may deem reasonable and appropriate;

(6) Within its area of operation, to purchase, obtain options upon, acquire by gift, grant, devise, eminent domain or otherwise, any real or personal property or any interest therein, together with any improvements thereon, necessary or incidental to a redevelopment project, except that eminent domain may only be used to take a blighted parcel; to hold, improve, clear or prepare for redevelopment any such property, and subject to the provisions of G.S. 160A-514, and with the approval of the local governing body sell, exchange, transfer, assign, subdivide, retain for its own use, mortgage, pledge, hypothecate or otherwise encumber or dispose of any real or personal property or any interest therein, either as an entirety to a single "redeveloper" or in parts to several redevelopers; provided that the commission finds that the sale or other transfer of any such part will not be prejudicial to the sale of other parts of the redevelopment area, nor in any other way prejudicial to the realization of the redevelopment plan approved by the governing body; to enter into contracts, either before or after the real property that is the subject of the contract is acquired by the Commission (although disposition of the property is still subject to G.S. 160A-514), with "redevelopers" of property containing covenants, restrictions, and conditions regarding the use of such property for residential, commercial, industrial, recreational purposes or for public purposes in accordance with the redevelopment plan and such other covenants, restrictions and conditions as the commission may deem necessary to prevent a recurrence of blighted areas or to effectuate the purposes of this Article; to make any of the covenants, restrictions or conditions of the foregoing contracts covenants running with the land, and to provide appropriate remedies for any breach of any such covenants or conditions, including the right to terminate such contracts and any interest in the property created pursuant thereto; to borrow money and issue bonds therefor and provide security for bonds; to insure or provide for the insurance of any real or personal property or operations of the commission against any risks or hazards, including the power to pay premiums on any such insurance; and to enter into any contracts necessary to effectuate the purposes of this Article;

State; to redeem its bonds at the redemption price established therein or to purchase its bonds at less than redemption price, all bonds so redeemed or purchased to be cancelled;

(8) To borrow money and to apply for and accept advances, loans evidenced by bonds, grants, contributions and any other form of financial assistance from the federal government, the State, county, municipality or other public body or from any sources, public or private for the purposes of this Article, to give such security as may be required and to enter into and carry out contracts in connection therewith; and, notwithstanding the provisions of any other law, may include in any contract for financial assistance with the federal government for a redevelopment project such conditions imposed pursuant to federal law as the commission may deem reasonable and appropriate and which are not inconsistent with the purposes of this Article;

(9) Acting through one or more commissioners or other persons designated by the commission, to conduct examinations and investigations and to hear testimony and take proof under oath at public or private hearings on any matter material for its information; to administer oaths, issue subpoenas requiring the attendance of witnesses or the production of books and papers;

(10) Within its area of operation, to make or have made all surveys, studies and plans (but not including the preparation of a general plan for the community) necessary to the carrying out of the purposes of this Article and in connection therewith to enter into or upon any land, building, or improvement thereon for such purposes and to make soundings, test borings, surveys, appraisals and other preliminary studies and investigations necessary to carry out its powers but such entry shall constitute no cause of action for trespass in favor of the owner of such land, building, or improvement except for injuries resulting from negligence, wantonness or malice; and to contract or cooperate with any and all persons or agencies public or private, in the making and carrying out of such surveys, appraisals, studies and plans.

A redevelopment commission is hereby specifically authorized to make (i) plans for carrying out a program of voluntary repair and rehabilitation of buildings and improvements and (ii) plans for the enforcement of laws, codes, and regulations relating to the use of land and the use and occupancy of buildings and improvements, and to the compulsory repair, rehabilitation, demolition, or of slums and urban blight.

(11) To make such expenditures as may be necessary to carry out the purposes of this Article; and to make expenditures from funds obtained from the federal government;

(12) To sue and be sued;

(13) To adopt a seal;

(14) To have perpetual succession;

(15) To make and execute contracts and other instruments necessary or convenient to the exercise of the powers of the commission; and any contract or instrument when signed by the chairman or vice-chairman and secretary or assistant secretary, or, treasurer or assistant treasurer of the commission shall be held to have been properly executed for and on its behalf;

(16) To make and from time to time amend and repeal bylaws, rules, regulations and resolutions;

(17) To make available to the government or municipality or any appropriate agency, board or commission, the recommendations of the commission affecting any area in its field of operation or property therein, which it may deem likely to promote the public health, morals, safety or welfare;

(18) To perform redevelopment project undertakings and activities in one or more contiguous or noncontiguous redevelopment areas which are planned and carried out on the basis of annual increments. (1951, c. 1095, s. 9; 1961, c. 837, ss. 5, 7; 1969, c. 254, s. 1; 1973, c. 426, s. 75; 1981 (Reg. Sess., 1982), c. 1276, s. 14; 2003-403, s. 17; 2006-224, s. 2.3; 2006-259, s. 47; 2011-284, s. 120.)

§ 160A-513. Preparation and adoption of redevelopment plans.

(a) A commission shall prepare a redevelopment plan for any area certified by the planning commission to be a redevelopment area. A redevelopment plan

improvements and the proposed land uses and building requirements in the redevelopment project area.

(b)   The planning commission's certification of a redevelopment area shall be made in conformance with its comprehensive general plan, if any (which may include, inter alia, a plan of major traffic arteries and terminals and a land use plan and projected population densities) for the area.

(c)   A commission shall not acquire real property for a development project unless the governing body of the community in which the redevelopment project area is located has approved the redevelopment plan, as hereinafter prescribed; provided, however, that the commission may acquire, through negotiation, specific pieces of property in the redevelopment area prior to the approval of such plan when the governing body finds that advance acquisition of such properties is in the public interest and specifically approves such action.

(d)   The redevelopment commission's redevelopment plan shall include, without being limited to, the following:

(1)   The boundaries of the area, with a map showing the existing uses of the real property therein;

(2)   A land use plan of the area showing proposed uses following redevelopment;

(3)   Standards of population densities, land coverage and building intensities in the proposed redevelopment;

(4)   A preliminary site plan of the area;

(5)   A statement of the proposed changes, if any, in zoning ordinances or maps;

(6)   A statement of any proposed changes in street layouts or street levels;

(7)   A statement of the estimated cost and method of financing redevelopment under the plan; provided, that where redevelopment activities are performed on the basis of annual increments, such statement to be

(8) A statement of such continuing controls as may be deemed necessary to effectuate the purposes of this Article;

(9) A statement of a feasible method proposed for the relocation of the families displaced.

(e) The commission shall hold a public hearing prior to its final determination of the redevelopment plan. Notice of such hearing shall be given once a week for two successive calendar weeks in a newspaper published in the municipality, or if there be no newspaper published in the municipality, by posting such notice at four public places in the municipality, said notice to be published the first time or posted not less than 15 days prior to the date fixed for said hearing.

(f) The commission shall submit the redevelopment plan to the planning commission for review. The planning commission, shall, within 45 days, certify to the redevelopment commission its recommendation on the redevelopment plan, either of approval, rejection or modification, and in the latter event, specify the changes recommended.

(g) Upon receipt of the planning commission's recommendation, or at the expiration of 45 days, if no recommendation is made by the planning commission, the commission shall submit to the governing body the redevelopment plan with the recommendation, if any, of the planning commission thereon. Prior to recommending a redevelopment plan to the governing body for approval, the commission shall consider whether the proposed land uses and building requirements in the redevelopment project area are designed with the general purpose of accomplishing, in conformance with the general plan, a coordinated, adjusted and harmonious development of the community and its environs, which will in accordance with present and future needs promote health, safety, morals, order, convenience, prosperity and the general welfare, as well as efficiency and economy in the process of development, including, among other things, adequate provision for traffic, vehicular parking, the promotion of safety from fire, panic and other dangers, adequate provision for light and air, the promotion of the healthful and convenient distribution of population, the provision of adequate transportation, water, sewerage and other public utilities, schools, parks, recreational and

slums, or conditions or blight.

(h)   The governing body, upon receipt of the redevelopment plan and the recommendation (if any) of the planning commission, shall hold a public hearing upon said plan. Notice of such hearing shall be given once a week for two successive weeks in a newspaper published in the municipality, or, if there be no newspaper published in the municipality, by posting such notice at four public places in the municipality, said notice to be published the first time or posted not less than 15 days prior to the date fixed for said hearing. The notice shall describe the redevelopment area by boundaries, in a manner designed to be understandable by the general public. The redevelopment plan, including such maps, plans, contracts, or other documents as form a part of it, together with the recommendation (if any) of the planning commission and supporting data, shall be available for public inspection at a location specified in the notice for at least 10 days prior to the hearing.

At the hearing the governing body shall afford an opportunity to all persons or agencies interested to be heard and shall receive, make known, and consider recommendations in writing with reference to the redevelopment plan.

(i)   The governing body shall approve, amend, or reject the redevelopment plan as submitted.

(j)   Subject to the proviso in subsection (c) of this section, upon approval by the governing body of the redevelopment plan, the commission is authorized to acquire property, to execute contracts for clearance and preparation of the land for resale, and to take other actions necessary to carry out the plan, in accordance with the provisions of this Article.

(k)   A redevelopment plan may be modified at any time by the commission; provided that, if modified after the sale of real property in the redevelopment project area, the modification must be consented to by the redeveloper of such real property or his successor, or their successors in interest affected by the proposed modification. Where the proposed modification will substantially change the redevelopment plan as previously approved by the governing body the modification must similarly be approved by the governing body as provided above. (1951, c. 1095, s. 10; 1961, c. 837, s. 8; 1965, c. 808; 1969, c. 254, s. 2; 1973, c. 426, s. 75.)

(a) A commission may privately contract for engineering, legal, surveying, professional or other similar services without advertisement or bid.

(b) In entering and carrying out any contract for construction, demolition, moving of structures, or repair work or the purchase of apparatus, supplies, materials, or equipment, a commission shall comply with the provisions of Article 8 of Chapter 143 of the General Statutes. In construing such provisions, the commission shall be considered to be the governing board of a "subdivision of the State," and a contract for demolition or moving of structures, shall be treated in the same manner as a contract for construction or repair. Compliance with such provisions shall not be required, however, where the commission enters into contracts with the municipality which created it for the municipality to furnish any such services, work, apparatus, supplies, materials, or equipment; the making of these contracts without advertisement or bids is hereby specifically authorized. Advertisement or bids shall not be required for any contract for construction, demolition, moving of structures, or repair work, or for the purchase of apparatus, supplies, materials, or equipment, where such contract involves the expenditure of public money in an amount less than five hundred dollars ($500.00).

(c) A commission may sell, exchange, or otherwise transfer the fee or any lesser interest in real property in a redevelopment project area to any redeveloper for any public or private use that accords with the redevelopment plan, subject to such covenants, conditions and restrictions as the commission may deem to be in the public interest and in furtherance of the purposes of this Article. In the sale, exchange, or transfer of property, the commission shall exercise the authority and procedure set out in G.S. 160A-268, 160A-269, 160A-270, 160A-271, or 160A-279 for the disposition of property by a city council. Provided, however, that all sales, exchanges, or other transfers of real property from July 9, 1985, to December 31, 1987, in accordance with the provisions of this section prior to its revision on July 9, 1985, shall be and are valid in all respects.

(d) A commission may sell personal property having a value of less than five hundred dollars ($500.00) at private sale without advertisement and bids.

(e) In carrying out a redevelopment project, the commission may:

ways.

(2)   With or without consideration, convey at private sale, grant, or dedicate easements and rights-of-way for public utilities, sewers, streets and other similar facilities, in accordance with the redevelopment plan.

(3)   With or without consideration and at private sale convey to the municipality, county or other appropriate public body such real property as, in accordance with the redevelopment plan, is to be used for parks, schools, public buildings, facilities or other public purposes.

(4)   In addition to other authority contained in this section, after a public hearing advertised in accordance with the provisions of G.S. 160A-513(e), and subject to the approval of the governing body of the municipality, convey to a nonprofit association or corporation organized and operated exclusively for educational, scientific, literary, cultural, charitable or religious purposes, no part of the net earnings of which inure to the benefit of any private shareholder or individual, such real property as, in accordance with the redevelopment plan, is to be used for the purposes of such associations or corporations. Such conveyance shall be for such consideration as may be agreed upon by the commission and the association or corporation, which shall not be less than the fair value of the property agreed upon by a committee of three professional real estate appraisers currently practicing in the State, which committee shall be appointed by the commission. All conveyances made under the authority of this subsection shall contain restrictive covenants limiting the use of property so conveyed to the purposes for which the conveyance is made.

(f)   After receiving the required approval of a sale from the governing body of the municipality, the commission may execute any required contracts, deeds, and other instruments and take all steps necessary to effectuate any such contract or sale. Any contract of sale between a commission and a redeveloper may contain, without being limited to, any or all of the following provisions:

(1)   Plans prepared by the redeveloper or otherwise and such other documents as may be required to show the type, material, structure and general character of the proposed redevelopment;

(3) A guaranty of completion of the proposed redevelopment within specified time limits;

(4) The amount, if known, of the consideration to be paid;

(5) Adequate safeguards for proper maintenance of all parts of the proposed redevelopment;

(6) Such other continuing controls as may be deemed necessary to effectuate the purposes of this Article.

Any deed to a redeveloper in furtherance of a redevelopment contract shall be executed in the name of the commission, by its proper officers, and shall contain in addition to all other provisions, such conditions, restrictions and provisions as the commission may deem desirable to run with the land in order to effectuate the purposes of this Article.

(g) The commission may temporarily rent or lease, operate and maintain real property in a redevelopment project area, pending the disposition of the property for redevelopment, for such uses and purposes as may be deemed desirable even though not in conformity with the redevelopment plan. (1951, c. 1095, s. 11; 1961, c. 837, s. 9; 1963, c. 1212, ss. 1, 2; 1965, c. 679, s. 2; 1967, c. 24, s. 18; c. 932, s. 1; 1973, c. 426, s. 75; 1985, c. 665, ss. 1, 2; 1987, c. 364; 1989, c. 413; 2003-66, ss. 1, 2.)

§ 160A-515. Eminent domain.

The commission may exercise the right of eminent domain in accordance with the provisions of Chapter 40A, but only where the property to be taken is a blighted parcel. (1951, c. 1095, s. 12; 1965, c. 679, s. 3; c. 1132; 1967, c. 932, ss. 2, 3; 1973, c. 426, s. 75; 1981, c. 919, s. 30; 2006-224, s. 2.4; 2006-259, s. 47.)

§ 160A-515.1. Project development financing.

Statutes, together with any other revenues that are available to the city. Before it receives the approval of the Local Government Commission for issuance of project development financing debt instruments, the city's governing body must define a development financing district and adopt a development financing plan for the district. The city may act jointly with a county to finance a project, define a development financing district, and adopt a development financing plan for the district.

(b) Development Financing District. - A development financing district shall comprise all or portions of one or more redevelopment areas defined pursuant to this Article. The total land area within development financing districts in a city, including development financing districts created pursuant to G.S. 158-7.3, may not exceed five percent (5%) of the total land area of the city. For purposes of this section, land in a district created by a county that subsequently becomes part of a city does not count against the city's five-percent (5%) limit unless the city and the county have entered into an agreement pursuant to G.S. 159-107(e).

(c) Development Financing Plan. - The development financing plan must be compatible with the redevelopment plan or plans for the redevelopment area or areas included within the district. The development financing plan must include all of the following:

(1) A description of the boundaries of the development financing district.

(2) A description of the proposed development of the district, both public and private.

(3) The costs of the proposed public activities.

(4) The sources and amounts of funds to pay for the proposed public activities.

(5) The base valuation of the development financing district.

(6) The projected incremental valuation of the development financing district.

public and private, will benefit the residents and business owners of the district in terms of jobs, affordable housing, or services.

(9) A description of the appropriate ameliorative activities which will be undertaken if the proposed projects have a negative impact on residents or business owners of the district in terms of jobs, affordable housing, services, or displacement.

(10) A requirement that the initial users of any new manufacturing facilities that will be located in the district and that are included in the plan will comply with the wage requirements in subsection (d) of this section.

(d) Wage Requirements. - A development financing plan shall include a requirement that the initial users of a new manufacturing facility to be located in the district and included in the plan must pay its employees an average weekly manufacturing wage that is either above the average manufacturing wage paid in the county in which the district will be located or not less than ten percent (10%) above the average weekly manufacturing wage paid in the State. The plan may include information on the wages to be paid by the initial users of a new manufacturing facility to its employees and any provisions necessary to implement the wage requirement. The issuing unit's governing body shall not adopt a plan until the Secretary of Commerce certifies that the Secretary has reviewed the average weekly manufacturing wage required by the plan to be paid to the employees of a new manufacturing facility and has found either (i) that the wages proposed by the initial users of a new manufacturing facility are in compliance with the amount required by this subsection or (ii) that the plan is exempt from the requirement of this subsection. The Secretary of Commerce may exempt a plan from the requirement of this subsection if the Secretary receives a resolution from the issuing unit's governing body requesting an exemption from the wage requirement and a letter from an appropriate State official, selected by the Secretary, finding that unemployment in the county in which the proposed district is to be located is especially severe. Upon the creation of the district, the unit of local government proposing the creation of the district shall take any lawful actions necessary to require compliance with the applicable wage requirement by the initial users of any new manufacturing facility included in the plan; however, failure to take such actions or obtain such compliance shall not affect the validity of any proceedings for the creation of the district, the existence of the district, or the validity of any debt instruments

facility" means any facility that is used in the manufacturing or production of tangible personal property, including the processing resulting in a change in the condition of the property.

(e) County Review. - Before adopting a plan for a development financing district, the city council shall send notice of the plan, by first-class mail, to the board of county commissioners of the county or counties in which the development financing district is located. The person mailing the notice shall certify that fact, and the date thereof, to the city council, and the certificate is conclusive in the absence of fraud. Unless the board of county commissioners (or either board, if the district is in two counties) by resolution disapproves the proposed plan within 28 days after the date the notice is mailed, the city council may proceed to adopt the plan.

(f) Environmental Review. - Before adopting a plan for development financing districts, the city council shall submit the plan to the Secretary of Environment and Natural Resources to review to determine if the construction and operation of any new manufacturing facility in the district will have a materially adverse effect on the environment and whether the company that will operate the facility has operated in substantial compliance with federal and State laws, regulations, and rules for the protection of the environment. If the Secretary finds that the new manufacturing facility will not have a materially adverse effect on the environment and that the company that will operate the facility has operated other facilities in compliance with environmental requirements, the Secretary shall approve the plan. In making the determination on environmental impact, the Secretary shall use the same criteria that apply to the determination under G.S. 159C-7 of whether an industrial project will have a materially adverse effect on the environment. The findings of the Secretary are conclusive and binding.

(g) Plan Adoption. - Before adopting a plan for a development financing district, the city council shall hold a public hearing on the plan. The council shall, no less than 30 days before the day of hearing, cause notice of the hearing to be mailed by first-class mail to all property owners and mailing addresses within the proposed development financing district. The council shall also, no more than 30 days and no less than 14 days before the day of the hearing, cause notice of the hearing to be published once in a newspaper of general circulation in the city. The notice shall state the time and place of the hearing, shall specify

proposed plan. Unless a board of county commissioners or the Secretary of Environment and Natural Resources has disapproved the plan pursuant to subsection (e) or (f) of this section, the council may adopt the plan, with or without amendment, at any time after the public hearing. However, the plan and the district do not become effective until the city's application to issue project development financing debt instruments has been approved by the Local Government Commission, pursuant to Article 6 of Chapter 159 of the General Statutes.

(h) Plan Modification. - Subject to the limitations of this subsection, a city council may, after the effective date of the district, amend a development financing plan adopted for a development financing district. Before making any amendment, the city council shall follow the procedures and meet the requirements of subsections (d) through (g) of this section. The boundaries of the district may be enlarged only during the first five years after the effective date of the district and only if the area to be added has been or is about to be developed and the development is primarily attributable to development that has occurred within the district, as certified by the Local Government Commission. The boundaries of the district may be reduced at any time, but the city may agree with the holders of any project development financing debt instruments to restrict its power to reduce district boundaries.

(i) Plan Implementation. - In implementing a development financing plan, a city may act directly, through a redevelopment commission, through one or more contracts with private agencies, or by any combination of these. A private agency that enters into a contract with a city for the implementation of a development financing plan is subject to the provisions of Article 8 of Chapter 143 of the General Statutes only to the extent specified in the contract. (2003-403, s. 18; 2005-238, s. 12; 2006-211, s. 4.)

§ 160A-516. Issuance of bonds.

(a) The commission shall have power to issue bonds from time to time for any of its corporate purposes including the payment of principal and interest upon any advances for surveys and plans for redevelopment projects. The commission shall also have power to issue refunding bonds for the purpose of paying or retiring or in exchange for bonds previously issued by it. The

(1) Exclusively from the income, proceeds, and revenues of the redevelopment project financed with the proceeds of such bonds; or

(2) Exclusively from the income, proceeds, and revenues of any of its redevelopment projects whether or not they are financed in whole or in part with the proceeds of such bonds; provided, that any such bonds may be additionally secured by a pledge of any loan, grant or contributions, or parts thereof, from the federal government or other source, or a mortgage of any redevelopment project or projects of the commission.

(b) Neither the commissioners of a commission nor any person executing the bonds shall be liable personally on the bonds by reason of the issuance of the bonds. The bonds and other obligations of the commission (and the bonds and obligations shall so state on their face) shall not be a debt of the municipality, the county, or the State and neither the municipality, the county, nor the State shall be liable on the bonds, nor in any event shall the bonds or obligations be payable out of any funds or properties other than those of the commission acquired for the purpose of this Article. The bonds shall not constitute an indebtedness of the municipality within the meaning of any constitutional or statutory debt limitation or restriction. Bonds of a commission are declared to be issued for an essential public and governmental purpose and to be public instrumentalities. The bonds are exempt from all State, county, and municipal taxation or assessment, direct or indirect, general or special, whether imposed for the purpose of general revenue or otherwise, excluding inheritance and gift taxes, income taxes on the gain from the transfer of the bonds and notes, and franchise taxes. The interest on the bonds is not subject to taxation as income. Bonds may be issued by a commission under this Article notwithstanding any debt or other limitation prescribed in any statute. This Article without reference to other statutes of the State shall constitute full and complete authority for the authorization and issuance of bonds by the commission under this Article and this authorization and issuance shall not be subject to any conditions, restrictions, or limitations imposed by any other statute whether general, special, or local, except as provided in subsection (d) of this section.

(c) Bonds of the commission shall be authorized by its resolution and may be issued in one or more series and shall bear such date or dates, be payable

priority, be executed in such manner, be payable in such medium of payment, at such place or places, and be subject to such terms of redemption (with or without premium) as such resolution, its trust indenture or mortgage may provide.

(d)   Bonds shall be sold by the redevelopment commission at either public or private sale upon such terms and in such manner, consistent with the provisions hereof, as the redevelopment commission may determine. Prior to the public sale of bonds hereunder, the redevelopment commission shall first cause a notice of the sale of the bonds to be published at least once at least 10 days before the date fixed for the receipt of bids for the bonds (i) in a newspaper having the largest or next largest circulation in the redevelopment commission's area of operation and (ii) in a publication that carries advertisements for the sale of State and municipal bonds published in the City of New York in the State of New York; provided, however, that in its discretion the redevelopment commission may cause any such notice of sale in the New York publication to be published as part of a consolidated notice of sale offering for sale the obligations of other public agencies in addition to the redevelopment commission's bonds, and provided, further, that any bonds may be sold by the redevelopment commission at private sale upon such terms and conditions as are mutually agreed upon between the commission and the purchaser. No bonds issued pursuant to this Article shall be sold at less than par and accrued interest. The provisions of the Local Government Finance Act shall not be applicable with respect to bonds sold or issued under this Article.

(e)   In case any of the commissioners or officers of the commission whose signatures appear on any bonds or coupons shall cease to be such commissioners or officers before the delivery of such bonds, such signatures shall, nevertheless, be valid and sufficient for all purposes, the same as if such commissioners or officers had remained in office until such delivery. Any provisions of any law to the contrary notwithstanding, any bonds issued pursuant to this Article shall be fully negotiable.

(f)   In any suit, action or proceedings involving the validity or enforceability of any bond of the commission or the security therefor, any such bond reciting in substance that it has been issued by the commission to aid in financing a redevelopment project, as herein defined, shall be conclusively deemed to have been issued for such purpose and such project shall be conclusively deemed to

(g) Bonds (including, without limitation, interim and long-term notes) may be issued or sold under this Article at private sale upon such terms and conditions as may be negotiated and mutually agreed upon by the commission and the purchaser (who may be the government or other public or private lender or purchaser). (1951, c. 1095, s. 13; 1961, c. 837, s. 10; 1971, c. 87, s. 3; 1973, c. 426, s. 75; 1981, c. 907, ss. 3, 4; 1995, c. 46, s. 20.)

§ 160A-517. Powers in connection with issuance of bonds.

(a) In connection with the issuance of bonds or the incurring of obligations and in order to secure the payment of such bonds or obligations, the commission, in addition to its other powers, shall have power:

(1) To pledge all or any part of its gross or net rents, fees or revenues to which its right then exists or may thereafter come into existence;

(2) To mortgage all or any part of its real or personal property, then owned or thereafter acquired;

(3) To covenant against pledging all or any part of its rents, fees and revenues, or against mortgaging all or any part of its real or personal property, to which its right or title then exists or may thereafter come into existence or against permitting or suffering any lien on such revenues or property; to covenant with respect to limitations on its right to sell, lease or otherwise dispose of any redevelopment project or any part thereof; and to covenant as to what other, or additional debts or obligations may be incurred by it;

(4) To covenant as to the bonds to be issued and as to the issuance of such bonds in escrow or otherwise, and as to the use and disposition of the proceeds thereof; to provide for the replacement of lost, destroyed or mutilated bonds, to covenant against extending the time for the payment of its bonds or interest thereon; and to covenant for the redemption of the bonds and to provide the terms and conditions thereof;

(5) To covenant (subject to the limitations contained in this Article) as to the amount of revenues to be raised each year or other period of time by rents, fees and other revenues, and as to the use and disposition to be made thereof; to

(6) To prescribe the procedure, if any, by which the terms of any contract with bondholders may be amended or abrogated, the amount of bonds the holders of which must consent thereto and the manner in which such consent may be given;

(7) To covenant as to the use, maintenance and replacement of any of or all of its real or personal property, the insurance to be carried thereon and the use and disposition of insurance moneys, and to warrant its title to such property;

(8) To covenant as to the rights, liabilities, powers and duties arising upon the breach by it of any covenants, conditions or obligations; and to covenant and prescribe as to events of default and terms and conditions upon which any or all of its bonds or obligations shall become or may be declared due before maturity and as to the terms and conditions upon which such declaration and its consequences may be waived;

(9) To vest in any obligees of the commissions the right to enforce the payment of the bonds or any covenants securing or relating to the bonds; to vest in any obligee or obligees holding a specified amount in bonds the right, in the event of a default to take possession of and use, operate and manage any redevelopment project or any part thereof, title to which is in the commission, or any funds connected therewith, and to collect the rents and revenues arising therefrom and to dispose of such moneys in accordance with the agreement with such obligees; to provide for the powers and duties of such obligees and to limit the liabilities thereof, and to provide the terms and conditions upon which such obligees may enforce any covenant or rights securing or relating to the bonds; and

(10) To exercise all or any part or combination of the powers herein granted; to make such covenants (other than and in addition to the covenants herein expressly authorized) and to do any and all such acts and things as may be necessary or convenient or desirable in order to secure its bonds, or, in the absolute discretion of said commission, as will tend to make the bonds more marketable notwithstanding that such covenants, acts or things may not be enumerated herein.

may otherwise be conferred), upon the happening of an event of default as defined in such resolution or instrument, by suit, action or proceeding in any court of competent jurisdiction:

(1) To cause possession of any redevelopment project or any part thereof title to which is in the commission, to be surrendered to any such obligee;

(2) To obtain the appointment of a receiver of any redevelopment project of said commission or any part thereof, title to which is in the commission and of the rents and profits therefrom. If such receiver be appointed, he may enter and take possession of, carry out, operate and maintain such project or any part therefrom and collect and receive all fees, rents, revenues, or other charges thereafter arising therefrom, and shall keep such moneys in a separate account or accounts and apply the same in accordance with the obligations of said commission as the court shall direct; and

(3) To require said commission and the commissioners, officers, agents and employees thereof to account as if it and they were the trustees of an express trust. (1951, c. 1095, s. 14; 1973, c. 426, s. 75.)

§ 160A-518. Right of obligee.

An obligee of the commission shall have the right in addition to all other rights which may be conferred on such obligee, subject only to any contractual restrictions binding upon such obligee:

(1) By mandamus, suit, action or proceeding at law or in equity to compel said commission and the commissioners, officers, agents or employees thereof to perform each and every term, provision and covenant contained in any contract of said commission with or for the benefit of such obligee, and to require the carrying out of any or all such covenants and agreements of said commission and the fulfillment of all duties imposed upon said commission by this Article; and

(2) By suit, action or proceeding in equity, to enjoin any acts or things which may be unlawful, or the violation of any of the rights of such obligee of said commission. (1951, c. 1095, s. 15; 1973, c. 426, s. 75.)

or carrying out of a redevelopment project located within the area in which it is authorized to act, any public body may, upon such terms, with or without consideration, as it may determine:

(1) Dedicate, sell, convey or lease any of its interest in any property, or grant easements, licenses or any other rights or privileges therein to a commission;

(2) Cause parks, playgrounds, recreational, community, educational, water, sewer or drainage facilities, or any other works which it is otherwise empowered to undertake, to be furnished in connection with a redevelopment project;

(3) Furnish, dedicate, close, vacate, pave, install, grade, regrade, plan or replan streets, roads, sidewalks, ways or other places, which it is otherwise empowered to undertake;

(4) Plan or replan, zone or rezone any part of the redevelopment;

(5) Cause administrative and other services to be furnished to the commission of the character which the public body is otherwise empowered to undertake or furnish for the same or other purposes;

(6) Incur the entire expense of any public improvements made by such public body in exercising the powers granted in this section;

(7) Do any and all things necessary or convenient to aid and cooperate in the planning or carrying out of a redevelopment plan.

(b) Any sale, conveyance, or agreement provided for in this section may be made by a public body without public notice, advertisement or public bidding. (1951, c. 1095, s. 16; 1973, c. 426, s. 75.)

§ 160A-520. Grant of funds by community.

Any municipality located within the area of operation of a commission may appropriate funds to a commission for the purpose of aiding such commission in carrying out any of its powers and functions under this Article. To obtain funds

§ 160A-521. Records and reports.

(a)   The books and records of a commission shall at all times be open and subject to inspection by the public.

(b)   A copy of all bylaws and rules and regulations and amendments thereto adopted by it, from time to time, shall be filed with the city clerk and shall be open for public inspection.

(c)   At least once each year a report of its activities for the preceding year and such other reports as may be required shall be made. Copies of such reports shall be filed with the mayor and governing body of the municipality. (1951, c. 1095, s. 18; 1973, c. 426, s. 75.)

§ 160A-522. Title of purchaser.

Any instrument executed by a commission and purporting to convey any right, title or interest in any property under this Article shall be conclusive evidence of compliance with the provisions of this Article insofar as title or other interest of any bona fide purchasers, lessees or transferees of such property is concerned. (1951, c. 1095, s. 19; 1973, c. 426, s. 75.)

§ 160A-523. Preparation of general plan by local governing body.

The governing body of any municipality or county, which is not otherwise authorized to create a planning commission with power to prepare a general plan for the development of the community, is hereby authorized and empowered to prepare such a general plan prior to the initiation and carrying out of a redevelopment project under this Article. (1951, c. 1095, s. 20; 1973, c. 426, s. 75.)

§ 160A-524. Inconsistent provisions.

§ 160A-525. Certain actions and proceedings validated.

All proceedings, resolutions, ordinances, motions, notices, findings, determinations, and other actions of redevelopment commissions, incorporated cities and towns, governing bodies, and planning boards and commissions, had and taken prior to January 1, 1965, pursuant to or purporting to comply with the Urban Redevelopment Law (G.S. 160A-500 to 160A-526) and incident to the creation and organization of redevelopment commissions and appointment of members thereof, designation of redevelopment and project areas, findings and determinations respecting conditions in redevelopment and project areas, preparation, development, review, processing and approval of urban redevelopment projects and plans, including redevelopment plans, calling and holding of public hearings, and the time and manner of giving and publishing notices thereof, are hereby in all respects legalized, ratified, approved, validated and confirmed, and all such actions are declared to be valid and lawfully authorized; provided, however, that no such action shall be legalized, ratified, approved, validated or confirmed, under this section if they appertain to any redevelopment or project area, the acquisition or taking of any property in any such area, any urban redevelopment project or any redevelopment plan respecting which any decree or judgment has been rendered by the Supreme Court of North Carolina prior to May 25, 1965. (1963, c. 194; 1965, c. 680; 1973, c. 426, s. 75.)

§ 160A-526. Contracts and agreements validated.

All contracts or agreements of redevelopment commissions heretofore entered into with the federal government or its agencies, and with municipalities or others relating to financial assistance for redevelopment projects in which it was required that loans or advances shall bear an interest rate in excess of six per centum (6%) per annum, or in which a municipality or others had agreed to pay funds equal to the interest in excess of six per centum (6%) per annum are hereby validated, ratified, confirmed, approved and declared legal with respect to the payment of interest in excess of six per centum (6%), and all things done or performed in reference thereto. The redevelopment commissions are hereby authorized to assume the full obligation of the municipalities under the contracts

§§ 160A-527 through 160A-534. Reserved for future codification purposes.

Article 23.

Municipal Service Districts.

§ 160A-535. Title; effective date.

This Article may be cited as "The Municipal Service District Act of 1973," and is enacted pursuant to Article V, Sec. 2(4) of the Constitution of North Carolina, effective July 1, 1973. (1973, c. 655, s. 1.)

§ 160A-536. Purposes for which districts may be established.

(a) Purposes. - The city council of any city may define any number of service districts in order to finance, provide, or maintain for the districts one or more of the following services, facilities, or functions in addition to or to a greater extent than those financed, provided or maintained for the entire city:

(1) Beach erosion control and flood and hurricane protection works.

(1a) (For applicability see note) Any service, facility, or function which the municipality may by law provide in the city, and including but not limited to placement of utility wiring underground, placement of period street lighting, placement of specially designed street signs and street furniture, landscaping, specialized street and sidewalk paving, and other appropriate improvements to the rights-of-way that generally preserve the character of an historic district; provided that this subdivision only applies to a service district which, at the time of its creation, had the same boundaries as an historic district created under Part 3A of Article 19 of this Chapter.

(2) Downtown revitalization projects.

(2a) Urban area revitalization projects.

(3) Drainage projects.

(3a) Sewage collection and disposal systems of all types, including septic tank systems or other on-site collection or disposal facilities or systems.

(3b) (For applicability see note) Lighting at interstate highway interchange ramps.

(4) Off-street parking facilities.

(5) Watershed improvement projects, including but not limited to watershed improvement projects as defined in General Statutes Chapter 139; drainage projects, including but not limited to the drainage projects provided for by General Statutes Chapter 156; and water resources development projects, including but not limited to the federal water resources development projects provided for by General Statutes Chapter 143, Article 21.

(6) Conversion of private residential streets to public streets as provided in subsection (e) of this section.

(b) Downtown Revitalization Defined. - As used in this section "downtown revitalization projects" are improvements, services, functions, promotions, and developmental activities intended to further the public health, safety, welfare, convenience, and economic well-being of the central city or downtown area. Exercise of the authority granted by this Article to undertake downtown revitalization projects financed by a service district do not prejudice a city's authority to undertake urban renewal projects in the same area. Examples of downtown revitalization projects include by way of illustration but not limitation all of the following:

(1) Improvements to water mains, sanitary sewer mains, storm sewer mains, electric power distribution lines, gas mains, street lighting, streets and sidewalks, including rights-of-way and easements.

(2) Construction of pedestrian malls, bicycle paths, overhead pedestrian walkways, sidewalk canopies, and parking facilities both on-street and off-street.

(4) Improvements to relieve traffic congestion in the central city and improve pedestrian and vehicular access to it.

(5) Improvements to reduce the incidence of crime in the central city.

(6) Providing city services or functions in addition to or to a greater extent than those provided or maintained for the entire city.

(7) Sponsoring festivals and markets in the downtown area, promoting business investment in the downtown area, helping to coordinate public and private actions in the downtown area, and developing and issuing publications on the downtown area.

(c) Urban Area Revitalization Defined. - As used in this section, the term "urban area revitalization projects" includes the provision within an urban area of any service or facility that may be provided in a downtown area as a downtown revitalization project under subdivision (a)(2) and subsection (b) of this section. As used in this section, the term "urban area" means an area that (i) is located within a city and (ii) meets one or more of the following conditions:

(1) It is the central business district of the city.

(2) It consists primarily of existing or redeveloping concentrations of industrial, retail, wholesale, office, or significant employment-generating uses, or any combination of these uses.

(3) It is located in or along a major transportation corridor and does not include any residential parcels that are not, at their closest point, within 150 feet of the major transportation corridor right-of-way or any nonresidentially zoned parcels that are not, at their closest point, within 1,500 feet of the major transportation corridor right-of-way.

(4) It has as its center and focus a major concentration of public or institutional uses, such as airports, seaports, colleges or universities, hospitals and health care facilities, or governmental facilities.

(c1) Transit-Oriented Development Defined. - As used in this section, the term "transit-oriented development" includes the provision within a public transit

transportation service operates or a busway or guideway dedicated to public transportation service. A busway is not a mass transit line if a majority of its length is also generally open to passenger cars and other private vehicles more than two days a week.

The following services and facilities are included in the definition of "transit-oriented development" if they are provided within a transit area:

(1) Any service or facility that may be provided in a downtown area as a downtown revitalization project under subdivision (a)(2) and subsection (b) of this section.

(2) Passenger stops and stations on a mass transit line.

(3) Parking facilities and structures associated with passenger stops and stations on a mass transit line.

(4) Any other service or facility, whether public or public-private, that the city may by law provide or participate in within the city, including retail, residential, and commercial facilities.

(d) Contracts. - A city may provide services, facilities, functions, or promotional and developmental activities in a service district with its own forces, through a contract with another governmental agency, through a contract with a private agency, or by any combination thereof. Any contracts entered into pursuant to this paragraph shall specify the purposes for which city moneys are to be used and shall require an appropriate accounting for those moneys at the end of each fiscal year or other appropriate period.

(e) Converting Private Residential Streets to Public Streets. - A city may establish a municipal service district for the purpose of converting private residential streets to public streets if the conditions of this subsection are met. The property tax levied in a municipal service district created for this purpose may be used only to pay the costs related to the transfer of ownership of the streets, evaluation of the condition of the private streets, and the design and construction costs related to improving the private streets to meet public street standards as approved by the governing board. Notwithstanding G.S. 160A-542, the property tax rate in a district created for this purpose may not be in excess

from the tax in the district, no further tax may be levied in the district, and the city council must abolish the municipal service district as provided by G.S. 160A-541.

Notwithstanding G.S. 160A-299, if a city abandons the streets and associated rights-of-way acquired pursuant to this subsection, the street-related common elements must be returned to the owners' association from which the city acquired them in a manner that makes the owners' association's holdings in common elements as they were prior to the establishment of the municipal service district.

For a city to create a municipal service district for the purpose of converting private residential streets to public streets, all of the following conditions must be met:

(1)   The private residential road must be nongated.

(2)   The city must receive a petition signed by at least sixty percent (60%) of the lot owners of the owners' association requesting the city to establish a municipal service district for the purpose of paying the costs related to converting private residential streets to public streets. The executive board of an owners' association for which the city has received a petition under this subsection may transfer street-related common elements to the city, notwithstanding the provisions of either the North Carolina Planned Community Act in Chapter 47F of the General Statutes or the North Carolina Condominium Act in Chapter 47C of the General Statutes, or related articles of declaration, deed covenants, or any other similar document recorded with the Register of Deeds.

(3)   The city must agree to accept the converted streets for perpetual public maintenance.

(4)   The city must meet one of the following requirements:

a.   Located primarily in a county that has a population of 750,000 or more according to the most recent decennial federal census, and also located in an adjacent county with a population of 250,000 or more according to the most recent decennial federal census.

recent decennial federal census. (1973, c. 655, s. 1; 1977, c. 775, ss. 1, 2; 1979, c. 595, s. 2; 1985, c. 580; 1987, c. 621, s. 1; 1999-224, s. 1; 1999-388, s. 1; 2004-151, s. 1; 2004-203, s. 5(m); 2009-385, s. 1; 2011-72, ss. 1, 2; 2011-322, s. 1; 2012-79, s. 1.11.)

§ 160A-537. Definition of service districts.

(a) Standards. - The city council of any city may by resolution define a service district upon finding that a proposed district is in need of one or more of the services, facilities, or functions listed in G.S. 160A-536 to a demonstrably greater extent than the remainder of the city.

(b) Report. - Before the public hearing required by subsection (c), the city council shall cause to be prepared a report containing:

(1) A map of the proposed district, showing its proposed boundaries;

(2) A statement showing that the proposed district meets the standards set out in subsection (a); and

(3) A plan for providing in the district one or more of the services listed in G.S. 160A-536.

The report shall be available for public inspection in the office of the city clerk for at least four weeks before the date of the public hearing.

(c) Hearing and Notice. - The city council shall hold a public hearing before adopting any resolution defining a new service district under this section. Notice of the hearing shall state the date, hour, and place of the hearing and its subject, and shall include a map of the proposed district and a statement that the report required by subsection (b) is available for public inspection in the office of the city clerk. The notice shall be published at least once not less than one week before the date of the hearing. In addition, it shall be mailed at least four weeks before the date of the hearing by any class of U.S. mail which is fully prepaid to the owners as shown by the county tax records as of the preceding January 1 (and at the address shown thereon) of all property located within the

(d) Effective Date. - Except as otherwise provided in this subsection, the resolution defining a service district shall take effect at the beginning of a fiscal year commencing after its passage, as determined by the city council. If the governing body in the resolution states that general obligation bonds or special obligation bonds are anticipated to be authorized for the project, it may make the resolution effective immediately upon its adoption or as otherwise provided in the resolution. However, no ad valorem tax may be levied for a partial fiscal year.

(e) In the case of a resolution defining a service district, which is adopted during the period beginning July 1, 1981, and ending July 31, 1981, and which district is for any purpose defined in G.S. 160A-536(1), the city council may make the resolution effective for the fiscal year beginning July 1, 1981. In any such case, the report under subsection (b) of this section need only have been available for public inspection for at least two weeks before the date of the public hearing, and the notice required by subsection (c) of this section need only have been mailed at least two weeks before the date of the hearing. (1973, c. 655, s. 1; 1981, c. 53, s. 1; c. 733, s. 1; 2006-162, s. 25; 2012-156, s. 4.)

§ 160A-538. Extension of service districts.

(a) Standards. - The city council may by resolution annex territory to any service district upon finding that:

(1) The area to be annexed is contiguous to the district, with at least one eighth of the area's aggregate external boundary coincident with the existing boundary of the district;

(2) That the area to be annexed requires the services of the district.

(b) Annexation by Petition. - The city council may also by resolution extend by annexation the boundaries of any service district when one hundred percent (100%) of the real property owners of the area to be annexed have petitioned the council for annexation to the service district.

(1) A map of the service district and the adjacent territory, showing the present and proposed boundaries of the district;

(2) A statement showing that the area to be annexed meets the standards and requirements of subsections (a) or (b); and

(3) A plan for extending services to the area to be annexed.

The report shall be available for public inspection in the office of the city clerk for at least two weeks before the date of the public hearing.

(d) Hearing and Notice. - The council shall hold a public hearing before adopting any resolution extending the boundaries of a service district. Notice of the hearing shall state the date, hour and place of the hearing and its subject, and shall include a statement that the report required by subsection (c) is available for inspection in the office of the city clerk. The notice shall be published at least once not less than one week before the date of the hearing. In addition, the notice shall be mailed at least four weeks before the date of the hearing to the owners as shown by the county tax records as of the preceding January 1 of all property located within the area to be annexed. The notice may be mailed by any class of U.S. mail which is fully prepaid. The person designated by the council to mail the notice shall certify to the council that the mailing has been completed, and his certificate shall be conclusive in the absence of fraud.

(e) Effective Date. - The resolution extending the boundaries of the district shall take effect at the beginning of a fiscal year commencing after its passage, as determined by the council.

(f) (For applicability see note) A service district which at the time of its creation had the same boundaries as an historic district created under Part 3A of Article 19 of this Chapter may only have its boundaries extended to include territory which has been added to the historic district. (1973, c. 655, s. 1; 1981, c. 53, s. 2; 1987, c. 621, s. 2.)

§ 160A-538.1. Reduction of service districts.

land which it has determined need no longer be included in said district. The city council shall hold a public hearing before adopting a resolution removing any tract or parcel of land from a district. Notice of the hearing shall state the date, hour and place of the hearing, and its subject, and shall be published at least once not less than one week before the date of the hearing.

(b) The removal of any tract or parcel of land from any service district shall take effect at the end of a fiscal year following passage of the resolution, as determined by the city council.

(c) (For applicability see note) A service district which at the time of its creation had the same boundaries as an historic district created under Part 3A of Article 19 of this Chapter may only have its boundaries reduced to exclude territory which has been removed from the historic district. (1977, c. 775, s. 3; 1987, c. 621, s. 3.)

§ 160A-539. Consolidation of service districts.

(a) The city council may by resolution consolidate two or more service districts upon finding that:

(1) The districts are contiguous or are in a continuous boundary; and

(2) The services provided in each of the districts are substantially the same; or

(3) If the services provided are lower for one of the districts, there is a need to increase those services for that district to the level of that enjoyed by the other districts.

(b) Report. - Before the public hearing required by subsection (c), the city council shall cause to be prepared a report containing:

(1) A map of the districts to be consolidated;

(2) A statement showing the proposed consolidation meets the standards of subsection (a); and

The report shall be available in the office of the city clerk for at least two weeks before the public hearing.

(c) Hearing and Notice. - The city council shall hold a public hearing before adopting any resolution consolidating service districts. Notice of the hearing shall state the date, hour, and place of the hearing and its subject, and shall include a statement that the report required by subsection (b) is available for inspection in the office of the city clerk. The notice shall be published at least once not less than one week before the date of the hearing. In addition, the notice shall be mailed at least four weeks before the hearing to the owners as shown by the county tax records as of the preceding January 1 of all property located within the consolidated district. The notice may be mailed by any class of U.S. mail which is fully prepaid. The person designated by the council to mail the notice shall certify to the council that the mailing has been completed, and his certificate shall be conclusive in the absence of fraud.

(d) Effective Date. - The consolidation of service districts shall take effect at the beginning of a fiscal year commencing after passage of the resolution of consolidation, as determined by the council. (1973, c. 655, s. 1; 1981, c. 53, s. 2.)

§ 160A-540. Required provision or maintenance of services.

(a) New District. - When a city defines a new service district, it shall provide, maintain, or let contracts for the services for which the residents of the district are being taxed within a reasonable time, not to exceed one year, after the effective date of the definition of the district.

(b) Extended District. - When a city annexes territory for a service district, it shall provide, maintain, or let contracts for the services provided or maintained throughout the district to the residents of the area annexed to the district within a reasonable time, not to exceed one year, after the effective date of the annexation.

(c) Consolidated District. - When a city consolidates two or more service districts, one of which has had provided or maintained a lower level of services,

of the consolidation. (1973, c. 655, s. 1.)

§ 160A-541. Abolition of service districts.

Upon finding that there is no longer a need for a particular service district, the city council may by resolution abolish that district. The council shall hold a public hearing before adopting a resolution abolishing a district. Notice of the hearing shall state the date, hour and place of the hearing, and its subject, and shall be published at least once not less than one week before the date of the hearing. The abolition of any service district shall take effect at the end of a fiscal year following passage of the resolution, as determined by the council. (1973, c. 655, s. 1.)

§ 160A-542. Taxes authorized; rate limitation.

A city may levy property taxes within defined service districts in addition to those levied throughout the city, in order to finance, provide or maintain for the district services provided therein in addition to or to a greater extent than those financed, provided or maintained for the entire city. In addition, a city may allocate to a service district any other revenues whose use is not otherwise restricted by law.

Property subject to taxation in a newly established district or in an area annexed to an existing district is that subject to taxation by the city as of the preceding January 1.

Property taxes may not be levied within any district established pursuant to this Article in excess of a rate on each one hundred dollar ($100.00) value of property subject to taxation which, when added to the rate levied city wide for purposes subject to the rate limitation, would exceed the rate limitation established in G.S. 160A-209(d), unless that portion of the rate in excess of this limitation is submitted to and approved by a majority of the qualified voters residing within the district. Any referendum held pursuant to this paragraph shall be held and conducted as provided in G.S. 160A-209.

§ 160A-543. Bonds authorized.

A city may incur debt under general law to finance services, facilities or functions provided within a service district. If a proposed general obligation bond issue is required by law to be submitted to and approved by the voters of the city, and if the proceeds of the proposed bond issue are to be used in connection with a service that is or, if the bond issue is approved, will be provided only for one or more service districts or at a higher level in service districts than city wide, the proposed bond issue must be approved concurrently by a majority of those voting throughout the entire city and by a majority of the total of those voting in all of the affected or to be affected service districts. (1973, c. 655, s. 1; 2004-151, s. 4.)

§ 160A-544. Exclusion of personal property of public service corporations.

There shall be excluded from any service district and the provisions of this Article shall not apply to the personal property of any public service corporation as defined in G.S. 160A-243(c); provided that this section shall not apply to any service district in existence on January 1, 1977. (1977, c. 775, s. 4.)

§§ 160A-545 through 160A-549. Reserved for future codification purposes.

Article 24.

Parking Authorities.

§ 160A-550. Short title.

This Article may be cited as the "Parking Authority Law." (1951, c. 779, s. 1; 1979, 2nd Sess., c. 1247, s. 44.)

from the context:

(1) The term "authority" shall mean a public body and a body corporate and politic organized in accordance with this Article for the purposes, with the powers and subject to the restrictions hereinafter set forth;

(2) The term "bonds" shall mean bonds authorized by this Article;

(3) The term "city" shall mean the city that is, or is about to be, included in the territorial boundaries of an authority when created hereunder;

(4) The term "city clerk" shall mean the clerk of the city or the officer thereof charged with the duties customarily imposed on the clerk;

(5) The term "city council" shall mean the legislative body, council, board of commissioners, or other body charged with governing the city;

(6) The term "commissioner" shall mean one of the members of an authority, appointed in accordance with the provisions of this Article;

(7) The term "parking project" shall mean any area or place operated or to be operated by the authority for the parking or storing of motor and other vehicles, open to public use for a fee, and shall without limiting the foregoing, include all real and personal property, driveways, roads, approaches, structures, garages, meters, mechanical equipment, and all appurtenances and facilities either on, above or under the ground which are used or usable in connection with such parking or storing of such vehicles, including on-street parking meters if so provided by the governing authority;

(8) The term "real property" shall mean lands, structures, franchises, and interest in lands, and any and all things usually included within the said term, and includes not only fees simple absolute but also any and all lesser interests, such as easements, rights-of-way, uses, leases, licenses, and all other incorporeal hereditaments and every estate, interest or right, legal or equitable, including terms of years, and liens thereon by way of judgments, mortgages or otherwise, and also claims for damage to real estate. (1951, c. 779, s. 2; 1965, c. 998, s. 1; 1979, 2nd Sess., c. 1247, s. 44.)

of 25 or more residents of the city, hold a public hearing on the question whether or not it is necessary for the city to organize an authority under the provisions of this Article. Notice of the time, place and purpose of such hearing shall be given by publication in a newspaper of general circulation in the city, at least once, at least 10 days before such hearing. At such hearing, an opportunity to be heard shall be granted to all residents and taxpayers of the city and all other interested persons. If, after such hearing, the city council shall by resolution determine that it is necessary for the city to organize an authority under the provisions of this Article, the city council shall appoint, as hereinafter provided, five commissioners to act as an authority. Said commission shall be a public body and a body corporate and politic upon the completion of the taking of the following proceedings:

The commissioners shall present or cause to be presented to the Secretary of State of North Carolina a written application signed by them, which shall set forth

(1) A statement that the city council has, pursuant to this Article, and after a public hearing held as herein required, determined that it is necessary for the city to organize an authority under the provisions of this Article, and has appointed the signers of such application as commissioners of such an authority;

(2) A statement that the commissioners desire the authority to become a public body and a body corporate and politic under this Article;

(3) The name, address and term of office of each of the commissioners;

(4) The name which is proposed for the corporation; and

(5) The location and the principal office of the proposed corporation.

The application shall be accompanied by a copy, certified by the city clerk, of the resolution or resolutions of the city council making such determination and appointments. The application shall be subscribed and sworn to by each of said commissioners before an officer authorized by law to take and certify oaths, who shall certify upon the application that he personally knows said commissioners and knows them to be the persons appointed as stated in the application, and

this State or so nearly similar as to lead to confusion and uncertainty, he shall receive and file it and shall record it in an appropriate book of record in his office.

When the application has been made, filed and recorded, as herein provided, the authority shall constitute a public body and body corporate and politic under the name proposed in the application; and the Secretary of State shall make and issue a certificate of incorporation pursuant to this Article, under the seal of the State, and shall record the same with the application.

The boundaries of such authority shall be coterminous with those of such city.

In any suit, action or proceeding involving the validity or enforcement of or relating to any contract of the authority, the authority shall be conclusively deemed to have been established in accordance with the provisions of this Article upon proof of the issuance of the aforesaid certificate by the Secretary of State. A copy of such certificate, duly certified by the Secretary of State, shall be admissible in evidence in any such suit, action or proceeding, and shall be conclusive proof of the filing and contents thereof. (1951, c. 779, s. 3; 1979, 2nd Sess., c. 1247, s. 44.)

§ 160A-553. Appointment, removal, etc., of commissioners; quorum; chairman; vice-chairman, agents and employees.

An authority shall consist of five commissioners appointed by the city council, and the city council shall designate the first chairman. No commissioner shall be a city official.

The commissioners who are first appointed shall be designated by the city council to serve for terms of one, two, three, four and five years respectively from the date of their appointment. Thereafter, the term of office shall be five years. A commissioner shall hold office until his successor has been appointed by the city council and has qualified. Vacancies shall be filled by the city council for the unexpired term. Three commissioners shall constitute a quorum. A commissioner shall receive no compensation for his services, but he shall be entitled to reimbursement for his actual and necessary expenses incurred in the performance of his official duties.

(who shall be executive director), technical experts and such other officers, agents and employees, permanent or temporary, as it may require, and shall determine their qualifications, duties and compensation. An authority may, with the consent of the city council call upon the city attorney or chief law officer of the city for such legal services as it may require, or it may employ its own counsel and legal staff. An authority may delegate to one or more of its agents or employees such powers or duties as it may deem proper. The city council may remove any member of the authority for inefficiency, neglect of duty or misconduct in office, giving him a copy of the charges against him and an opportunity of being heard in person, or by counsel, in his defense upon not less than 10 days' notice. (1951, c. 779, s. 4; 1979, 2nd Sess., c. 1247, ss. 42, 44.)

§ 160A-554. Duty of authority and commissioners.

The authority and its commissioners shall be under a statutory duty to comply or cause compliance strictly with all provisions of this Article and, in addition thereto, with each and every term, provision and covenant in any contract of the authority on its part to be kept or performed. (1951, c. 779, s. 5; 1979, 2nd Sess., c. 1247, s. 44.)

§ 160A-555. Interested commissioners or employees.

No commissioner or employee of an authority shall acquire any interest direct or indirect in any parking project or in any property included or planned to be included in any parking project, nor shall he have any interest direct or indirect in any contract or proposed contract for materials or services to be furnished or used in connection with any parking project. If any commissioner or employee of an authority owns or controls an interest direct or indirect in any property included or planned to be included in any parking project, he shall immediately disclose the same in writing to the authority and such disclosure shall be entered upon the minutes of the authority. Failure to so disclose such interest shall constitute misconduct in office. (1951, c. 779, s. 6; 1979, 2nd Sess., c. 1247, s. 44.)

body corporate and politic, exercising public powers as an agency or instrumentality of the city with which it is coterminous. The purpose of the authority shall be to relieve traffic congestion of the streets and public places in the city by means of parking facilities, and to that end to acquire, construct, improve, operate and maintain one or more parking projects in the city. To carry out said purpose, the authority shall have power:

(1) To sue and be sued;

(2) To have a seal and alter the same at pleasure;

(3) To acquire, hold and dispose of personal property for its corporate purposes, including the power to purchase prospective or tentative awards in connection with the condemnation of real property;

(4) To acquire by purchase or condemnation, and use real property necessary or convenient. All real property acquired by the authority by condemnation shall be acquired in the manner provided by law for the condemnation of land by the city;

(5) To make bylaws for the management and regulation of its affairs, and subject to agreements with bondholders, for the regulation of parking projects;

(6) To make contracts and leases, and to execute all instruments necessary or convenient;

(7) To construct such buildings, structures and facilities as may be necessary or convenient;

(8) To construct, reconstruct, improve, maintain and operate parking projects;

(9) To accept grants, loans or contributions from the United States, the State of North Carolina, or any agency or instrumentality of either of them, or the city, and to expend the proceeds for any purposes of the authority;

(11) To do all things necessary or convenient to carry out the purpose of the authority and the powers expressly given to it by this Article;

(12) To issue revenue bonds under the Local Government Revenue Bond Act. (1951, c. 779, s. 7; 1965, c. 998, s. 2; 1971, c. 780, s. 18; 1979, 2nd Sess., c. 1247, s. 44.)

§ 160A-557. Conveyance of property by the city to the authority; acquisition of property by the city or by the authority.

(a) The city may convey, with or without consideration, to the authority real and personal property owned by the city for use by the authority as a parking project or projects or a part thereof. In case of real property so conveyed, the instrument of conveyance shall contain a provision for reversion of the property to the city upon the termination of the corporate existence of the authority or upon the termination of the use of the property for the corporate purpose of the authority. Such conveyance of property by the city to the authority may be made without regard to the provisions of other laws regulating sales of property by the city or requiring previous advertisement of sales of property by the city.

(b) The city may acquire by purchase or condemnation real property in the name of the city for the authority or for the widening of existing roads, streets, parkways, avenues or highways or for new roads, streets, parkways, avenues or highways to any of the parking projects, or partly for such purposes and partly for other city purposes, by purchase or condemnation in the manner provided by law for the acquisition of real property by the city. The city may close such streets, roads, parkways, avenues, or highways as may be necessary or convenient.

(c) Contracts may be entered into between the city and the authority providing for the property to be conveyed by the city to the authority, the additional property to be acquired by the city and so conveyed, the streets, roads, parkways, avenues and highways to be closed by the city, and the amounts, terms and conditions of payment to be made by the authority. Such contracts may contain covenants by the city as to the road, street, parkway, avenue and highway improvements to be made by the city, including provisions

part of the revenues of on-street parking meters to the authority for a period of not to exceed the period during which bonds of the authority shall be outstanding; provided, that the total amount of such revenues which may be paid pursuant to such a pledge shall not exceed the total of the principal of and interest on such bonds which become due and payable during such period. Such contracts may also contain provisions limiting or prohibiting the construction and operation by the city or any agency thereof in designated areas of public parking facilities and parking meters whether or not a fee or charge is made therefor. Any such contracts between the city and the authority may be pledged by the authority to secure its bonds and may not be modified thereafter except as provided by the terms of the contracts or by the terms of the pledge. The city council may authorize such contracts on behalf of the city and no other authorization on the part of the city for such contracts shall be necessary.

(d) The authority may itself acquire real property for a parking project at the cost and expense of the authority by purchase or condemnation pursuant to the laws relating to the condemnation of land by the city.

(e) In case the authority shall acquire any real property which it shall determine is no longer required for a parking project, then, if such real property was acquired at the cost and expense of the city, the authority shall have power to convey it without consideration to the city, or, if such real property was acquired at the cost and expense of the authority, then the authority shall have power to sell, lease or otherwise dispose of said real property and shall retain and have the power to use the proceeds of sale, rentals or other moneys derived from the disposition thereof for its purposes. (1951, c. 779, s. 8; 1965, c. 998, s. 3; 1979, 2nd Sess., c. 1247, s. 44.)

§ 160A-558. Contracts.

The authority shall let contracts in the manner provided by law for contracts of the city. (1951, c. 779, s. 9; 1979, 2nd Sess., c. 1247, s. 44.)

§ 160A-559. Moneys of the authority.

separate bank account or accounts. The moneys in such accounts shall be paid out on checks of the treasurer on written requisition of the chairman of the authority or of such other person or persons as the authority may authorize to make such requisitions. All deposits of such moneys shall be secured in the manner provided by law for securing deposits of moneys of the city. The city accountant of the city and his legally authorized representatives are authorized and empowered from time to time to examine the accounts and books of the authority, including its receipts, disbursements, contracts, leases, sinking funds, investments and any other records and papers relating to its financial standing. The authority shall cause an annual audit of its accounts to be made by a certified public accountant or firm of certified public accountants, and shall cause a copy of the report of each such audit to be filed with the city clerk, who shall present the same to the city council. The authority shall have power, notwithstanding the provisions of this section to contract with the holders of any of its bonds as to the custody, collection, securing, investment and payment of any moneys of the authority or any moneys held in trust or otherwise for the payment of bonds or in any way to secure bonds, and to carry out any such contract notwithstanding that such contract may be inconsistent with the previous provisions of this section. Moneys held in trust or otherwise for the payment of bonds or in any way to secure bonds and deposits of such moneys may be secured in the same manner as moneys of the authority, and all banks and trust companies are authorized to give such security for such deposits. (1951, c. 779, s. 10; 1979, 2nd Sess., c. 1247, s. 44.)

§ 160A-560. Bonds legal investments for public officers and fiduciaries.

The bonds are hereby made securities in which all public officers and bodies of this State and all municipalities and municipal subdivisions, all insurance companies and associations and other persons carrying on an insurance business, all banks, bankers, trust companies, savings banks and savings associations, including savings and loan associations, investment companies and other persons carrying on a banking business and all other persons whatsoever, except as hereinafter provided, who are now or may hereafter be authorized to invest in bonds or other obligations of the State, may properly and legally invest funds including capital in their control or belonging to them; provided that, notwithstanding the provisions of any other general or special law to the contrary, such bonds shall not be eligible for the investment of funds, may be received by all public officers and bodies of this State and all municipalities and municipal subdivisions for any purpose for which the deposit of bonds or other obligations of this State is now or may hereafter be authorized. (1951, c. 779, s. 15; 1979, 2nd Sess., c. 1247, s. 44.)

§ 160A-561. Exemptions from taxation.

It is hereby found, determined and declared that the creation of the authority and the carrying out of its corporate purposes is in all respects for the benefit of the people of the State of North Carolina, for the improvement of their health, welfare and prosperity, and for the promotion of their traffic, and is a public purpose, and that the authority will be performing an essential governmental function in the exercise of the powers conferred upon it by this Article, and the State of North Carolina covenants with the holders of the bonds that the authority shall be required to pay no taxes or assessments upon any of the property acquired by it or under its jurisdiction, control, possession or supervision or upon its activities in the operation and maintenance of the project or any tolls, revenues or other income received by the authority and that the bonds of the authority and the income therefrom shall at all times be exempt from taxation, except for transfer and estate taxes. (1951, c. 779, s. 16; 1979, 2nd Sess., c. 1247, s. 44.)

§ 160A-562. Tax contract by the State.

The State of North Carolina covenants with the purchasers and with all subsequent holders and transferees of bonds issued by the authority pursuant to this Article, in consideration of the acceptance of and payment for the bonds, that the bonds of the authority issued pursuant to this Article and the income therefrom, and all moneys, funds and revenues pledged to pay or secure the payment of such bonds, shall at all times be free from taxation except for transfer and estate taxes. (1951, c. 779, s. 17; 1979, 2nd Sess., c. 1247, s. 44.)

§ 160A-563. Actions against the authority.

the demand, claim or claims upon which such action is founded were presented to a member of the authority, or to its secretary, or to its chief executive officer and that the authority has neglected or refused to make an adjustment or payment thereof for 30 days after such presentment. (1951, c. 779, s. 19; 1979, 2nd Sess., c. 1247, s. 44.)

§ 160A-564. Termination of authority.

The city council shall have the authority to terminate the existence of the authority at any time. In the event of such termination, all property and assets of the authority shall automatically become the property of the city and the city shall succeed to all rights, obligations and liabilities of the authority. (1951, c. 779, s. 20; 1979, 2nd Sess., c. 1247, ss. 43, 44.)

§ 160A-565. Inconsistent provisions in other acts superseded.

Insofar as the provisions of this Article are inconsistent with the provisions of any other act, general or special, the provisions of this Article shall be controlling. This Article shall not repeal or modify any other act providing a different method of financing parking projects in cities, the powers conferred hereby being intended to be in addition to and not in substitution for the powers conferred by other acts. (1951, c. 779, s. 22; 1979, 2nd Sess., c. 1247, s. 44.)

§§ 160A-566 through 160A-574. Reserved for future codification purposes.

Article 25.

Public Transportation Authorities.

§ 160A-575. Title.

This Article shall be known and may be cited as the "North Carolina Public Transportation Authorities Act." (1977, c. 465; 1979, 2nd Sess., c. 1247, s. 45.)

(1) "Authority" means a body corporate and politic organized in accordance with the provisions of this Article for the purposes, with the powers and subject to the restrictions hereinafter set forth.

(2) "Governing body" means the board, commission, council or other body, by whatever name it may be known, in which the general legislative powers of the municipality are vested.

(3) "Municipality" means any county, city, or town of this State, and any other political subdivision, public corporation, authority, or district in this State, which is or may be authorized by law to acquire, establish, construct, enlarge, improve, maintain, own, and operate public transportation systems.

(4) "Municipality's chief administrative official" means the county manager, city manager, town manager, or other person, by whatever title he shall be known, in whom the responsibility for the municipality's administrative duties is vested.

(5) "Public transportation" means transportation of passengers whether or not for hire by any means of conveyance, including but not limited to a street railway, elevated railway or guideway, subway, motor vehicle or motor bus, either publicly or privately owned and operated, holding itself out to the general public for the transportation of persons within the territorial jurisdiction of the authority, including charter service.

(6) "Public transportation system" means, without limitation, a combination of real and personal property, structures, improvements, buildings, equipment, vehicle parking or other facilities, and rights-of-way, or any combination thereof, used or useful for the purposes of public transportation. (1977, c. 465; 1979, 2nd Sess., c. 1247, s. 45.)

§ 160A-577. Creation; membership.

A municipality may, by resolution or ordinance, create a transportation authority, hereinafter sometimes referred to as the "authority." It shall be a body corporate

Members of the authority shall reside within the territorial jurisdiction of the authority as hereinafter set out. They shall be appointed by the governing body of the municipality. The terms of the members shall be fixed by the governing body. Appointments to fill vacancies occurring during the regular terms shall be made by the governing body. The appointments of all members shall run until their successors are appointed and qualified.

The members of the authority shall elect a chairman and vice-chairman from the membership of the authority. They shall also elect a secretary who may, or may not, be a member of the authority.

A majority of the members shall constitute a quorum for the transaction of business and an affirmative vote of the majority of the members present at a meeting of the authority shall be required to constitute action of the authority. Members of the authority shall receive such compensation, if any, as may be fixed by the governing body of the municipality. (1977, c. 465; 1979, 2nd Sess., c. 1247, s. 45.)

§ 160A-578. Purpose of the authority.

The purpose of the authority shall be to provide for a safe, adequate and convenient public transportation system for the municipality creating the authority and for its immediate environs, through the granting of franchises, ownership and leasing of terminals, buses and other transportation facilities and equipment, and otherwise through the exercise of the powers and duties conferred upon it. (1977, c. 465; 1979, 2nd Sess., c. 1247, s. 45.)

§ 160A-579. General powers of the authority.

The general powers of the authority shall include any or all of the following:

(1)   To sue and be sued;

(2)   To have a seal;

(4) To employ persons deemed necessary to carry out the management functions and duties assigned to them by the authority and to fix their compensation, within the limit of available funds;

(5) With the approval of the municipality's chief administrative official, to use officers, employees, agents and facilities of the municipality for such purposes and upon such terms as may be mutually agreeable;

(6) To retain and employ counsel, auditors, engineers and private consultants on an annual salary, contract basis, or otherwise for rendering professional or technical services and advice;

(7) To acquire, maintain and operate such lands, buildings, structures, facilities, and equipment as may be necessary or convenient for the operations of the authority and for the operation of a public transportation system;

(8) To make or enter into contracts, agreements, deeds, leases, conveyances or other instruments, including contracts and agreements with the United States and the State of North Carolina;

(9) To surrender to the municipality any property no longer required by the authority;

(10) To make plans, surveys and studies of public transportation facilities within the territorial jurisdiction of the authority and to prepare and make recommendations in regard thereto;

(11) To enter into and perform contracts with public transportation companies with respect to the operation of public passenger transportation;

(12) To issue certificates of public convenience and necessity; and to grant franchises and enter into franchise agreements and in all respects to regulate the operation of buses, taxicabs and other methods of public passenger transportation which originate and terminate within the territorial jurisdiction of the authority as fully as the municipality is now or hereafter empowered to do within the territorial jurisdiction of the municipality;

rent, lease or otherwise sell the right to do so to any person, public or private; further, to the extent authorized by resolution or ordinance of the municipality to obtain grants, loans and assistance from the United States, the State, any public body, or any private source whatsoever;

(14) To enter into and perform contracts and agreements with other public transportation authorities pursuant to the provisions of G.S. 160A-460 through 160A-464 of Part 1 of Article 20 of Chapter 160A of the General Statutes; in addition, to enter into and perform contracts with other units of local government when specifically authorized by the governing body, pursuant to the provisions of G.S. 160A-460 through 160A-464 of Part 1 of Article 20 of Chapter 160A of the General Statutes;

(15) To do all things necessary or convenient to carry out its purpose and to exercise the powers granted to the authority. (1977, c. 465; 1979, 2nd Sess., c. 1247, s. 45.)

§ 160A-580. Authority of Utilities Commission not affected.

Except as otherwise provided herein, nothing in this Article shall be construed to limit or otherwise affect the power or authority of the North Carolina Utilities Commission or the right of appeal to the North Carolina Utilities Commission as provided by law. (1977, c. 465; 1979, 2nd Sess., c. 1247, s. 45.)

§ 160A-581. Territorial jurisdiction.

The jurisdiction of the authority shall extend to all local public passenger transportation operating within the municipality. Said jurisdiction shall also extend up to 30 miles outside of the corporate limits of the municipality where the municipality is a town or city, and up to five miles outside of the boundaries of the municipality where the municipality is a county or up to five miles outside of the combined boundaries of a group of counties. The authority shall not have jurisdiction over public transportation subject to the jurisdiction of and regulated by the I.C.C., nor shall it have jurisdiction over intrastate public transportation classified as common carriers of passengers by the North Carolina Utilities Commission. A public transportation authority shall not extend service into a

§ 160A-582. Fiscal accountability.

The authority shall be fiscally accountable to the municipality, and the municipality's governing body shall have authority to examine all records and accounts of the authority at any time. (1977, c. 465; 1979, 2nd Sess., c. 1247, s. 45.)

§ 160A-583. Funds.

The establishment and operation of a transportation authority as herein authorized are governmental functions and constitute a public purpose, and the municipality is hereby authorized to appropriate funds to support the establishment and operation of the transit authority. The municipality may also dedicate, sell, convey, donate or lease any of its interest in any property to the authority. Further, the authority is hereby authorized to establish such license and regulatory fees and charges as it may deem appropriate, subject to the approval of the governing body of the municipality. If the governing body finds that the funds otherwise available are insufficient, it may call a special election without a petition and submit to the qualified voters of the municipality the question of whether or not a special tax shall be levied and/or bonds issued, specifying the maximum amount thereof, for the purpose of acquiring lands, buildings, equipment and facilities and for the operations of the transit authority. Any special election shall be conducted in accordance with G.S. 163-287. (1977, c. 465; 1979, 2nd Sess., c. 1247, s. 45; 2013-381, s. 10.29.)

§ 160A-584. Effect on existing franchises and operations.

In the event a transportation authority is established under the authority of this Article, any existing franchises granted by the municipality shall continue in full force and effect until legally terminated; further, all ordinances and resolutions of the municipality regulating bus operations and taxicabs shall continue in full force and effect until superseded by regulations of the transportation authority. (1977, c. 465; 1979, 2nd Sess., c. 1247, s. 45.)

existence of the authority at any time. In the event of such termination, all property and assets of the authority shall automatically become the property of the municipality and the municipality shall succeed to all rights, obligations and liabilities of the authority. (1977, c. 465; 1979, 2nd Sess., c. 1247, s. 45.)

§ 160A-586. Controlling provisions.

Insofar as the provisions of this Article are not consistent with the provisions of any other law, public or private, the provisions of this Article shall be controlling. (1977, c. 465; 1979, 2nd Sess., c. 1247, s. 45.)

§ 160A-587. Consolidation of public transportation authority and parking authority.

The municipality may, by resolution or ordinance, vest in a single body corporate and politic both the powers of a public transportation authority in accordance with the provisions of this Article and the powers of a parking authority in accordance with the provisions of Article 38 of Chapter 160 of the General Statutes. Notwithstanding the membership provisions of G.S. 160A-553, the members of a consolidated body created pursuant to this section shall be selected according to the provisions of G.S. 160A-577. (1977, c. 465; 1979, 2nd Sess., c. 1247, s. 45.)

§ 160A-588. Joint provision of services.

Two or more municipalities may cooperate in the exercise of any power granted by this Article according to the procedures and provisions of G.S. 160A-460 through 160A-464 of Part 1 of Article 20 of Chapter 160A of the General Statutes. Additional municipalities may join an existing transportation authority upon making satisfactory arrangements pursuant to the provisions of G.S. 160A-460 through 160A-464 of Part 1 of Article 20 of Chapter 160A of the General Statutes. (1977, c. 465; 1979, 2nd Sess., c. 1247, s. 45.)

Article 26.

Regional Public Transportation Authority.

§ 160A-600. Title.

This Article shall be known and may be cited as the "Regional Public Transportation Authority Act." (1989, c. 740, s. 1.)

§ 160A-601. Definitions.

As used in this Article, unless the context otherwise requires:

(1) "Authority" means a Regional Public Transportation Authority as defined by subdivision (6) of this section.

(2) "Board of Trustees" means the governing board of the Authority, in which the general legislative powers of the Authority are vested.

(3) "Population" means the number of persons residing in respective areas as defined and enumerated in the most recent decennial federal census.

(4) "Public transportation" means transportation of passengers whether or not for hire by any means of conveyance, including but not limited to a street or elevated railway or guideway, subway, motor vehicle or motor bus, carpool or vanpool, either publicly or privately owned and operated, holding itself out to the general public for the transportation of persons within or working within the territorial jurisdiction of the Authority, excluding charter, tour, or sight-seeing service.

(5) "Public transportation system" means, without limitation, a combination of real and personal property, structures, improvements, buildings, equipment, vehicle parking or other facilities, railroads and railroad rights-of-way whether held in fee simple by quitclaim or easement, and rights-of-way, or any combination thereof, used or useful for the purposes of public transportation. "Public transportation system" however, does not include streets, roads, or highways except those for ingress and egress to vehicle parking.

(7) "Unit of local government" means any county, city, town or municipality of this State, and any other political subdivision, public corporation, Authority, or district in this State, which is or may be authorized by law to acquire, establish, construct, enlarge, improve, maintain, own, and operate public transportation systems.

(8) "Unit of local government's chief administrative official" means the county manager, city manager, town manager, or other person, by whatever title he shall be known, in whom the responsibility for the unit of local government's administrative duties is vested. (1989, c. 740, s. 1.)

§ 160A-602. Definition of territorial jurisdiction of Authority.

An authority may be created for any area of the State that, at the time of creation of the authority, meets the following criteria:

(1) The area consists of three counties:

(2) At least one of those counties contains at least part of a County Research and Production Service District established pursuant to Part 2 of Article 16 of Chapter 153A of the General Statutes; and

(3) The other two counties each:

a. Contain at least one unit of local government that is designated by the Governor of the State of North Carolina as a recipient pursuant to Section 9 of the Urban Mass Transportation Act of 1964, as amended; and

b. Are adjacent to at least one county that contains at least part of a County Research and Production Service District established pursuant to Part 2 of Article 16 of Chapter 153A of the General Statutes. (1989, c. 740, s. 1.)

§ 160A-603. Creation of Authority.

provisions of this Article. Each of such resolutions shall be adopted after a public hearing thereon, notice of which hearing shall be given by publication at least once, not less than 10 days prior to the date fixed for such hearing, in a newspaper having a general circulation in the county. Such notice shall contain a brief statement of the substance of the proposed resolution, shall set forth the proposed articles of incorporation of the Authority and shall state the time and place of the public hearing to be held thereof. No county shall be required to make any other publication of such resolution under the provisions of any other law.

(b)   Each such resolution shall include articles of incorporation which shall set forth:

(1)   The name of the authority;

(2)   A statement that such authority is organized under this Article; and

(3)   The names of the three organizing counties.

(c)   A certified copy of each of such resolutions signifying the determination to organize an authority under the provisions of this Article shall be filed with the Secretary of State, together with proof of publication of the notice of hearing on each of such resolutions. If the Secretary of State finds that the resolutions, including the articles of incorporation, conform to the provisions of this Article and that the notices of hearing were properly published, he shall file such resolutions and proofs of publication in his office and shall issue a certificate of incorporation under the seal of the State and shall record the same in an appropriate book of record in his office. The issuance of such certificate of incorporation by the Secretary of State shall constitute the Authority a public body and body politic and corporate of the State of North Carolina. Said certificate of incorporation shall be conclusive evidence of the fact that such authority has been duly created and established under the provisions of this Article.

(d)   When the Authority has been duly organized and its officers elected as herein provided the secretary of the Authority shall certify to the Secretary of State the names and addresses of such officers as well as the address of the principal office of the Authority.

§ 160A-604. Territorial jurisdiction of the Authority.

(a) The territorial jurisdiction of any authority created pursuant to this Article shall be coterminous with the boundaries of the three counties that organized it.

(b) Except as provided by this Article, the jurisdiction of the Authority may include all local public passenger transportation operating within the territorial jurisdiction of the Authority, but the Authority may not take over the operation of any existing public transportation without the consent of the owner.

(c) The Authority shall not have jurisdiction over public transportation subject to the jurisdiction of and regulated by the Interstate Commerce Commission, nor shall it have jurisdiction over intrastate public transportation classified as common carriers of passengers by the North Carolina Utilities Commission. (1989, c. 740, s. 1.)

§ 160A-605. Membership; officers; compensation.

(a) The governing body of an authority is the Board of Trustees. The Board of Trustees shall consist of 13 members, appointed as follows:

(1) The county with the greatest population shall be allocated five members to be appointed as follows:

a. Two by the board of commissioners of that county;

b. Two by the city council of the city containing the largest population within that county; and

c. One by the city council of the city containing the second largest population within that county;

(2) The county with the next greatest population shall be allocated three members to be appointed as follows:

that county; and

c.   One jointly by that board of commissioners and city council, by procedures agreed on between them;

(3)   The county with the least population shall be allocated two members to be appointed as follows:

a.   One by the board of commissioners of that county; and

b.   One by the city council of the city containing the largest population within that county; and

(4)   Three members of the Board of Transportation appointed by the Secretary of Transportation, to serve as ex officio nonvoting members.

(b)   Voting members of the Board of Trustees shall serve for terms of four years, provided that one-half of the initial appointments shall be for two-year terms, to be determined by lot at the first meeting of the Board of Trustees. Initial terms of office shall commence upon approval by the Secretary of State of the articles of incorporation. The members appointed by the Secretary of Transportation shall serve at his pleasure.

(c)   An appointing authority may appoint one of its members to the Board of Trustees. Service on the Board of Trustees may be in addition to any other office which a person is entitled to hold. Each voting member of the Board of Trustees may hold elective public office as defined by G.S. 128-1.1(d).

(d)   Members of the Board of Trustees shall reside within the territorial jurisdiction of the Authority as defined by G.S. 160A-604.

(e)   The Board of Trustees shall annually elect from its membership a Chairperson, and a Vice-Chairperson, and shall annually elect a Secretary, and a Treasurer.

(f)   Members of the Board of Trustees shall receive the sum of fifty dollars ($50.00) as compensation for attendance at each duly conducted meeting of the Authority. (1989, c. 740, s. 1.)

transaction of business. Except as provided by G.S. 160A-605(a)(4), each member shall have one vote.

(b)   Each member of the Board of Trustees may be removed with or without cause by the appointer(s). If the appointment was made jointly by two boards, the removal must be concurred in by both.

(c)   Appointments to fill vacancies shall be made for the remainder of the unexpired term by the respective appointer(s) charged with the responsibility for making such appointments pursuant to G.S. 160A-605. All members shall serve until their successors are appointed and qualified, unless removed from office. (1989, c. 740, s. 1.)

§ 160A-607. Advisory committees.

The Board of Trustees may provide for the selection of such advisory committees as it may find appropriate, which may or may not include members of the Board of Trustees. (1989, c. 740, s. 1.)

§ 160A-607.1. Special tax board.

(a)   The special tax board of an authority shall be composed of two representatives from each of the counties organizing the authority appointed annually by the board of commissioners of each of those counties' members at the first regular meeting thereof in January, except that the initial members shall serve a term beginning on the date that the initial terms of the board of trustees of that authority begin under G.S. 160A-605(b), and ending on the last day of December of that year. Each member of the special tax board must be a member of the board of commissioners of the county by which he was appointed. Membership on the special tax board may be held in addition to the offices authorized by G.S. 128-1 or G.S. 128-1.1. Said representatives shall hold office from their appointment until their successors are appointed and qualified, except that when any member of the special tax board ceases for any reason to be a member of the board of commissioners of the county by which he was appointed, he shall simultaneously cease to be a member of said special tax board. Upon the occurrence of any vacancy on said special tax

take and subscribe an oath or affirmation to support the Constitution and laws of the United States and of this State and to discharge faithfully the duties of his office; and a record of each such oath shall be filed in the minutes of the respective participating units of local government.

(b)   The special tax board shall meet regularly at such places and on such dates as are determined by the special tax board. The initial meeting shall be called jointly by the chairmen of the boards of commissioners of the counties organizing the authority. Special meetings may be called by the chairman of the special tax board on his own initiative and shall be called by him upon request of two or more members of the board. All members shall be notified in writing at least 24 hours in advance of such meeting. A majority of the members of the special tax board shall constitute a quorum. No vacancy in the membership of the special tax board shall impair the right of a quorum to exercise all the rights and perform all the duties of the special tax board. No action, other than an action to recess or adjourn, shall be taken except upon a majority vote of the entire authorized membership of said special tax board. Each member, including the chairman, shall be entitled to vote on any question.

(c)   The special tax board shall elect annually in January from among its members a chairman, vice-chairman, secretary and treasurer, except that initial officers shall be elected at the first meeting of the special tax board. (1989, c. 740, s. 1.)

§ 160A-608. Purpose of the Authority.

The purpose of the Authority shall be to finance, provide, operate, and maintain for a safe, clean, reliable, adequate, convenient, energy efficient, economically and environmentally sound public transportation system for the service area of the Authority through the granting of franchises, ownership and leasing of terminals, buses and other transportation facilities and equipment, and otherwise through the exercise of the powers and duties conferred upon it, in order to enhance mobility in the region and encourage sound growth patterns.

Such a service, facility, or function shall be financed, provided, operated, or maintained in the service area of the Authority either in addition to or to a greater or lesser extent than services, facilities, or functions are financed,

§ 160A-609. Service area of the Authority.

The service area of the Authority shall be as determined by the Board of Trustees consistent with its purpose, but shall not exceed the territorial jurisdiction of the authority and any area it may provide service to under G.S. 160A-610. (1989, c. 740, s. 1.)

§ 160A-610. General powers of the Authority.

The general powers of the Authority shall include any or all of the following:

(1)   To sue and be sued;

(2)   To have a seal;

(3)   To make rules and regulations, not inconsistent with this Chapter, for its organization and internal management;

(4)   To employ persons deemed necessary to carry out the functions and duties assigned to them by the Authority and to fix their compensation, within the limit of available funds;

(5)   With the approval of the unit of local government's chief administrative official, to use officers, employees, agents and facilities of the unit of local government for such purposes and upon such terms as may be mutually agreeable;

(6)   To retain and employ counsel, auditors, engineers and private consultants on an annual salary, contract basis, or otherwise for rendering professional or technical services and advice;

(7)   To acquire, lease as lessee with or without option to purchase, hold, own, and use any franchise, property, real or personal, tangible or intangible, or any interest therein and to sell, lease as lessor with or without option to purchase, transfer (or dispose thereof) whenever the same is no longer required for purposes of the Authority, or exchange same for other property or rights

(7a) To enhance mobility within the region and promote sound growth patterns through joint transit development projects as generally described by Federal Transit Administration (FTA) policy at 62 Fed. Reg. 12266 (1997) and implementing guidelines in FTA Circular 9300.1A, Appendix B, as the policy and guidance may be amended; and, with respect to the planning, construction, and operation of joint transit development projects, upon the governing board's adoption of policies and procedures to ensure fair and open competition, to select developers or development teams in substantially the same manner as permitted by G.S. 143-129(h); and to enter into development agreements with public, private, or nonprofit entities to undertake the planning, construction, and operation of joint transit development projects.

(8) To acquire by gift, purchase, lease as lessee with or without option to purchase or otherwise to construct, improve, maintain, repair, operate or administer any component parts of a public transportation system or to contract for the maintenance, operation or administration thereof or to lease as lessor the same for maintenance, operation, or administration by private parties, including but not necessarily limited to parking facilities;

(9) To make or enter into contracts, agreements, deeds, leases with or without option to purchase, conveyances or other instruments, including contracts and agreements with the United States, the State of North Carolina, and units of local government;

(9a) To purchase or finance real or personal property in the manner provided for cities and counties under G.S. 160A-20;

(10) To surrender to the State of North Carolina any property no longer required by the Authority;

(11) To develop and make data, plans, information, surveys and studies of public transportation facilities within the territorial jurisdiction of the Authority, to prepare and make recommendations in regard thereto;

(12) To enter in a reasonable manner lands, waters or premises for the purpose of making surveys, soundings, drillings, and examinations whereby such entry shall not be deemed a trespass except that the Authority shall be liable for any actual and consequential damages resulting from such entries;

public transportation companies with respect to the management and operation of public passenger transportation;

(15) To make, enter into, and perform contracts with any public utility, railroad or transportation company for the joint use of property or rights, for the establishment of through routes, joint fares or transfer of passengers;

(16) To make, enter into, and perform agreements with governmental entities for payments to the Authority for the transportation of persons for whom the governmental entities desire transportation;

(17) With the consent of the unit of local government which would otherwise have jurisdiction to exercise the powers enumerated in this subdivision: to issue certificates of public convenience and necessity; and to grant franchises and enter into franchise agreements and in all respects to regulate the operation of buses, taxicabs and other methods of public passenger transportation which originate and terminate within the territorial jurisdiction of the Authority as fully as the unit of local government is now or hereafter empowered to do within the territorial jurisdiction of the unit of local government;

(18) To operate public transportation systems and to enter into and perform contracts to operate public transportation services and facilities and to own or lease property, facilities and equipment necessary or convenient therefor, and to rent, lease or otherwise sell the right to do so to any person, public or private; further, to obtain grants, loans and assistance from the United States, the State of North Carolina, any public body, or any private source whatsoever, but may not operate or contract for the operation of public transportation systems outside the territorial jurisdiction of the Authority except as provided by subdivision (20) of this section;

(19) To enter into and perform contracts and agreements with other public transportation authorities, regional public transportation authorities or units of local government pursuant to the provisions of G.S. 160A-460 through 160A-464 (Part 1 of Article 20 of Chapter 160A of the General Statutes); further to enter into contracts and agreements with private transportation companies, but this subdivision does not authorize the operation of, or contracting for the operation of, service of a public transportation system outside the service area of the Authority;

government operating its own public transportation system or franchising the operation of a public transportation system by majority vote of its governing board, shall deny consent, but such service may not extend more than 10 miles outside of the territorial jurisdiction of the authority, except that vanpool and carpool service shall not be subject to that mileage limitation;

(21) Except as restricted by covenants in bonds, notes, or equipment trust certificates, to set in its sole discretion rates, fees and charges for use of its public transportation system;

(22) To do all things necessary or convenient to carry out its purpose and to exercise the powers granted to the Authority;

(23) To collect or contract for the collection of taxes which it is authorized by law to levy;

(24) To issue bonds or other obligations of the Authority as provided by law and apply the proceeds thereof to the financing of any public transportation system or any part thereof and to refund, whether or not in advance of maturity or the earliest redemption date, any such bonds or other obligations; and

(25) To contract for, or to provide and maintain, with respect to the facilities and property owned, leased with or without option to purchase, operated or under the control of the Authority, and within the territory thereof, a security force to protect persons and property, dispense unlawful or dangerous assemblages and assemblages which obstruct full and free passage, control pedestrian and vehicular traffic, and otherwise preserve and protect the public peace, health, and safety; for these purposes a member of such force shall be a peace officer and, as such, shall have authority equivalent to the authority of a police officer of the city or county in which said member of such force is discharging such duties.

(26) To contract for the purchase, lease, or other acquisition of any apparatus, supplies, materials, or equipment for public transit purposes with any person or entity that, within the previous 60 months, after having completed a public formal bid process substantially similar to that required by Article 8 of Chapter 143 of the General Statutes or through the competitive proposal method provided in G.S. 143-129(h), has contracted to furnish the apparatus,

with the other unit or agency. Any purchase made under this section shall be approved by the Board of Trustees as provided in G.S. 143-129(g). (1989, c. 740, s. 1; 1998-70, s. 2; 2000-67, s. 25.6; 2003-197, s. 2.)

§ 160A-611. Authority of Utilities Commission not affected.

(a) Except as otherwise provided in this Article, nothing in this Article shall be construed to limit or otherwise affect the power or authority of the North Carolina Utilities Commission or the right of appeal to the North Carolina Utilities Commission as provided by law.

(b) The North Carolina Utilities Commission shall not have jurisdiction over rates, fees, charges, routes, and schedules of an Authority for service within its territorial jurisdiction. (1989, c. 740, s. 1.)

§ 160A-612. Fiscal accountability.

An Authority is a public authority subject to the provisions of Chapter 159 of the General Statutes. (1989, c. 740, s. 1.)

§ 160A-613. Funds.

(a) The establishment and operation of an Authority are governmental functions and constitute a public purpose, and the State of North Carolina and any unit of local government may appropriate funds to support the establishment and operation of the Authority. The State of North Carolina and any unit of local government may also dedicate, sell, convey, donate or lease any of their interests in any property to the Authority. An authority may apply for grants from the State of North Carolina, or from the United States or any department, agency, or instrumentality thereof. The Department of Transportation may allocate to an authority any funds appropriated for public transportation, or any funds whose use is not restricted by law.

(b) Repealed by Session Laws 2010-95, s. 41, effective July 17, 2010.

authorized purpose of the Authority. Notwithstanding any provision of G.S. 159-19 or G.S. 159-22, the Board of Trustees may, by amendment to the resolution establishing a capital reserve fund, withdraw moneys accumulated in a fund for noncapital purposes if the capital outlay purpose for which the fund was created is no longer viable, as determined by a majority of the Board of Trustees. Except as otherwise provided in this subsection, the provisions of Part 2 of Article 3 of Chapter 159 of the General Statutes shall control the establishment of capital reserve funds by the Authority. (1989, c. 740, s. 1; 1991, c. 666, s. 1; 2001-424, s. 27.28; 2010-95, s. 41.)

§ 160A-613.1. Competition.

No equipment of the authority may be used for charter, tour, or sight-seeing service. (1989, c. 740, s. 1.)

§ 160A-614. Effect on existing franchises and operations.

Creation of the Authority shall not have an effect on any existing franchises granted by any unit of local government; such existing franchises shall continue in full force and effect until legally terminated; further, all ordinances and resolutions of the unit of local government regulating local public transportation systems, bus operations, and taxicabs shall continue in full force and effect now and in the future, unless superseded by regulations of the Authority; such superseding, if any, may occur only on the basis of prior mutual agreement between the Authority and the respective unit of local government. (1989, c. 740, s. 1.)

§ 160A-615. Termination.

The Board of Trustees may terminate the existence of the Authority at any time when it has no outstanding indebtedness. In the event of such termination, all property and assets of the Authority not otherwise encumbered shall automatically become the property of the State of North Carolina, and the State of North Carolina shall succeed to all rights, obligations, and liabilities of the Authority. (1989, c. 740, s. 1.)

any other law, public or private, the provisions of this Article shall be controlling. (1989, c. 740, s. 1.)

§ 160A-617. Bonds and notes authorized.

In addition to the powers granted by this Article, the Authority may issue bonds and notes pursuant to the provisions of the Local Government Bond Act and the Local Government Revenue Bond Act for the purpose of financing public transportation systems or any part thereof and to refund such bonds and notes, whether or not in advance of their maturity or earliest redemption date. Any bond order must be approved by resolution adopted by the special tax board of the Authority and in the case of a bond order under the Local Government Bond Act also by the board of county commissioners of each county organizing the authority. To pay any bond or note issued under the Local Government Bond Act, the Authority may not pledge the levy of any ad valorem tax, but only a tax or taxes it is authorized to levy. (1989, c. 740, s. 1; 1989 (Reg. Sess., 1990), c. 1024, s. 41; 1991, c. 666, s. 5.)

§ 160A-618. Equipment trust certificates.

In addition to the powers here and before granted, the Authority shall have continuing power to purchase equipment, and in connection therewith execute agreements, leases with or without option to purchase, or equipment trust certificates. All money required to be paid by the Authority under the provisions of such agreements, leases with or without option to purchase, and equipment trust certificates shall be payable solely from the fares, fees, rentals, charges, revenues, and earnings of the Authority, monies derived from the sale of any surplus property of the Authority and gifts, grants, and contributions from any source whatever. Payment for such equipment or rentals therefore, may be made in installments; the deferred installments may be evidenced by equipment trust certificates payable solely from the aforesaid revenues or receipts and title to such equipment may or may not vest in the Authority until the equipment trust certificates are paid. (1989, c. 740, s. 1.)

devise, exchange, purchase, lease with or without option to purchase, or any other lawful method, including but not limited to the power of eminent domain, the fee or any lesser interest in real or personal property for use by the Authority.

(b)   Exercise of the power of eminent domain by the Authority shall be in accordance with Chapter 40A of the General Statutes. (1989, c. 740, s. 1; 2011-284, s. 121.)

§ 160A-620. Tax exemption.

The property of the Authority, both real and personal, its acts, activities and income shall be exempt from any tax or tax obligation; in the event of any lease of Authority property, or other arrangement which amounts to a leasehold interest, to a private party, this exemption shall not apply to the value of such leasehold interest nor shall it apply to the income of the lessee. Otherwise, however, for the purpose of taxation, when property of the Authority is leased to private parties solely for the purpose of the Authority, the acts and activities of the lessee shall be considered as the acts and activities of the Authority and the exemption. The interest on bonds or obligations issued by the Authority shall be exempt from State taxes. (1989, c. 740, s. 1.)

§ 160A-621. Removal and relocation of utility structures.

(a)   The Authority shall have the power to require any public utility, railroad, or other public service corporation owning or operating any installations, structures, equipment, apparatus, appliances or facilities in, upon, under, over, across or along any ways on which the Authority has the right to own, construct, operate or maintain its public transportation system, to relocate such installation, structures, equipment, apparatus, appliances or facilities from their locations, or, in the sole discretion of the affected public utility, railroad, or other public service corporation, to remove such installations, structures, equipment, apparatus, appliances or facilities from their locations.

(b)   If the owner or operator thereof fails or refuses to relocate them, the Authority may proceed to do so.

new locations shall not be in, on or above, a public highway; the Authority may also acquire the necessary new locations by purchase or otherwise.

(b2) Any affected public utility, railroad or other public service corporation shall be compensated for any real estate interest taken in a manner consistent with G.S. 160A-619, subject to the right of the Authority to reduce the compensation due by the value of any property exchanged under this section.

(b3) The method and procedures of a particular adjustment to the facilities of a public utility, railroad or other public service corporation shall be covered by an agreement between the Authority and the affected party or parties.

(c) The Authority shall reimburse the public utility, railroad or other public service corporation, for the cost of relocations or removals which shall be the entire amount paid or incurred by the utility properly attributable thereto after deducting the cost of any increase in the service capacity of the new installations, structures, equipment, apparatus, appliances or facilities and any salvage value derived from the old installations, structures, equipment, apparatus or appliances. (1989, c. 740, s. 1.)

§ 160A-622. Reserved for future codification purposes.

§ 160A-623. Regional Transportation Authority registration tax.

In accordance with Article 51 of Chapter 105 of the General Statutes, an Authority organized under this Article may levy an annual license tax upon any motor vehicle with a tax situs within its territorial jurisdiction as defined by G.S. 160A-602. A tax levied under this section before the enactment of Article 51 of Chapter 105 of the General Statutes is considered a tax levied under Article 51 of Chapter 105 of the General Statutes. (1991, c. 666, s. 2; 1993, c. 382, s. 1; c. 485, s. 28; 1993 (Reg. Sess., 1994), c. 761, s. 34; 1997-417, s. 5.)

§ 160A-624. Recommendation of additional revenue sources.

The Authority may make recommendations to the General Assembly concerning additional revenue sources, including, but not limited to:

(3)   Local land transfer taxes;

(4)   Drivers license fees;

(5)   Sales taxes on automobile parts and accessories; and

(6)   Motor fuels taxes.

Any additional revenue sources for an Authority must be approved by the General Assembly. (1991, c. 666, s. 4.)

§ 160A-625. Reports to the General Assembly.

The Authority shall annually submit to the General Assembly, on or before February 1, its annual operating report, including a report of its administrative expenditures, and its audited financial report. In odd-numbered years, the report shall be submitted to the Senate and House Transportation Committees. In even-numbered years, the report shall be submitted to the Joint Legislative Transportation Oversight Committee. (1993, c. 382, s. 2.)

§ 160A-626. Limitations on rail transportation liability.

(a)   As used in this section:

(1)   "Claim" means a claim, action, suit, or request for damages, whether compensatory, punitive, or otherwise, made by any person or entity against:

a.   The Authority, a railroad, or an operating rights railroad; or

b.   An officer, director, trustee, employee, parent, subsidiary, or affiliated corporation as defined in G.S. 105-130.2, or agent of: the Authority, a railroad, or an operating rights railroad.

Railroad Company under a claim of right over or adjacent to facilities used by or on behalf of the Authority.

(3)   "Passenger rail services" means the transportation of rail passengers by or on behalf of the Authority and all services performed by a railroad pursuant to a contract with the Authority in connection with the transportation of rail passengers, including, but not limited to, the operation of trains; the use of right of way, trackage, public or private roadway and rail crossings, equipment, or station areas or appurtenant facilities; the design, construction, reconstruction, operation, or maintenance of rail related equipment, tracks, and any appurtenant facilities; or the provision of access rights over or adjacent to lines owned by the Authority or a railroad, or otherwise occupied by the Authority or a railroad, pursuant to charter grant, fee simple deed, lease, easement, license, trackage rights, or other form of ownership or authorized use.

(4)   "Railroad" means a railroad corporation or railroad company, including a State-Owned Railroad Company as defined in G.S. 124-11, that has entered into any contracts or operating agreements of any kind with the Authority concerning passenger rail services.

(b)   Contracts Allocating Financial Responsibility Authorized. - The Authority may contract with any railroad to allocate financial responsibility for passenger rail services claims, including, but not limited to, the execution of indemnity agreements, notwithstanding any other statutory, common law, public policy, or other prohibition against same, and regardless of the nature of the claim or the conduct giving rise to such claim.

(c)   Insurance Required. -

(1)   If the Authority enters into any contract authorized by subsection (b) of this section, the contract shall require the Authority to secure and maintain, upon and after the commencement of the operation of trains by or on behalf of the Authority, a liability insurance policy covering the liability of the parties to the contract, a State-Owned Railroad Company as defined in G.S. 124-11 that owns or claims an interest in any real property subject to the contract, and any operating rights railroad for all claims for property damage, personal injury, bodily injury, and death arising out of or related to passenger rail services. The policy shall name the parties to the contract, a State-Owned Railroad Company

($200,000,000) per single accident or incident, and may include a self insured retention in an amount of not more than five million dollars ($5,000,000).

(2) If the Authority does not enter into any contract authorized by subsection (b) of this section, upon and after the commencement of the operation of trains by or on behalf of the Authority, the Authority shall secure and maintain a liability insurance policy, with policy limits and a self-insured retention consistent with subdivision (1) of this subsection, for all claims for property damage, personal injury, bodily injury, and death arising out of or related to passenger rail services.

(d) Liability Limit. - The aggregate liability of the Authority, the parties to the contract or contracts authorized by subsection (b) of this section, a State-Owned Railroad Company as defined in G.S. 124-11, and any operating rights railroad for all claims arising from a single accident or incident related to passenger rail services for property damage, personal injury, bodily injury, and death is limited to two hundred million dollars ($200,000,000) per single accident or incident or to any proceeds available under any insurance policy secured pursuant to subsection (c) of this section, whichever is greater.

(e) Effect on Other Laws. - This section shall not affect the damages that may be recovered under the Federal Employers' Liability Act, 45 U.S.C. § 51, et seq., (1908); or under Article 1 of Chapter 97 of the General Statutes. (2002-78, s. 1; 2012-79, s. 1.14(g).)

§ 160A-627. Civil liability.

Except as provided in G.S. 160A-626, the Authority shall be deemed a city for purposes of civil liability pursuant to G.S. 160A-485. Governmental immunity of the Authority is waived to a minimum of twenty million dollars ($20,000,000) per single accident or incident. The Authority shall maintain a minimum of twenty million dollars ($20,000,000) per single accident or incident of liability insurance. Participation in a local government risk pool pursuant to Article 23 of Chapter 58 of the General Statutes shall be deemed to be the purchase of insurance for the purpose of this section. (2005-160, s. 1.)

Article 27.

Regional Transportation Authority.

§ 160A-630. Title.

This Article shall be known and may be cited as the "Regional Transportation Authority Act." (1997-393, s. 1.)

§ 160A-631. Definitions.

As used in this Article, unless the context otherwise requires:

(1)   "Authority" means a Regional Transportation Authority as defined by subdivision (6) of this section.

(2)   "Board of Trustees" means the governing board of the Authority, in which the general legislative powers of the Authority are vested.

(3)   "Population" means the number of persons residing in respective areas as defined and enumerated in the most recent decennial federal census.

(4)   "Public transportation" means transportation of passengers whether or not for hire by any means of conveyance, including, but not limited to, a street or elevated railway or guideway, subway, motor vehicle or motor bus, carpool or vanpool, either publicly or privately owned and operated, holding itself out to the general public for the transportation of persons within or working within the territorial jurisdiction of the Authority, excluding charter, tour, or sight-seeing service.

(5)   "Public transportation system" means, without limitation, a combination of real and personal property, structures, improvements, buildings, equipment, vehicle parking, or other facilities, railroads and railroad rights-of-way whether held in fee simple by quitclaim or easement, and rights-of-way, or any combination thereof, used or useful for the purposes of public transportation.

(6) "Regional Transportation Authority," means a body corporate and politic organized in accordance with the provisions of this Article for the purposes, with the powers and subject to the restrictions hereinafter set forth.

(7) "Unit of local government" means any county, city, town or municipality of this State, and any other political subdivision, public corporation, Authority, or district in this State, which is or may be authorized by law to acquire, establish, construct, enlarge, improve, maintain, own, and operate public transportation systems.

(8) "Unit of local government's chief administrative official" means the county manager, city manager, town manager, or other person, by whatever title he shall be known, in whom the responsibility for the unit of local government's administrative duties is vested. (1997-393, s. 1.)

§ 160A-632. Definition of territorial jurisdiction of Authority.

An authority may be created for the area of any Metropolitan Planning Organization of the State that, at the time of creation of the authority, meets the following criteria, such area being the initial territorial jurisdiction of the Authority:

(1) The area consists of all or part of five counties, all five counties of which form a contiguous territory;

(2) At least two of those counties are contiguous to each other and each have a population of 250,000 or over; and

(3) The other three counties each have a population of 100,000 or over. (1997-393, s. 1.)

§ 160A-633. Creation of Authority.

(a) The city councils of the four largest cities within an area for which an authority may be created as defined in G.S. 160A-632 may by resolution signify their determination to organize an authority under the provisions of this Article. Each of such resolutions shall be adopted after a public hearing thereon, notice

substance of the proposed resolution, shall set forth the proposed articles of incorporation of the Authority and shall state the time and place of the public hearing to be held thereof. No city shall be required to make any other publication of such resolution under the provisions of any other law.

(b)   Each such resolution shall include articles of incorporation which shall set forth:

(1)   The name of the authority;

(2)   A statement that such authority is organized under this Article; and

(3)   The names of the four organizing cities.

(c)   A certified copy of each of such resolutions signifying the determination to organize an authority under the provisions of this Article shall be filed with the Secretary of State, together with proof of publication of the notice of hearing on each of such resolutions. If the Secretary of State finds that the resolutions, including the articles of incorporation, conform to the provisions of this Article and that the notices of hearing were properly published, he shall file such resolutions and proofs of publication in his office and shall issue a certificate of incorporation under the seal of the State and shall record the same in an appropriate book of record in his office. The issuance of such certificate of incorporation by the Secretary of State shall constitute the Authority, a public body and body politic and corporate of the State of North Carolina. Said certificate of incorporation shall be conclusive evidence of the fact that such authority has been duly created and established under the provisions of this Article.

(d)   When the Authority has been duly organized and its officers elected as herein provided, the secretary of the Authority shall certify to the Secretary of State the names and addresses of such officers as well as the address of the principal office of the Authority.

(e)   The Authority may become a Designated Recipient pursuant to the Urban Mass Transportation Act of 1964, as amended. (1997-393, s. 1.)

determined by the Board of Trustees consistent with its purpose, but shall initially consist of those areas included within the Metropolitan Planning Organization boundaries. With the consent by resolution of the affected board of county commissioners, the jurisdiction and area may be expanded to include contiguous areas, but the total jurisdiction and service area shall not exceed part or all of 12 counties. The jurisdiction and area include the entire area of the county if the Board of Trustees has been expanded to include the chair or other member of the board of commissioners of that county pursuant to G.S. 160A-635(a)(4).

(b) Except as provided by this Article, the jurisdiction of the Authority may include all local public passenger transportation operating within the territorial jurisdiction of the Authority, but the Authority may not take over the operation of any existing public transportation without the consent of the owner.

(c) The Authority shall not have jurisdiction over public transportation subject to the jurisdiction of and regulated by the United States Department of Transportation, nor shall it have jurisdiction over intrastate public transportation classified as common carriers of passengers by the North Carolina Utilities Commission. (1997-393, s. 1; 1999-445, s. 1.)

§ 160A-635. Membership; officers; compensation.

(a) The governing body of an authority is the Board of Trustees. The Board of Trustees shall consist of:

(1) The mayor of the four cities within the service area that have the largest population, or a member of the city council designated by the city council to serve in the absence of the mayor.

(2) Two members of the Board of Transportation appointed by the Secretary of Transportation, to serve as ex officio nonvoting members.

(3) The chair of each Metropolitan Planning Organization or a member of the Metropolitan Planning Organization designated by the Metropolitan Planning Organization in the territorial jurisdiction.

by resolution has expanded the Board of Trustees to include the chair of the board of commissioners of that county and the board of commissioners of that county has consented by resolution.

(5) The chair of the principal airport authority or airport commission of each of the two most populous counties within the territorial jurisdiction, as determined by the most recent decennial federal census. The chair of the airport authority or airport commission may appoint a designee. The designee is not required to be a member of the airport authority or airport commission.

(b) The members appointed by the Secretary of Transportation shall serve at the pleasure of the Secretary.

(c) Service on the Board of Trustees may be in addition to any other office which a person is entitled to hold. Each voting member of the Board of Trustees may hold elective public office as defined by G.S. 128-1.1(d).

(d) Members of the Board of Trustees shall reside within the territorial jurisdiction of the Authority as defined by G.S. 160A-634.

(e) The Board of Trustees shall annually elect from its membership a Chairperson, and a Vice-Chairperson, and shall annually elect a Secretary, and a Treasurer.

(f) Members of the Board of Trustees shall receive the sum of fifty dollars ($50.00) as compensation for attendance at each duly conducted meeting of the Authority. (1997-393, s. 1; 1999-445, s. 2; 2004-203, s. 56; 2005-322, s. 1.)

§ 160A-636. Voting.

A majority of the members of the Board of Trustees shall constitute a quorum for the transaction of business. Except as provided by G.S. 160A-635(a)(2), each member shall have one vote. (1997-393, s. 1.)

§ 160A-637. Advisory committees.

§ 160A-638. Purpose of the Authority.

The purpose of the authority is to enhance the quality of life in its territorial jurisdiction by promoting the development of sound transportation systems which provide transportation choices, enhance mobility, accessibility, and safety, encourage economic development and sound growth patterns, and protect the man-made and natural environments of the region. (1997-393, s. 1.)

§ 160A-639. General powers of the Authority.

The general powers of the Authority shall include any or all of the following:

(1)   To sue and be sued;

(2)   To have a seal;

(3)   To make rules and regulations, not inconsistent with this Chapter, for its organization and internal management;

(4)   To employ persons deemed necessary to carry out the functions and duties assigned to them by the Authority and to fix their compensation, within the limit of available funds;

(5)   With the approval of the unit of local government's chief administrative official, to use officers, employees, agents, and facilities of the unit of local government for such purposes and upon such terms as may be mutually agreeable;

(6)   To retain and employ counsel, auditors, engineers, and private consultants on an annual salary, contract basis, or otherwise for rendering professional or technical services and advice;

(7)   To acquire, lease as lessee with or without option to purchase, hold, own, and use any franchise, property, real or personal, tangible or intangible, or any interest therein, and to sell, lease as lessor with or without option to

limited to parking facilities;

(8) To acquire by gift, purchase, lease as lessee with or without option to purchase or otherwise to construct, improve, maintain, repair, operate, or administer any component parts of a public transportation system or to contract for the maintenance, operation or administration thereof, or to lease as lessor the same for maintenance, operation, or administration by private parties, including, but not necessarily limited to, parking facilities;

(9) To make or enter into contracts, agreements, deeds, leases with or without option to purchase, conveyances or other instruments, including contracts and agreements with the United States, the State of North Carolina, and units of local government;

(9a) To purchase or finance real or personal property in the manner provided for cities and counties under G.S. 160A-20;

(10) To surrender to the State of North Carolina any property no longer required by the Authority;

(11) To develop and make data, plans, information, surveys and studies of public transportation facilities within the territorial jurisdiction of the Authority and to prepare and make recommendations in regard thereto;

(12) To enter in a reasonable manner lands, waters, or premises for the purpose of making surveys, soundings, drillings, and examinations whereby such entry shall not be deemed a trespass except that the Authority shall be liable for any actual and consequential damages resulting from such entries;

(13) To develop and carry out demonstration projects;

(14) To make, enter into, and perform contracts with private parties, and public transportation companies with respect to the management and operation of public passenger transportation;

(15) To make, enter into, and perform contracts with any public utility, railroad or transportation company for the joint use of property or rights, for the establishment of through routes, joint fares, or transfer of passengers;

(17)   With the consent of the unit of local government which would otherwise have jurisdiction to exercise the powers enumerated in this subdivision: to issue certificates of public convenience and necessity; and to grant franchises and enter into franchise agreements, and in all respects to regulate the operation of buses, taxicabs, and other methods of public passenger transportation which originate and terminate within the territorial jurisdiction of the Authority as fully as the unit of local government is now or hereafter empowered to do within the territorial jurisdiction of the unit of local government;

(18)   To operate public transportation systems and to enter into and perform contracts to operate public transportation services and facilities, and to own or lease property, facilities and equipment necessary or convenient therefor, and to rent, lease or otherwise sell the right to do so to any person, public or private; further, to obtain grants, loans, and assistance from the United States, the State of North Carolina, any public body, or any private source whatsoever, but may not operate or contract for the operation of public transportation systems outside the territorial jurisdiction of the Authority except as provided by subdivision (20) of this section;

(19)   To enter into and perform contracts and agreements with other public transportation authorities, regional public transportation authorities, or units of local government pursuant to the provisions of G.S. 160A-460 through G.S. 160A-464 (Part 1 of Article 20 of Chapter 160A of the General Statutes); further to enter into contracts and agreements with private transportation companies, but this subdivision does not authorize the operation of, or contracting for the operation of, service of a public transportation system outside the service area of the Authority;

(20)   To operate public transportation systems extending service into any political subdivision of the State of North Carolina unless a particular unit of local government operating its own public transportation system or franchising the operation of a public transportation system by majority vote of its governing board, shall deny consent, but such service may not extend more than 10 miles outside of the territorial jurisdiction of the authority, except that vanpool and carpool service shall not be subject to that mileage limitation;

(22) To do all things necessary or convenient to carry out its purpose and to exercise the powers granted to the Authority;

(23) To facilitate the coordination of transportation plans in the service area and the activities of the member Metropolitan Planning Organizations;

(24) To maintain databases for the projection of future travel demands in the region;

(25) To provide and operate regional ridesharing and vanpool operations;

(26) To provide and operate regional transportation services for the elderly and handicapped;

(27) To provide other transportation related services, including air quality monitoring and analysis, as determined by the Board of Trustees;

(28) To issue bonds or other obligations of the Authority as provided by law and apply the proceeds thereof to the financing of any public transportation system or any part thereof and to refund, whether or not in advance of maturity or the earliest redemption date, any such bonds or other obligations; and

(29) To contract for, or to provide and maintain, with respect to the facilities and property owned, leased with or without option to purchase, operated or under the control of the Authority, and within the territory thereof, a security force to protect persons and property, dispense unlawful or dangerous assemblages and assemblages which obstruct full and free passage, control pedestrian and vehicular traffic, and otherwise preserve and protect the public peace, health, and safety; for these purposes a member of such force shall be a peace officer and, as such, shall have authority equivalent to the authority of a police officer of the city or county in which said member of such force is discharging such duties. (1997-393, s. 1; 1998-70, s. 3.)

§ 160A-640. Authority of Utilities Commission not affected.

Commission as provided by law.

(b) The North Carolina Utilities Commission shall not have jurisdiction over rates, fees, charges, routes, and schedules of an Authority for service within its territorial jurisdiction. (1997-393, s. 1.)

§ 160A-641. Fiscal accountability.

An Authority is a public authority subject to the provisions of Chapter 159 of the General Statutes. (1997-393, s. 1.)

§ 160A-642. Funds.

The establishment and operation of an Authority are governmental functions and constitute a public purpose, and the State of North Carolina and any unit of local government may appropriate funds to support the establishment and operation of the Authority. The State of North Carolina and any unit of local government may also dedicate, sell, convey, donate, or lease any of their interests in any property to the Authority. An Authority may apply for grants from the State of North Carolina, or from the United States or any department, agency, or instrumentality thereof. The Department of Transportation may allocate to an Authority any funds appropriated for transportation, or any funds whose use is not restricted by law. (1997-393, s. 1.)

§ 160A-643. Competition.

No equipment of the Authority may be used for charter, tour, or sight-seeing service. (1997-393, s. 1.)

§ 160A-644. Effect on existing franchises and operations.

Creation of the Authority shall not have an effect on any existing franchises granted by any unit of local government; such existing franchises shall continue in full force and effect until legally terminated; further, all ordinances and

superseding, if any, may occur only on the basis of prior mutual agreement between the Authority and the respective unit of local government. (1997-393, s. 1.)

§ 160A-645. Termination.

The Board of Trustees may terminate the existence of the Authority at any time when it has no outstanding indebtedness. In the event of such termination, all property and assets of the Authority not otherwise encumbered shall automatically become the property of the State of North Carolina, and the State of North Carolina shall succeed to all rights, obligations, and liabilities of the Authority. (1997-393, s. 1.)

§ 160A-646. Controlling provisions.

Insofar as the provisions of this Article are not consistent with the provisions of any other law, public or private, the provisions of this Article shall be controlling. (1997-393, s. 1.)

§ 160A-647. Bonds and notes authorized.

In addition to the powers granted by this Article, the Authority may issue bonds and notes pursuant to the provisions of The State and Local Government Revenue Bond Act, Article 5 of Chapter 159 of the General Statutes, for the purpose of financing public transportation systems or any part thereof and to refund such bonds and notes, whether or not in advance of their maturity or earliest redemption date. (1997-393, s. 1.)

§ 160A-648. Equipment trust certificates.

In addition to the powers here and before granted, the Authority shall have continuing power to purchase equipment, and in connection therewith execute agreements, leases with or without option to purchase, or equipment trust certificates. All money required to be paid by the Authority under the provisions

surplus property of the Authority and gifts, grants, and contributions from any source whatever. Payment for such equipment or rentals therefore, may be made in installments; the deferred installments may be evidenced by equipment trust certificates payable solely from the aforesaid revenues or receipts, and title to such equipment may or may not vest in the Authority until the equipment trust certificates are paid. (1997-393, s. 1.)

§ 160A-649. Power of eminent domain.

(a) The Authority shall have continuing power to acquire, by gift, grant, devise, exchange, purchase, lease with or without option to purchase, or any other lawful method, including, but not limited to, the power of eminent domain, the fee or any lesser interest in real or personal property for use by the Authority.

(b) Exercise of the power of eminent domain by the Authority shall be in accordance with Chapter 40A of the General Statutes. (1997-393, s. 1; 2011-284, s. 122.)

§ 160A-650. Tax exemption.

The property of the Authority, both real and personal, its acts, activities, and income shall be exempt from any tax or tax obligation; in the event of any lease of Authority property, or other arrangement which amounts to a leasehold interest, to a private party, this exemption shall not apply to the value of such leasehold interest nor shall it apply to the income of the lessee. Otherwise, however, for the purpose of taxation, when property of the Authority is leased to private parties solely for the purpose of the Authority, the acts and activities of the lessee shall be considered as the acts and activities of the Authority and the exemption. The interest on bonds or obligations issued by the Authority shall be exempt from State taxes. (1997-393, s. 1.)

§ 160A-651. Removal and relocation of utility structures.

across or along any ways on which the Authority has the right to own, construct, operate, or maintain its public transportation system, to relocate such installation, structures, equipment, apparatus, appliances, or facilities from their locations, or, in the sole discretion of the affected public utility, railroad, or other public service corporation, to remove such installations, structures, equipment, apparatus, appliances, or facilities from their locations.

(b)   If the owner or operator thereof fails or refuses to relocate them, the Authority may proceed to do so.

(c)   The Authority shall provide any necessary new locations and necessary real estate interests for such relocation, and for that purpose the power of eminent domain as provided in G.S. 160A-649 may be exercised provided the new locations shall not be in, on or above, a public highway; the Authority may also acquire the necessary new locations by purchase or otherwise.

(d)   Any affected public utility, railroad, or other public service corporation shall be compensated for any real estate interest taken in a manner consistent with G.S. 160A-649, subject to the right of the Authority to reduce the compensation due by the value of any property exchanged under this section.

(e)   The method and procedures of a particular adjustment to the facilities of a public utility, railroad, or other public service corporation shall be covered by an agreement between the Authority and the affected party or parties.

(f)   The Authority shall reimburse the public utility, railroad, or other public service corporation, for the cost of relocations or removals which shall be the entire amount paid or incurred by the utility properly attributable thereto after deducting the cost of any increase in the service capacity of the new installations, structures, equipment, apparatus, appliances, or facilities and any salvage value derived from the old installations, structures, equipment, apparatus or appliances. (1997-393, s. 1.)

§§ 160A-652 through 160A-659. Reserved for future codification purposes.

§ 160A-660. Title.

This Article is the "Regional Natural Gas District Act" and may be cited by that name. (1997-426, s. 2.)

§ 160A-661. Purpose; definitions.

(a) The purpose of a district created under this Article is to enhance the quality of life in its territorial jurisdiction by promoting the development of natural gas systems to enhance the economic development of the area.

(b) The following definitions apply in this Article:

(1) Board of Trustees. - The governing board of the district in which the general legislative powers of the district are vested.

(2) District. - A regional natural gas district.

(3) Natural gas system. - A gas production, storage, transmission and distribution system, or any part or parts thereof.

(4) Regional natural gas district. - A public body and body politic and corporate of the State of North Carolina organized in accordance with the provisions of this Article exercising public and essential governmental functions to provide for the preservation and promotion of the public welfare for the purposes, with the powers, and subject to the restrictions set forth in this Article.

(5) Unit of local government. - Any county, city, town, or municipality of this State, and any other political subdivision, public corporation, or district in this State, that is or may be authorized by law to acquire, establish, construct, enlarge, improve, maintain, own, or operate natural gas systems.

(6) Unit of local government's chief administrative official. - The county manager, city manager, town manager, or other person, by whatever title known, in whom the responsibility for the unit of local government's administrative duties is vested. (1997-426, s. 2.)

unserved with natural gas and in which a specific natural gas project has not been approved by the Utilities Commission at the time of creation of the district. A letter from the Utilities Commission to this effect shall conclusively establish that the area is totally unserved and that a project has not been approved. This area is the territorial jurisdiction and the service area of the district.

(b) The creation of a district does not confer on the district the exclusive right to provide natural gas service in that territorial jurisdiction. (1997-426, s. 2.)

§ 160A-663. Creation of district.

(a) The boards of commissioners of any one or more counties within an area for which a district may be created as provided by G.S. 160A-662, and the governing body of any city geographically located within one or more of these counties and that chooses to join in the organization of a district, may by resolution signify their determination to organize a district under the provisions of this Article. Each of these resolutions shall be adopted after a public hearing thereon, notice of which hearing shall be given by publication at least once, not less than 10 days prior to the date fixed for the hearing, in a newspaper having a general circulation in the county. The notice shall contain a brief statement of the substance of the proposed resolution, shall set forth the proposed articles of incorporation of the district, and shall state the time and place of the public hearing. A copy of the notice shall be mailed not later than the first day of newspaper publication to the business office of any public utility that holds a franchise from the North Carolina Utilities Commission to serve any part of the proposed district with natural gas service. No county or city shall be required to make any other publication of the resolution under the provisions of any other law.

(b) Each resolution shall include articles of incorporation which shall set forth all of the following:

(1) The name of the district.

(2) The composition of the board of trustees, terms of office, and the manner of making appointments and filling vacancies.

(5)   Provision for the distribution of assets in the event the district is terminated.

(c)   A certified copy of each of the resolutions signifying the determination to organize a district under the provisions of this Article shall be filed with the Secretary of State, together with proof of publication and mailing of the notice of hearing on each of the resolutions. If the Secretary of State finds that the resolutions, including the articles of incorporation, conform to the provisions of this Article and that the notices of hearing were properly published and mailed, the Secretary of State shall file the resolutions and proofs of publication and mailing, shall issue a certificate of incorporation under the seal of the State, and shall record the certificate in an appropriate book of record. The issuance of this certificate of incorporation by the Secretary of State shall constitute the district a public body and body politic and corporate of the State of North Carolina. The certificate of incorporation shall be conclusive evidence of the fact that the district has been duly created and established under this Article.

(d)   When the district has been duly organized and its officers elected, the secretary of the district shall certify to the Secretary of State the names and addresses of the officers, the name and address of the registered agent, and the address of the principal office of the district. The district shall be subject to the provisions of Article 5 of Chapter 55A of the General Statutes. (1997-426, s. 2.)

§ 160A-664. Membership; officers; compensation.

(a)   The governing body of a district is the Board of Trustees. The Board of Trustees shall consist of members as provided in the articles of incorporation.

(b)   Service on the Board of Trustees may be in addition to any other office which a person is entitled to hold. Each voting member of the Board of Trustees may hold elective public office as defined by G.S. 128-1.1(d).

(c)   Members of the Board of Trustees shall reside within the territorial jurisdiction of the district as defined by G.S. 160A-662.

(e) Members of the Board of Trustees shall receive a sum not to exceed fifty dollars ($50.00) as compensation for attendance at each duly conducted meeting of the district. (1997-426, s. 2.)

§ 160A-665. Quorum.

A majority of the members of the Board of Trustees shall constitute a quorum for the transaction of business. (1997-426, s. 2.)

§ 160A-666. Advisory committees.

The Board of Trustees may provide for the selection of any advisory committees that it finds appropriate, which may or may not include members of the Board of Trustees. (1997-426, s. 2.)

§ 160A-667. General powers of the district.

The general powers of the district include all of the following:

(1) To sue and be sued.

(2) To have a seal.

(3) To make rules not inconsistent with this Article, for its organization and internal management.

(4) To employ persons deemed necessary to carry out the functions and duties assigned to them by the district and to fix their compensation, within the limit of available funds.

(5) With the approval of the unit of local government's chief administrative official, to use officers, employees, agents, and facilities of the unit of local government for such purposes and upon such terms as may be mutually agreeable.

(7) To acquire, lease as lessee with or without option to purchase, hold, own, and use any franchise, property, real or personal, tangible or intangible, or any interest therein and to sell, lease as lessor with or without option to purchase, transfer (or dispose thereof) whenever the property is no longer required for purposes of the district, or exchange it for other property or rights which are useful for the district's purposes. Except as provided in any covenant or debt instrument designed to protect the creditor, if any loans or grants by the Department of Commerce have not been repaid, all or a substantial part of an operating natural gas district may not be disposed of without the approval of the Department of Commerce. If the sale is approved by the Department of Commerce, the district shall repay the State the lesser of the amount of any capital grant made by the State or one-half of the amount of the proceeds.

(8) To acquire by gift, purchase, lease as lessee with or without option to purchase or otherwise to construct, improve, maintain, repair, operate, or administer any component parts of a natural gas system. The district also may contract for the maintenance, operation, or administration thereof or to lease as lessor the same for maintenance, operation, or administration by private parties.

(9) To make or enter into contracts, agreements, deeds, leases with or without option to purchase, conveyances, or other instruments, including contracts and agreements with the United States, the State of North Carolina, and units of local government.

(10) To develop and make data, plans, information, surveys, and studies of natural gas systems within the territorial jurisdiction of the district and to prepare and make recommendations in regard thereto.

(11) To enter in a reasonable manner lands, waters, or premises for the purpose of making surveys, soundings, drillings, and examinations. This entry shall not be deemed a trespass except that the district shall be liable for any actual and consequential damages resulting from the entry.

(12) To develop and carry out demonstration projects.

(14) To make, enter into, and perform contracts with any public utility, railroad, or transportation company for the joint use of property or rights.

(15) To own, lease, and operate natural gas systems. These systems may also include the purchase or lease, or both, of natural gas fields and natural gas reserves within the State, and the purchase of natural gas supplies within or without the State. A district may operate that part of a gas system involving the purchase or lease, or both, of natural gas fields, natural gas reserves, and natural gas supplies, in an operating agreement, partnership or joint venture arrangement with natural gas utilities and private enterprise. The district may acquire, purchase, construct, receive, own, operate, maintain, enlarge, and improve natural gas systems and transport and sell at wholesale all or any part of its gas supply.

(16) To purchase or finance real or personal property under G.S. 160A-20.

(17) To obtain grants, loans, and assistance from the United States, the State of North Carolina, any public body, or any private source.

(18) To enter into and perform contracts and agreements with other natural gas districts, regional natural gas districts, or units of local government pursuant to the provisions of Part 1 of Article 20 of Chapter 160A of the General Statutes and to enter into contracts and agreements with private natural gas companies, but this subdivision does not authorize the operation of, or contracting for the operation of, service of a natural gas system outside the service area of the district. A district may provide service or contract for the providing of service to a city geographically located within a district, notwithstanding that the city did not join the district pursuant to G.S. 160A-663(a) or G.S. 160A-672.

(19) Except as restricted by covenants in bonds, notes, security interests, or trust certificates, to set in its sole discretion rates, fees, and charges for use of its natural gas system in accordance with G.S. 160A-676.

(20) To do all related things necessary to carry out its purpose and to exercise the powers granted to the district.

§ 160A-668. Fiscal accountability.

A district is a public authority subject to the provisions of Chapter 159 of the General Statutes. (1997-426, s. 2.)

§ 160A-669. Funds.

The establishment and operation of a district is a public purpose, and the State of North Carolina and any unit of local government may appropriate funds to support the establishment and operation of the district. The State of North Carolina and any unit of local government may also dedicate, sell, convey, donate, or lease any of their interests in any property to the district. A district may apply for grants from the State of North Carolina, or from the United States or any department, agency, or instrumentality thereof. The Department of Commerce may allocate to a district any funds appropriated for natural gas. (1997-426, s. 2.)

§ 160A-670. Effect on existing franchises and operations.

Creation of the district does not affect any existing franchises granted by any unit of local government. Those existing franchises shall continue in full force and effect until legally terminated, and all ordinances and resolutions of the unit of local government regulating local natural gas systems shall continue in full force and effect unless superseded by rules of the district. This superseding, if any, may occur only on the basis of prior mutual agreement between the district and the respective unit of local government. (1997-426, s. 2.)

§ 160A-671. Termination of district.

The Board of Trustees, after providing for the continued availability of natural gas service to its customers, if any, may terminate the existence of the district at any time when it has no outstanding indebtedness. The Board of Trustees shall file notification of the termination with the Secretary of State. (1997-426, s. 2.)

Article, a county as defined in G.S. 160A-662(a) or a city within that county, or a city that did not join in the organization of a district but is geographically located within the district may, with the consent of the district as evidenced by a resolution adopted by a majority of the members of the Board of Trustees of the district, join the district.

(b) A county or city desiring to join an existing district shall signify its desire by resolution adopted after a public hearing thereon, notice of which hearing shall be given in the manner and at the time provided in G.S. 160A-663. Such notice shall contain a brief statement of the substance of said resolution and shall state the time and place of the public hearing.

(c) A certified copy of each resolution signifying the desire of a county or city to join an existing district, together with proof of publication of the notice of hearing on the resolution, and a certified copy of the resolution of the Board of Trustees of the district consenting to the joining shall be filed with the Secretary of State. If the Secretary of State finds that the resolutions conform to the provisions of this Article and that the notices of hearing were properly published, the Secretary of State shall file such resolutions and proofs of publication in the office of the Secretary of State, shall issue a certificate of joinder, and shall record the certificate in the appropriate book of record. The issuance of the certificate shall be conclusive evidence of the joinder of the county or city to the district. (1997-426, s. 2.)

§ 160A-673. Bonds and notes authorized.

The district may issue revenue bonds and revenue bond anticipation notes pursuant to the provisions of the State and Local Government Revenue Bond Act, Article 5 of Chapter 159 of the General Statutes, and Article 9 of Chapter 159 for the purposes provided in this Article. If and to the extent any provisions of Articles 5 and 9 of Chapter 159 are inconsistent with the provisions of this Article, the provisions of this Article shall be controlling. A district may proceed with the issuance of bonds and notes under Articles 5 and 9 of Chapter 159 notwithstanding that, to the extent of any inconsistency only, the district complies with the provisions of this Article and not the provisions of Articles 5 and 9 of Chapter 159. (1997-426, s. 2.)

exchange, purchase, lease with or without option to purchase, or any other lawful method including, but not limited to, the power of eminent domain, the fee or any lesser interest in real or personal property for use by the district.

(b)   Exercise of the power of eminent domain by the district shall be as a private condemnor in accordance with Chapter 40A of the General Statutes. Notwithstanding Chapter 40A of the General Statutes, before final judgment may be entered in any action of condemnation initiated by the district, the district shall furnish proof that the board of commissioners of the county where the land is located has consented by resolution or ordinance to the taking. (1997-426, s. 2; 2011-284, s. 123.)

§ 160A-675. Tax exemption.

A district, and its property, bonds and notes, and income, are exempt from property taxes and income taxes to the same extent as if it were a city. A district is subject to gross receipts tax under G.S. 105-116. (1997-426, s. 2.)

§ 160A-676. Authority to fix and enforce rates.

(a)   A district may establish and revise from time to time schedules of rents, rates, fees, charges, and penalties made applicable throughout the district for the gas services. Schedules of rents, rates, fees, charges, or penalties may vary according to classes of service. Before it establishes or revises a schedule of rents, rates, fees, charges, or penalties, the district Board of Trustees shall hold a public hearing on the matter. A notice of the hearing shall be given at least once in a newspaper having general circulation in the area, not less than seven days before the public hearing.

(b)   A district may collect delinquent accounts by any remedy provided by law for collecting and enforcing private debts. A district may also discontinue service to any customer whose account remains delinquent for more than 30 days. When service is discontinued for delinquency, it shall be unlawful for any person other than a duly authorized agent or employee of the district to do any act that results in a resumption of services. If a delinquent customer is not the owner of the premises to which the services are delivered, the payment of the

services are measured by the same meter.

(c) Rents, rates, fees, charges, and penalties for services shall be legal obligations of the person contracting for them and shall in no case be a lien upon the property or premises served.

(d) Rents, rates, fees, charges, and penalties for services shall be legal obligations of the owner of the premises served when the property or premises are leased or rented to more than one tenant and services rendered to more than one tenant are measured by the same meter. (1997-426, s. 2.)

Chapter 160B.

Consolidated City-County Act.

Article 1.

Title and Definition.

§ 160B-1. Title; effective date.

This Chapter shall be cited as the "Consolidated City-County Act of 1973" and is enacted pursuant to Article V, Sec. 2(4) of the North Carolina Constitution, effective July 1, 1973. (1973, c. 537, s. 1.)

§ 160B-2. Definitions.

In this Chapter:

(1) "Consolidated city-county" means any county where the largest municipality in the county has been abolished and its powers, duties, rights, privileges and immunities consolidated with those of the county. Other municipalities in the county, if any, may or may not have been abolished and their powers, duties, rights, privileges and immunities consolidated with those of the county.

Article 1A.

Consolidated City-County Powers and Governance.

§ 160B-2.1. Powers of consolidated city-county.

(a) A consolidated city-county shall have and may exercise or may hereafter be authorized or required to exercise the powers, duties, functions, rights, privileges, and immunities granted to:

(1) A county under the Constitution and the general laws of the State of North Carolina, throughout its jurisdiction; and

(2) A city under the Constitution and the general laws of the State of North Carolina, within an urban service district.

(b) Outside the boundaries of an urban service district, the consolidated city-county shall have and may exercise or may hereafter be authorized or required to exercise the same powers, duties, functions, rights, privileges, and immunities granted to a city under the Constitution and the general laws of the State of North Carolina that can be exercised or may hereafter be authorized or required to exercise outside of city boundaries. (1995, c. 461, s. 1.)

§ 160B-2.2. Dissolution of consolidated city-county; establishment of study commission; purposes and powers of study commission.

(a) The governing board of a consolidated city-county may by resolution establish a governmental study commission to study all matters pertaining to the dissolution of the consolidated city-county and reestablishment of separate city and county government. The study commission may:

(1) Prepare a report of its findings and conclusions.

(2) Prepare drafts of any agreements or legislation necessary to effect the dissolution of a consolidated city-county.

(1) Adopt rules and regulations for the conduct of its business.

(2) Employ personnel.

(3) Contract with consultants.

(4) Hold hearings in the furtherance of its business.

(5) Take any other action necessary or expedient to the furtherance of its business. (1995, c. 461, s. 1.)

§ 160B-2.3. Ethics.

(a) The governing board shall adopt a resolution or policy containing a code of ethics, as required by G.S. 160A-86.

(b) All members of the governing board, whether elected or appointed, shall receive the ethics education required by G.S. 160A-87. (2009-403, s. 5.)

§ 160B-2.4. Reserved for future codification purposes.

§ 160B-2.5. Reserved for future codification purposes.

§ 160B-2.6. Reserved for future codification purposes.

Article 2.

Defining Urban Service Districts.

§ 160B-3. Authority; purpose; administration.

(a) The governing board may define any number of urban service districts in order to finance, provide or maintain for the districts services, facilities and

(b) The powers, duties, functions, rights, privileges, and immunities of an urban service district shall be exercised or administered by the governing board of the consolidated city-county. Any revenues, distributions, or other funds due an urban service district shall be paid to the governing board of the consolidated city-county. (1973, c. 537, s. 1; 1995 (Reg. Sess., 1996), c. 646, ss. 22(a), 22(b).)

§ 160B-4. Definition of urban service districts to replace municipalities abolished at the time of consolidation.

(a) The governing board, by resolution, may define an urban service district within the boundaries of the largest municipality that existed in the county before consolidation and within the boundaries of any other municipality abolished at the time of the establishment of the consolidated city-county. Notwithstanding the provisions of G.S. 160B-7, the resolution may also define an urban service district to include areas proposed for inclusion in an urban service district and identified in a plan for consolidation prepared by a consolidation study commission pursuant to Article 20 of Chapter 153A of the General Statutes or a plan approved by the General Assembly. Any urban service district so defined shall comprise the total area of the abolished municipality as it existed immediately before the effective date of consolidation. As determined by the governing board, the resolution shall take effect as to the areas included therein either upon its adoption or at the beginning of a fiscal year commencing after its passage.

(b) Prior to the effective date of consolidation, an interim governing board of a consolidated city-county by resolution may define an urban service district. The resolution defining the urban service district shall take effect upon the effective date of the consolidation.

(c) Recodified as § 160B-3(b) by Session Laws 1995 (Reg. Sess., 1996), c. 646, s. 22(a). (1973, c. 537, s. 1; 1995, c. 461, s. 2; 1995 (Reg. Sess., 1996), c. 646, s. 22(a).)

The governing board, by resolution, may define an urban service district within the boundaries of any municipality within the consolidated city-county the citizens of which, subsequent to the establishment of the consolidated city-county, have voted in a referendum to abolish their municipality and consolidate its powers, duties, rights, privileges and immunities with those of the consolidated city-county. An urban service district so defined shall comprise the total area of the municipality as it existed immediately before the effective date of its abolition. The resolution shall take effect at the beginning of the fiscal year next occurring after its adoption. (1973, c. 537, s. 1.)

§ 160B-6. Definition of urban service districts where no municipality existed.

(a) Standards. - The governing board, by resolution, may define an urban service district upon finding that a proposed district:

(1) Has a resident population of at least 1,000;

(2) Has a resident population density of at least one person per acre;

(3) Has an assessed valuation of at least two and one-half million dollars ($2,500,000);

(4) Requires one or more of the services, facilities and functions that are provided or maintained only or to a greater extent for an urban service district; and

(5) Does not include any territory within an active incorporated municipality.

(b) Report. - Prior to the public hearing required by subsection (c), the consolidated city-county shall prepare a report containing:

(1) A map of the proposed district, showing its proposed boundaries;

(2) A statement showing that the proposed district meets the standards of subsection (a); and

The report shall be available in the office of the clerk of the consolidated city-county for at least two weeks prior to the date of the public hearing.

(c)   Hearing and Notice. - The governing board shall hold a public hearing prior to adoption of any resolution defining a new urban service district. Notice of the hearing shall state the date, hour and place of the hearing and its subject, and shall include a statement that the report required by subsection (b) is available for inspection in the office of the clerk of the consolidated city-county. The notice shall be published in a newspaper of general circulation in the county at least once and not less than one week prior to the date of the hearing. In addition it shall be mailed at least four weeks prior to the date of the hearing to the owners as shown by the tax records of the consolidated city-county of all property located within the proposed district. The person designated by the governing board to mail the notice shall certify to the governing board that the mailing has been completed and his certificate shall be conclusive in the absence of fraud. The hearing may be held within the proposed district.

(d)   Effective Date. - The resolution defining an urban service district shall take effect at the beginning of a fiscal year commencing after its passage, as determined by the governing board. (1973, c. 537, s. 1.)

§ 160B-7. Extension of urban service districts.

(a)   Standards. - The governing board, by resolution, may extend by annexation the boundaries of any urban service district upon finding that:

(1)   The area to be annexed is contiguous to the district, with at least one eighth of the area's aggregate external boundary coincident with the existing boundary of the district;

(2)   The area to be annexed has a resident population density of at least one person per acre and an assessed valuation of at least one thousand dollars ($1,000) per resident person; or the area to be annexed is so developed that at least sixty per cent (60%) of the total number of lots and tracts in the area at the time of annexation are used for residential, commercial, industrial, institutional or governmental purposes and at least sixty percent (60%) of the total acreage of the area at the time of annexation is devoted to these uses; and

(b) Annexation by Petition. - The governing board also, by resolution, may extend by annexation the boundaries of any urban service district when one hundred percent (100%) of the real property owners of the area to be annexed have petitioned the governing board for annexation to the service district.

(c) Report. - Prior to the public hearing required by subsection (d), the consolidated city-county shall prepare a report containing:

(1) A map of the urban service district and the adjacent territory, showing the present and proposed boundaries of the district;

(2) A statement showing that the area to be annexed meets the standards of subsection (a) or comes before the governing board by petition as provided by subsection (b); and

(3) A plan for extending urban services, facilities and functions to the area to be annexed.

The report shall be available in the office of the clerk of the consolidated city-county for at least two weeks prior to the date for the public hearing.

(d) Hearing and Notice. - The governing board shall hold a public hearing prior to adoption of any resolution extending the boundaries of an urban service district. Notice of the hearing shall state the date, hour and place of the hearing and its subject, and shall include a statement that the report required by subsection (c) is available for inspection in the office of the clerk of the consolidated city-county. Notice shall be published in a newspaper of general circulation in the county at least once and not less than one week prior to the date of the hearing. In addition notice shall be mailed at least four weeks prior to the date of the hearing to the owners as shown by the tax records of the consolidated city-county of all property located within the area to be annexed. The person designated by the governing board to mail the notice shall certify to the governing board that the mailing has been completed, and his certificate shall be conclusive in the absence of fraud.

(d1) Alternative Notice. - Notwithstanding the provisions of subsection (d) of this section, first-class mail notice shall not be required where a plan for consolidation prepared by a consolidation study committee pursuant to Article

(e) Effective Date. - The resolution extending the boundaries of the district shall take effect at the beginning of a fiscal year commencing after its passage, as determined by the governing board.

(f) A consolidated city-county may not utilize the procedures of this section to annex to an urban service district territory within the boundaries of an active incorporated municipality. (1973, c. 537, s. 1; 1995, c. 461, s. 3.)

§ 160B-8. Consolidation of urban service districts.

(a) Standards. - The governing board, by resolution, may consolidate two or more urban service districts upon finding that:

(1) The districts are contiguous or are in a continuous boundary; and

(2) The provision or maintenance of urban services, facilities and functions for each of the districts is substantially the same; or

(3) If the provision or maintenance of urban services, facilities and functions is lower for one of the districts, there is a need to increase those services, facilities and functions for that district. However, no urban service district providing electric or telephone services may be consolidated with any other urban service district unless the voters of the district providing these utility services approve the consolidation in a referendum held for that purpose. Any consolidated city-county may hold these referendums.

(b) Report. - Prior to the public hearing required by subsection (c), the consolidated city-county shall prepare a report containing:

(1) A map of the districts to be consolidated;

(2) A statement showing the proposed consolidation meets the standards of subsection (a); and

The report shall be available in the office of the clerk of the consolidated city-county for at least two weeks prior to the date of the public hearing.

(c) Hearing and Notice. - The governing board shall hold a public hearing prior to adoption of any resolution consolidating urban service districts. Notice of the hearing shall state the date, hour and place of the hearing and its subject, and shall include a statement that the report required by subsection (b) is available for inspection in the office of the clerk of the consolidated city-county. Notice shall be published in a newspaper of general circulation in the county at least once and not less than two weeks prior to the date of the hearing. In addition, if the services, facilities and functions for one of the districts will be substantially increased as a result of the consolidation, notice shall be mailed at least four weeks prior to the date of the hearing to the owners as shown by the tax records of the consolidated city-county of all property located within the district. The person designated by the governing board to mail the notice shall certify to the governing board that the mailing has been completed and his certificate shall be conclusive in the absence of fraud.

(d) Effective Date. - The consolidation of urban service districts shall take effect at the beginning of a fiscal year commencing after passage of the resolution of consolidation, as determined by the governing board. (1973, c. 537, s. 1.)

§ 160B-9. Required provision or maintenance of services, facilities and functions.

(a) New District. - When a consolidated city-county defines a new urban service district, it shall provide or maintain the services, facilities and functions for which the residents of the district are being taxed within a reasonable time, not to exceed one year, after the effective date of the definition of the district.

(b) Extended District. - When a consolidated city-county annexes territory to an urban service district, it shall provide or maintain the services, facilities and functions provided or maintained throughout the district to the residents of the area annexed to the district within a reasonable time not to exceed one year, after the effective date of the annexation.

lower level of urban services, it shall increase the services, facilities and functions within that district to a level comparable to those provided or maintained elsewhere in the consolidated district within a reasonable time, not to exceed one year, after the effective date of the consolidation. (1973, c. 537, s. 1.)

§ 160B-10. Abolition of urban service districts.

Upon finding that there is no longer a need for a particular urban service district, the governing board, by resolution, may abolish that district. The governing board shall hold a public hearing prior to adoption of a resolution abolishing a district. Notice of the hearing shall state the date, hour and place of the hearing, and its subject, and shall be published in a newspaper of general circulation in the county at least once a week for two successive weeks prior to the date of the hearing. The abolition of any urban service district shall take effect at the end of a fiscal year following passage of the resolution, as determined by the governing board. (1973, c. 537, s. 1.)

Article 3.

Levy of Taxes in Urban Service Districts.

§ 160B-11. Taxes authorized; limits.

A consolidated city-county may levy the following taxes within defined urban service districts in addition to those levied throughout the county, in order to finance, provide or maintain for the districts services, facilities and functions in addition to or to a greater extent than those financed, provided or maintained for the entire county.

(1) Property Taxes. - A consolidated city-county may levy within any urban service district a tax on property at a rate not to exceed one dollar and fifty cents ($1.50) on the one hundred dollars ($100.00) of appraised valuation. This rate limitation does not apply to property taxes levied (i) for debt service on general obligation bonds of the consolidated city-county, (ii) for the support of the public schools or (iii) for any purpose approved by a special vote of the people.

taxes authorized in G.S. 20-97.

(3) Privilege License Taxes. - A consolidated city-county may levy within any urban service district privilege license taxes as authorized for cities and towns under the general law of the state. (1973, c. 537, s. 1.)

Article 4.

Allocation of Other Revenues.

§ 160B-12. Other allocation authorized.

A consolidated city-county may allocate to any urban service district it creates any other revenues of the consolidated government whose use is not otherwise restricted by law. (1973, c. 537, s. 1.)

§ 160B-13. Authority to borrow money and issue bonds.

A consolidated city-county may borrow money and issue its bonds under Chapter 159, Subchapter IV, and for those purposes shall be considered a unit of local government under Article 4 thereof and a municipality under Article 5 thereof. A consolidated city-county may borrow money and issue its bonds for any purpose for which either a city or a county may do so. (1973, c. 537, s. 1.)

§ 160B-14. Procedure for issuing general obligation and revenue bonds.

In issuing its general obligation and revenue bonds, a consolidated city-county, except as expressly modified by this chapter, is subject to the provisions of Chapter 159 of the General Statutes of North Carolina.

If a proposed bond issue is required by law to be submitted to and approved by the voters of the consolidated government, and if the proceeds of the proposed bond issue are to be used in connection with a service, facility or function that is or, if the bond issue is approved, will be financed, provided or maintained only for one or more urban service districts, the proposed bond issue must be

§ 160B-15. Debt limitations.

The net indebtedness in the form of general obligations of a consolidated city-county for school purposes may not exceed eight percent (8%) of the appraised valuation of taxable property in the county. The net indebtedness in the form of general obligations of a consolidated city-county for all purposes other than for schools or water, sewerage, gas and electric purposes may not exceed eight percent (8%) of the appraised valuation of taxable property in the county. No other debt limitations applying to counties and municipalities in North Carolina apply to a consolidated city-county. (1973, c. 537, s. 1.)

Article 5.

Assumption of Obligations and Debt Secured By a Pledge of Faith and Credit.

Part 1. General Provisions.

§ 160B-16. Applicability of this Article.

(a)   This Article applies to any county that has (i) a population over 120,000 according to the most recent federal decennial census and (ii) an area of less than 200 square miles.

(b)   If this section is declared unconstitutional or invalid by the courts, it does not affect the validity of the Article as a whole or any part other than the part so declared to be unconstitutional or invalid. (1995, c. 461, s. 4.)

Part 2. Assumption of Obligations and Debt.

§ 160B-17. Organizational meeting; preparation of budget.

The governing board of a consolidated city-county shall have its first organizational meeting as provided in the charter or applicable local acts of the General Assembly, but not later than the first business day following the

to the effective date of consolidation, any interim governing board designated or appointed in the charter or applicable local acts may meet to discuss business and take action as appropriate, including preparation of a proposed budget for the next ensuing fiscal year. In addition, any such interim governing board may take any action which is specifically authorized by this Chapter to be taken by an interim governing board. Meetings of any interim governing board during this period are subject to all applicable notice and meeting procedures required by general law. (1995, c. 461, s. 4.)

§ 160B-18. Referendum approval of certain debt assumption required for consolidation; effective date of consolidation.

(a)   Referendum Approval of Certain Debt Assumption Required for Consolidation. - For the consolidation of a city with a county to be effective in accordance with the provisions hereof, the assumption by the consolidated city-county of all debt secured by a pledge of faith and credit of said city outstanding at the effective date of consolidation must have been approved by referendum (which referendum approval may occur at different times for different portions of said debt).

(b)   Effective Date of Consolidation. - Subject to the requirement of referendum approval of certain debt assumption for consolidation as provided by subsection (a) of this section, the consolidation of a city with a county shall be effective upon the later of:

(1)   Sixty days following publication of notice of the enactment of the consolidation by the General Assembly;

(2)   Sixty days following publication of the statement of result of the latest referendum relating to the consolidation or to the assumption of debt secured by a pledge of faith and credit in connection with the consolidation; or

(3)   Any effective date of the consolidation set by the General Assembly.

In addition, upon adoption of concurrent resolutions by the governing board of each unit to be consolidated, or by the interim governing board of the

(c) Limitation of Local Acts. - No special, private, or local act, including any enactment of a consolidation of a city with a county, enacted after July 1, 1995, may be construed to modify, amend, or repeal any portion of this section unless it expressly so provides by specific reference to this section. (1995, c. 461, s. 4.)

§ 160B-19. Referendum on consolidation and on assumption of certain debt secured by a pledge of faith and credit; right to issue certain authorized but unissued debt secured by a pledge of faith and credit.

(a) In connection with a city-county consolidation, if there exists at the effective date of the consolidation (i) any outstanding debt secured by a pledge of faith and credit of a consolidating city or (ii) the right to issue any authorized but unissued debt of said city that is to be secured by a pledge of faith and credit and is proposed to be assumed by the consolidated city-county, then there shall have been held a favorable referendum on the question of the assumption of that debt secured by a pledge of faith and credit and, if applicable, there shall have been held a referendum on the assumption of the right to issue that authorized but unissued debt secured by a pledge of faith and credit.

(b) The referendum on the question of the assumption of debt secured by a pledge of faith and credit or, if applicable, the assumption of the right to issue authorized but unissued debt secured by a pledge of faith and credit may be included in the proposition submitted to the voters in a referendum called by a consolidation study commission under G.S. 153A-405.

(c) If the General Assembly provided for a referendum on the question of consolidation instead of a referendum called by a consolidation study commission under G.S. 153A-405, the governing bodies of the units proposed to be consolidated, by resolution, may add to the ballot proposition the assumption of debt secured by a pledge of faith and credit question and, if applicable, the assumption of the right to issue authorized but unissued debt secured by a pledge of faith and credit question. In either event, the proposition shall be substantially as provided in G.S. 153A-405.

or, if applicable, the question of the assumption of the right to issue any authorized but unissued faith and credit debt, then the governing bodies of the units proposed to be consolidated, by resolution, may provide for a referendum on said questions. In addition, any interim governing board for the consolidated city-county, by resolution, also may provide for such a referendum. The proposition submitted to the voters shall be substantially in the following form (and may include part or all of the bracketed language as appropriate and any other modifications as may be needed to reflect the issued debt secured by a pledge of faith and credit of any of the consolidating units or the portion of the authorized but unissued debt secured by a pledge of faith and credit of any of the consolidating units, the right to issue which is proposed to be assumed by the consolidated city-county):

"Shall, in connection with the consolidation of the City of   with the County of   , the consolidated unit assume the debt of each secured by a pledge of faith and credit, [the right to issue authorized but unissued debt to be secured by a pledge of faith and credit [(including any such debt as may be authorized for said city or county on the date of this referendum)] and any of said authorized but unissued debt as may be hereafter issued,] and be authorized to levy taxes in an amount sufficient to pay the principal of and the interest on said debt secured by a pledge of faith and credit?

[ ] YES   [ ] NO"

(e)   To be approved the proposition must receive the votes of a majority of those voting in the referendum. In connection with the proposed consolidation of one or more cities with a county, if the assumption by the consolidated city-county of outstanding debt secured by a pledge of faith and credit of the consolidating city and, if applicable, the right to issue authorized but unissued debt secured by a pledge of faith and credit of the consolidating city was approved by the votes of a majority of those voting in the referendum, the vote on that referendum shall constitute the approval by a majority of the qualified voters who vote thereon as required by Article V, Section 4(2) of the Constitution of North Carolina.

(f)   Any such referendum on the question of consolidation or the assumption of debt secured by a pledge of faith and credit or the right to issue authorized but unissued debt secured by a pledge of faith and credit may be held on the

board of elections conducting the referendum and already validly called or scheduled by law.

(g)   A notice of a referendum on consolidation or on the assumption of debt secured by a pledge of faith and credit or, if applicable, the right to issue authorized but unissued debt secured by a pledge of faith and credit shall be published at least twice in a newspaper of general circulation in the county. The first publication shall be not less than 14 days and the second publication not less than seven days before the last day on which voters may register for the referendum. The notice shall state the date of the referendum, a statement as to the last date for registration for the referendum under the election laws then in effect, and substantially the text of the proposition to be voted upon. The notice shall be published by the governing bodies of the units proposed to be consolidated or, if applicable, the interim governing board of the consolidated city-county by their respective clerks or by such other person as shall be designated by each applicable governing body or board.

(h)   The board of elections shall canvass any referendum on consolidation and any referendum on the assumption of debt secured by a pledge of faith and credit or, if applicable, the right to issue authorized but unissued debt secured by a pledge of faith and credit and shall certify the results to the governing bodies of the units proposed to be consolidated or, if applicable, the interim governing board of the consolidated city-county which shall then certify and declare the result of the referendum and shall publish a statement of the result once in a newspaper of general circulation in the county, with the following statement appended:

"Any action or proceeding challenging the regularity or validity of this referendum must be begun within 30 days after the date of publication of this statement of result."

(i)   Any action or proceeding in any court to set aside a referendum on consolidation or a referendum on assumption of debt secured by a pledge of faith and credit or, if applicable, the right to issue authorized but unissued debt secured by a pledge of faith and credit in connection with consolidation, or to obtain any other relief, upon the grounds that the referendum is invalid or was irregularly conducted, must be begun within 30 days after the publication of the statement of the result of the referendum. After the expiration of this period of

in an action or proceeding begun within the period of limitation prescribed in this section. (1995, c. 461, s. 4.)

§ 160B-20. Local Government Commission review of assumption of debt secured by a pledge of faith and credit; assumption of debt secured by a pledge of faith and credit and right to issue authorized but unissued debt secured by a pledge of faith and credit upon consolidation.

(a) Review by Local Government Commission. - At the date specified in the following sentence if any consolidating city or county has outstanding any debt secured by a pledge of faith and credit or, if applicable, any authorized but unissued debt secured by a pledge of faith and credit which is proposed to be assumed by the consolidated city-county or has outstanding or pending approval any debt secured by a pledge of faith and credit the issuance of which was or is subject to approval by the Local Government Commission, then the assumption of any such debt and, if applicable, the assumption of the right to issue such authorized but unissued debt, if any, shall be subject to review by the Local Government Commission. The finance officers of the units proposed to be consolidated shall use their best efforts to notify the secretary of the Local Government Commission of the proposed consolidation and assumption of debt secured by a pledge of faith and credit or, if applicable, the right to issue authorized but unissued debt secured by a pledge of faith and credit at least two months before the introduction in the General Assembly of legislation proposing to enact the consolidation into law, provided that time allows. The Local Government Commission, to such extent it deems appropriate, may conduct a review of the proposed consolidation and assumption of debt secured by a pledge of faith and credit or, if applicable, the right to issue authorized but unissued debt secured by a pledge of faith and credit and may report the results of its review to the presiding officer of each house of the General Assembly to be provided to the respective committees to which the legislation to enact the consolidation shall be referred.

(b) Assumption of Debt Secured by a Pledge of Faith and Credit by Consolidated City-County. - Subject to the requirement of referendum approval of certain debt assumption for consolidation provided in G.S. 160B-18(a), upon enactment of the consolidation by the General Assembly and effective upon the effective date of the consolidation provided in G.S. 160B-18(b), the debt assumed by, and becomes a binding obligation of the consolidated city-county, and the faith and credit of the consolidated city-county is pledged to secure any such assumed debt secured by a pledge of faith and credit. In addition, any debt secured by a pledge of faith and credit of the county at the effective date of the consolidation shall become a binding obligation of the consolidated city-county and the faith and credit of the consolidated city-county is pledged to secure any such debt.

(c) Right to Issue Authorized but Unissued Debt Secured by a Pledge of Faith and Credit. - Subject to the passage of a referendum relating to the assumption by the consolidated city-county of the right to issue any authorized but unissued debt of the consolidating city to be secured by a pledge of faith and credit that is proposed to be assumed by the consolidated city-county, upon enactment of the consolidation by the General Assembly and effective upon the effective date of the consolidation as provided in G.S. 160B-18(b), the right to issue the authorized but unissued debt secured by a pledge of faith and credit of the consolidating city at the effective date of the consolidation is assumed by, and upon issuance such obligations become binding obligations of, the consolidated city-county, and, upon issuance, the faith and credit of the consolidated city-county is pledged to secure any such debt secured by a pledge of faith and credit. In addition, the right to issue the authorized but unissued debt secured by a pledge of faith and credit of the county at the effective date of the consolidation shall be vested in the consolidated city-county and, upon issuance, such debt secured by a pledge of faith and credit becomes a binding obligation of the consolidated city-county and, upon issuance, the faith and credit of the consolidated city-county is pledged to secure any such debt. (1995, c. 461, s. 4; 1995 (Reg. Sess., 1996), c. 742, s. 40.)

§ 160B-21. Notice of enactment of consolidation; limitation of actions.

(a) Publication of Notice of Enactment. - Following ratification of an act of the General Assembly authorizing consolidation, there shall be published once in a newspaper of general circulation in the county a notice of said enactment and, if applicable, the fact that in connection with said enactment there is an assumption by the consolidated city-county of the debt secured by a pledge of faith and credit of the consolidating city and, if applicable, assumption of the right to issue authorized but unissued debt secured by a pledge of faith and

authorized but unissued debt secured by a pledge of faith and credit of the county with the following statement appended:

"Any action or proceeding challenging the regularity or validity of this enactment must be begun within 30 days after the date of publication of this notice."

The notice shall be published by the governing bodies of the units proposed to be consolidated or, if applicable, the interim governing board of the consolidated city-county by their respective clerks or by such other persons as shall be designated by each applicable governing body or board.

(b) Limitation on Action Contesting Validity of Enactment of Consolidation. - Any action or proceeding in any court to set aside enactment of a city-county consolidation by the General Assembly, or to obtain any other relief, upon the grounds that the enactment is invalid or was irregularly enacted, must be begun within 30 days after the publication of the notice of the enactment. After the expiration of this period of limitation, no right of action or defense based upon the invalidity of the enactment or any irregularity in the enactment shall be asserted, nor shall the validity of the enactment be open to question in any court upon any grounds whatever, except in an action or proceeding begun within the period of limitation prescribed in this section. (1995, c. 461, s. 4; 1995 (Reg. Sess., 1996), c. 742, s. 41.)

Fax Orders:	1-980-299-5965
Phone Orders:	1-704-898-0770
E-mail Orders:	www.visionbooks.org
Mail Orders:	Vision Books, LLC P.O. Box 42406 Charlotte, NC 28215

Shipp To:
Name_____
Address_____
City_____State_____Zip_____
Phone_____Fax_____
Email_____@_____

Bill To: We can bill a third party on your behalf.
Name_____
Address_____
City_____State_____Zip_____
Phone___(_____)_____Fax_____
Email_____@_____

Pamphlet Number ($15.00 Each)	Qty	Total Cost
_____	_____	_____
_____	_____	_____
_____	_____	_____
_____	_____	_____
_____	_____	_____
_____	_____	_____
_____	_____	_____
<u>Full Volume Set 1-92</u>	<u>92 Pamphlets</u>	<u>1,380.00</u>

Free Shipping & Handling on Full Volume Orders
Add $1.00 Shipping & Handling Per Pamphlet $_____

Total Cost $_____

Thak you your support. Management!

been fasely imprisoned, we would like to hear your story. If the 'North Carolina Criminal Law and Procedure' has had an effect in your life or if you have suggestions, we would like to hear from you. Send your letters to:

Vision Books, LLC
Attn: Staff Writers
P.O. Box 42406
Charlotte, NC 28215
Email: staff@visionbooks.org

Order Additional Copies:

Fax Orders:	1-980-299-5965
Phone Orders:	1-704-898-0770
E-mail Orders:	www.visionbooks.org
Mail Orders:	Vision Books, LLC P.O. Box 42406 Charlotte, NC 28215

www.ingramcontent.com/pod-product-compliance
Lightning Source LLC
Chambersburg PA
CBHW051631170526
45167CB00001B/146